Praise for *100 Great Catholic Poems*

"The current Catholic literary revival takes a huge leap forward with this essential new book. *100 Great Catholic Poems* not only lives up to its ambitious title but exceeds it. Editor Sally Read presents an arresting cross section of the best poems from antiquity to the modern age; then she adds a useful and engaging note for each selection. This anthology helps restore a lost legacy to the Church. Whether you are a student, a teacher, or a cardinal, you will want this book on your shelf."

—**Dana Gioia**, former California Poet Laureate and Chairman of the National Endowment for the Arts

"What an extraordinary gift Sally Read's *100 Great Catholic Poems* is! Even with poems many of us may already know—the Magnificat, Dante, Shakespeare, Crashaw, Hopkins, and, yes, Wallace Stevens—her commentaries on each of these blessed one hundred are so vivid and insightful that we find ourselves wrapped again and again in an aura of stunning, grace-filled light. And then there are those poems we may never have come across before, shining here like the hidden diamonds they are. What a treasure this book is! Read it. I promise you will indeed be changed by the encounter."

—**Paul Mariani**, University Professor of English Emeritus at Boston College

"In this superb anthology, Sally Read has somehow taken the vast sweep of Catholic wisdom and civilization and distilled it as a single volume. With poems spanning the centuries, from Mary's Magnificat to the stuttering prophetic joy of David Jones and beyond, *100 Great Catholic Poems* will make not only a fine initiation into the Catholic literary tradition for many readers but also a portal into the profound vision and mystery of the Church. Read's helpful commentaries illuminate the poems and draw even the most wary reader into the sacramental imagination."

—**James Matthew Wilson**, author of *The Strangeness of the Good* and Professor of Humanities at the University of St. Thomas

"A truly absorbing anthology! Sally Read brings to the poems selected—an impressive sweep over two millennia—an originality of insight that opens the door for the reader into a new world of vision, refreshing our understanding not only of some of the great classics of the tradition but also of work much less familiar yet no less compelling. For any serious lover of sacred verse, this is a must-have anthology."

—**Fr. Paul Murray, OP**, author of *Light at the Torn Horizon*

100 Great Catholic Poems

100 Great Catholic Poems

EDITED AND WITH COMMENTARY
BY SALLY READ

Published by Word on Fire, Elk Grove Village, IL 60007
© 2023 by Word on Fire Catholic Ministries
Printed in the United States of America
All rights reserved

Cover design by Michael Stevens, typesetting by Marlene Burrell,
and interior art direction by Michael Stevens

Second printing, November 2023
First published November 2023

ISBN: 978-1-68578-074-6

Library of Congress Control Number: 2023911449

To Fabio

Contents

CONTENTS

Acknowledgments

No one man or woman can commentate on two thousand years of poetry, across multiple cultures and languages, without help from a number of people. I am immensely grateful to the following:

To Dr. Mark Doerksen for his assistance with Middle English, to Dr. Matthew Genung for answering my biblical queries, to Dr. Helena Tomko for telling me about Gertrud von Le Fort's poetry, to Dana Gioia for so generously introducing me to Mario Luzi, to Bevil Luck for introducing me to FT Prince and sharing so much of his knowledge, to Tim Bete for helpful suggestions and tracking down texts, to Pelé Cox for reminding me that in poetry you never stop learning and you should always take risks, to Pat Destito for his support and enthusiasm, to Rosaleen Howard and Paul Flynn for their willingness to help on Irish language matters, to Marta Prados for giving me insights into the Spanish of Saint Teresa, to Dr. Marie Cabaud Meaney for being an ever-willing pair of eyes and ears, to Kerry Lee Crabbe for being, as ever, a wellspring of knowledge, advice and grist, particularly about Shakespeare, to Father Paul Murray, OP, for sharing both his books and his wisdom, to Father Gregory Hrynkiw for being my on-call theologian and teaching me so much about Gregory of Nazianzus over the years, to my mum for photographing hundreds of pages from books back home, to Matthew Becklo and the team at Word on Fire for their vision, kindness, and expertise, and to my daughter Celia Bottone for her unerring sagacity and guiding me through *La Commedia*.

All lapses in judgment are my own.

Introduction

Before we begin our journey, it might be as well to define our terms: *poems*, *Catholic*, and *great*. If anyone wonders why certain poems or poets are included in this anthology, the answer should be contained in this introduction—and, of course, in the works that follow.

Poems

I was twenty-five years old when I had my first encounter with a poem in this book. I was working as a nurse in London, and while tending to the variously tested and battered hearts on a hospital ward, my own had been broken. The minutes of the frenetic London days were painful in their passing. The city—it has been said many times before—was lonely in its endless succession of faces and meetings. But sitting in my flat one evening I read this line: "It is late last night the dog was speaking of you."

I was struck at once by its strangeness (the "error" in the tenses, the talking animal when this was obviously no poem for children). There was much more I did not understand as I read on. The images were outlandish to me, the context alien. And yet it spoke to my heart. I was soothed, but electrified. The poem would travel with me for a long time.

My early days as a lover of poetry were marked by similar feelings of elation, bewilderment, and the feeling that I had stumbled on the truth. No other literary genre is so concerned with truth—not only in the sense of writing about true things, as the Irish bards did, or as the confessional poets do as they dish us their personal lives, but in the scalpel-precise rendering of things that humans cannot otherwise articulate. This, perhaps, is what sets poetry apart from other genres: by using image and metaphor and the music of language, poets lift the human senses beyond the everyday. They show us the woven relationships between all things. They link heaven and earth and leave enough space for the silence of mystery, for the truth that remains wordless on human tongues.

In the years that followed my poetic encounter with that first line of "Donal Og" (Young Donald),[1] I began, incrementally, to devote my life to poetry. In whatever job or country I found myself, I would inevitably turn to poems to make sense of my situation—and to try and help others to make sense of theirs. I have used poetry with dementia sufferers and schoolchildren, retreatants and English language students. My biggest challenge has always been in persuading participants that they did not need to understand, word for word, everything that a poem said. Poems were not riddles: there was not one answer that clever readers understood. I have tried to convince people that poetry is like music: we should let it wash over us, listening to the sounds and responding instinctively. And over the years, I have witnessed similar experiences to my own occurring again and again. Even people who professed no interest in poetry, who did not understand it, or who had never read it would ask if they could photocopy a page, or stay after a session to write out some lines. Educated or not, poetry lover or no, in my experience, anyone with a story of their own is hungry for the truth and consolation that poetry can bring.

1. See page 39.

What has all this to do with Catholicism?

Well, that same bewildered yet convinced sensation would come upon me during my conversion to the Catholic faith. As I stood on the threshold of churches watching the symmetry and beauty of the Mass unfold before me, with its symbols (the candles, the incense), its images and figurative language ("the Body of Christ," the "dewfall" of the Spirit), I did not understand every word, nor every action at the altar. But I was arrested by the Mass' structure. As any man knows when listening to Bach's *Saint Matthew Passion* that there is not one note amiss, I knew the Church's rightness as I witnessed its liturgy and prayer. I saw it as a poem: the seamless working of form and meaning within the Mass was reminiscent to me of the tight interrelation of shape and content in a piece of poetry. Every word, every gesture of every liturgy mattered. What I also understood, as a convert poet, was that God the Father was *the* poet. By sending his Son into the world through Jesus Christ, he put flesh on the ineffable. He made tangible the ungraspable. He explained the inexplicable. And, fundamentally, that is what any poet is trying to do.

As I lined up in those early days to receive the Eucharist, I thought about how being in the Church is like stepping into a poem. Take a famous line like "Shall I compare thee to a summer's day?" Shakespeare conjures, in his perfect words, the colors, flowers, and beauty of a day. In a poetic sense, the beloved of that sonnet then *becomes* the day, and the day becomes her. The poet will never know a summer day without thinking of her, nor her without thinking of a summer's day. This is what metaphors do: they couple two separate entities by what they have in common. But in reality, the woman and day remain distinct.

Similarly (not identically), Catholics know, as they walk up to the altar, that the bread (which is white as flesh) and the wine (which is red as blood) *have become* the Flesh and Blood of Christ. But *this* becoming (unlike Shakespeare's metaphor) is literal. The bread and wine are not "like" flesh and blood anymore; after the consecration, they *are* Flesh and Blood. The mechanism of what happens at the altar is truly poetic—it has the same engagement with what things are like, and how they become linked—but then it goes further. It fulfills what every poem promises. In the Eucharist, "types and shadows have their ending," as Thomas Aquinas wrote in "Pange Lingua."[2] The Mass rips through simile and metaphor and leads us to reality.

It stands to reason that poetry is evident everywhere in the Catholic faith. Humankind is always resorting to metaphor to understand, even partially, what is ineffable. So, Catholics speak poetry from Matins to Compline, in every Psalm, prayer, and song. They live it in every litany to Our Lady (who is expressed in metaphorical terms like no one else in history—read Walter of Wimborne's extravagant "Ave Virgo Mater Christi"[3]). Poetry is the language of Catholicism.

"I don't read poetry," several devout, practicing Catholics have remarked to me over the years. "I don't get it." Although they may not be reading poems in poetry books, they are, nonetheless, picking up a poem with their first coffee of the day (a Psalm). When they recite the Litany of Loreto or the Magnificat, they are also engaging with the genre. The truths of the faith have *always* been transmitted through poetry, because it is memorable; because its images embed in our hearts and minds; because some things are too complex for stark prose.

2. Thomas Aquinas, "Pange lingua," in Paul Murray, *Aquinas at Prayer: The Bible, Mysticism and Poetry* (London: Bloomsbury, 2013), 192.
3. See page 95.

Thomas Aquinas, who was ambivalent about poetry's ability to speak truth (though he wrote poetry himself), knew that it shares theology's reliance on metaphor: "The hiding of truth in figures is useful for the exercise of thoughtful minds."[4] Poetry shows us the world's invisible connections and subtleties. It whispers past our consciousness to the place where we also stand in prayer, barely beginning to apprehend mystery. "Her concealment," writes Hadewijch about God's love within these pages, "reveals what can be known of her."[5]

Very much aware of the copious use of poetry within the Catholic faith, the great challenge for me in selecting these poems was in discerning where to draw my lines!

Prayer

Early on, I realized that prayers should not be included, for the simple reason that if they were, the book would quickly become a book of prayer. Prayers, though often beautifully worded and full of poetry's characteristic uses of image, linguistic music, and even rhyme, are written for direct communication with God, not for our fellow men and women. When choosing these poems, this was the first of my self-imposed boundaries, the following of which shaped the book like a sculptor with a modeling knife. I often grieved the off-cuts that fell to the floor. But I saw that my ruthlessness was bringing forth an extraordinary and unique shape.

Yet all rules have exceptions. The Fathers of the Church wrote poetry as a way of teaching the faith, and the form of their poems is often very similar to prayer, with address to God, petition, etc. It would be foolish to cast these aside as

4. Thomas Aquinas, *Summa theologiae* 1.1.9 ad 2.
5. Hadewijch, "The Paradoxes of Love." See page 88.

non-poems. Early Christian poetry was often indistinguishable from theology. In fact, St. Gregory the Theologian was named as such for his poetry. St. Patrick's later prayer, "The Deer's Cry," is so poetic that it is anthologized in secular books and has been set to music many times.[6] Its direction is "out" to men and women as well as "up" to God. It is even possible that the saint's original prayer was shaped into the poem's compelling form by another poetic pen (and certainly, in turn, by the translator). Later, Anne Porter and Caryll Houselander, among others, would deliberately blur the lines between poetry and prayer, as Thomas Aquinas did so many years before them. This is a very Catholic art, a very Catholic way of praying, a very Catholic way of writing poetry. So, although most prayers had to be excluded, I have brought in several that sufficiently cross the boundary into poetry, taking into account both the author's aim in writing the piece and the historical-literary context.

Hymns

Another consideration for an editor of a Catholic anthology is the hymn. Can songs be included? The earliest lyric poetry in Greece was often set to music, and St. Ephrem and St. Ambrose later used tunes to make their didactic poetry memorable for their flocks. Hildegard of Bingen liked to write musical settings for her poems. Many other poetic works, like John Henry Newman's "The Pillar of the Cloud," were set to music later.[7] All of these poets I included. However, my modeling knife twitched, and I threw out hymns more specifically composed for sung worship. A determining attribute of poetry is that it stands alone. It does not need accompaniment; the language makes its

6. See page 27.
7. See page 242.

own unpredictable music. (It is worth bearing in mind that the word "hymn," particularly as applied to the work of Gregory of Nazianzus, Ephrem, and Clement of Alexandria, means poem, as well as song, of praise.)

Prose

The next cut with the modeling knife when considering the word "poetry" was, of course, prose. How much glorious, shimmering prose has been written by Julian of Norwich, St. Catherine of Siena, St. Clare of Assisi, and St. Augustine! Dozens of sections of their writings could be chopped up on the page and a poem created (and the internet routinely does just that). But, in the interests of the form that was revealing itself to me, I stuck with *poetry*. The reader will by now not be surprised to hear that there are grey areas surrounding this rule. William Shakespeare sometimes abandoned blank verse in his plays, not only as a means of signaling less exalted thought and speech, but also—especially in later works—as a way of changing pace and emotional register and drawing *more* attention, not less, to the words. A prose speech from *Hamlet* (a play that Harold Bloom described as "of no genre" and "the most unlimited" of all poems[8]) is therefore included.[9] (The issue of including Shakespeare as a Catholic poet is discussed in the next section.)

A passage from St. Augustine's *Confessions* is also here.[10] These are famous lines so poetically wrought, written with such symmetry and form, that it would be a crime against Catholic poetry not to include them. Their inclusion is testimony to the fact that the genres sometimes blur and that true poetry can live in diverse places.

8. Harold Bloom, *Hamlet: Poem Unlimited* (New York: Riverhead Books, 2003).
9. "I have of late . . ." from act 2, scene 2, of *Hamlet*. See page 217.
10. See page 22.

Scripture

The most important of those places, of course, is Scripture. The
Bible is packed with poetry. The Psalms and Song of Solomon
are, themselves, the most wondrous religious verse ever written.
But their inclusion would have made for a biblical anthology
and dwarfed the efforts of men and women in the two thousand
years since the birth, death, and Resurrection of Christ. The
coming of Jesus seemed a good chronological place to begin a
Catholic anthology, and as an acknowledgment of God's poetry,
we begin with Our Lady's spontaneous song as she exalts the
Poem within her.[11] Mary is, in a very real sense, the Mother of
poetry, and in a clear way she heralds the poetic endeavors of
those to come.

Catholic Poems

It is tempting to say that every poem is a Catholic poem. Any
fully realized poem is intimately engaged with, as Flannery
O'Connor said of fiction, the salvation or damnation of the
soul.[12] Whereas O'Connor was talking more of her characters'
souls, the poet is concerned with the human imagination pitted
against chaos. Poets are looking for form and connection—a
search that, more often than not, leads them to beauty and
truth. They are—whether religious or not—striving to see
the integrity of creation. In this sense, they (and their poems)
are reaching out to the divine. In their clear-sightedness,
their industrious quest for meaning, poets are, as Percy Bysshe

---

11. "The Magnificat." See page 3.
12. Flannery O'Connor, "Novelist and Believer," in *Mystery and Manners* (New York:
Farrar, Straus and Giroux, 1969), 167.

Shelley once wrote, "the unacknowledged legislators of the world."[13]

As they create order out of chaos, poets are also like Adam in the garden of Eden, naming each plant and creature. Poets name to know the world better—to illuminate things, emotions, and events and their place in creation. There are no other themes for writers of living poems—even if they do not believe in God.

Transcendent Poetry

But there is no poet on the planet worth his or her salt who does not admit that a good poem comes from some place over which they have no control. The atheistic might say it is their unconscious that does the work: writing poetry is only a matter of relaxing the consciousness and allowing the unplumbed depths of the mind to throw up astonishing matter onto the page. The more vaguely spiritual, though, will point to a transcendent force that inspires them. W.B. Yeats called it the *Spiritus Mundi*. Ted Hughes believed that poets were shamanic: poems were a means of healing. When the atheist Shelley wrote "Adonais," a eulogy for his dear friend John Keats, he reached for the imagery of the gods. It was always this way. For the Romans, poets were seers. No one believed that the weight of poetic words came from one man or woman's fallible brain. In other words, poetry, above all literary genres, has a special relationship not only with truth but with *transcendent* truth.

It should not surprise us, therefore, that references to God, and even Catholicism, show up regularly in the work of non-Catholic poets. The Virgin Mary and Christ are both

13. Percy Bysshe Shelley, *A Defence of Poetry* (Indianapolis, IN: Bobbs-Merrill Company, 1904), 90.

mentioned a surprising number of times in Sylvia Plath's work. Anne Sexton, who arguably sailed near to actual conversion, wrote extensively about God and her spiritual journey. More controversially, for the edits of my ruthless modeling knife, the poetry of Anglicans John Donne, George Herbert, and T.S. Eliot, to name but a few, is known as being among the most sublime religious poetry ever written.

So what do we gain by losing all of these fine names in a *Catholic* anthology? At first I was diffident. I stood before my vast mass of clay (the entire number of great Christian poems written in the last two thousand years) and could see no method in seeking out what was purely "Catholic." I was not alone. Numerous anthologies of Christian or spiritual poetry have been published and are being published, and for the most part, editors are content to see God in many places (rightly) and to see the post-Reformation division as a matter unfit for the classification of poems. This view has my sympathy. But as I began to cut, to pare, to shape the clay in search of truly *Catholic* poetry, my breath was taken by the form that continued to emerge.

A Communion of Poetic Saints

The song that began on Mary's lips was taken up by the early saints, who plunged deep into God's poetry to teach the new faith, to express its joy, to correct heresy, and to understand themselves within the great drama of salvation. Catholic poetry quickly became, also, a historical record—of mysticism, persecution, martyrdom, ecstasy, conversion, and renewal. A good proportion of the poets here were not solely poets. They were reformers (Teresa of Avila and John of the Cross), popes (Pope John Paul II), mystics (Teresa and John again, but also

Hildegard of Bingen, Hadewijch, Caryll Houselander, Symeon the New Theologian). They were men and women who, in pain, had recourse only to their faith, and their expression of this was poetry (Takashi Nagai, Henry Walpole). They were journalists and essayists (G.K. Chesterton and Hilaire Belloc). They were theologians and philosophers, whose finest thought was sometimes best rendered in verse (Sts. Thomas, Symeon, Ambrose, Gregory, Ephrem, and Edith Stein). They were also poets so steeped in the religion of their age that the signs and concerns of their works were effortlessly Catholic (William Langland, Geoffrey Chaucer).

The Beating Catholic Heart

But not all the poems in this book have obviously Catholic (rather than simply Christian) themes, like the Blessed Virgin, the Blessed Sacrament, or purgatory. As I read hundreds of poems, I tentatively began to be able to identify what we mean by a "Catholic poem." *It beats with a Catholic heart*, I started to hear myself think when I found a candidate text. But I had to define what I meant by that. It often seemed to hinge on a physicality that could only ever be found in the poetry of a faith that believes that its adherents take God in their mouths. "I have felt for His Wounds," David Jones cries in "A, a, a Domine Deus."[14] "It is her tenderness / Heats the dead world," says Thomas Merton of Mary.[15] "I trembled as His arms went round me," says the cross itself in an eighth-century dream poem.[16] This physicality is sensuous; it is erotic in the vein of the great forerunner Song of Solomon. "Upon my flowering

---

14. See page 417.
15. "The Annunciation." See page 411.
16. "The Dream of the Rood." See page 43.

breast / Which I kept wholly for him alone," sings St. John of the Cross.[17] "His lifeless sacred skin [will be] my page," says Vittoria Colonna, taking this intimate relationship with the Word directly into the literary realm.[18] Gregory of Narek sees *himself* as his devotional book.[19] Meanwhile, Edith Sitwell envisions the entire city of London as the body of Christ, pelted by 1940 nails.[20] For Catholic poets, the relationship between Word and poem, Word and body, and Word and place is powerful.

But this beating Catholic heart goes beyond the obviously sensual in poetry. The Catholic poet takes God's own poetry—of the Scriptures, of intimacy through the sacraments, of sacrifice and redemption—and runs with it. Even poems that do not have primarily religious themes can spring from this Catholic imagination and beat with a Catholic heart. "Donal Og," the poem that so arrested me as a young woman, is steeped in the language of divine and human love. "O Rosary that Recalled my Tear" is a poem of grief, spoken through the sacramental rosary.[21] A simple ninth-century poem about a monk and his cat might, at first glance, not contain much specifically Catholic, but it, too, springs from the Catholic imagination in its simple understanding of the interconnected web of creation.[22]

Working within this creative and spiritual palette, our poets often call out to each other, sometimes unknowingly, across the centuries. The deer of Psalm 42 pops up in John Dryden.[23] Richard Crashaw's "Flaming Heart" belongs to Teresa of Avila.[24]

---

17. "The Dark Night." See page 192.
18. "Too Long My Chaste Love." See page 177.
19. "Prayer 54e" of the *Book of Lamentations*. See note on page 63.
20. "Still Falls the Rain." See page 345.
21. Aithbhreac Inghean Corcadail, "O Rosary that Recalled my Tear." See page 161.
22. "Pangur Bàn." See page 54.
23. "The Hind and the Panther." See page 228.
24. "The Flaming Heart, Upon the Book and Picture of the Seraphical Saint Teresa." See page 222.

The jeweled cross of "The Dream of the Rood" echoes in Will's dream in *Piers Plowman*.[25] Christ is a swan to an anonymous medieval poet, a pelican to Thomas Aquinas, and a windhover to Gerard Manley Hopkins.[26] To Roy Campbell, Michelangelo, and the tenth-century author of "The Seafarer," the Catholic life is best described by a voyage at sea.[27] Catholic poetry is a vibrant millennia-long conversation. The challenge for the Catholic poet is to stay rooted in this great conversation but at the same time to strike out, clear-eyed as Adam.

Making It New in the Tradition

This is because poetry "purges from our inward sight the film of familiarity," as Shelley also said.[28] A poem should always, in some way, shock. It should discomfit. It has to be *new*, as Ezra Pound exhorted.[29] The normal reaction to a fine poem in the mind of the reader should usually be a silent question mark, followed by a shiver of recognition.

That, potentially, puts Catholic poets into a bit of a bind. They inhabit a world already highly structured in poetic terms. (The symbols have been taken—a rock, a candle, a chalice, wine, bread, water. The metaphorical landscape is ingrained. Even the figure of Jesus Christ himself is so laden with resonance that placing him in a poem spins the wheel for any poet.) Whereas the poet's job is usually to stand in an empty field beside a bleak hedgerow and somehow transport the reader to

25. See "The Dream of the Rood," page 41, and excerpt Passus 20 of *Piers Plowman*, page 148.

26. See "The Crucifixion," page 72; "Adoro Te Devote," page 90; and "The Windhover," page 261.

27. See "Mass at Dawn," page 338; "Arrived from Across a Stormy Sea," page 178; and "The Seafarer," page 58.

28. Percy Bysshe Shelley, *A Defence of Poetry*, 83.

29. Ezra Pound, *Make it New* (London: Faber & Faber, 1934).

epiphany through incisive insight, Catholic poets, like Robert Southwell, Alexander Pope, and Denise Levertov, were already standing in the most finely articulated collection of symbols and order known to man. The cradle Catholic, lapsed Catholic, and deathbed revert Kathleen Raine wrote that she, personally, could never have tangled with ecclesiastical symbols in her poems. That water was muddied through millennia of use. *That poem was already written.*[30]

Others managed it. They not only managed it; they added to our understanding of God's poetry by swimming in it, seeing it with new eyes, presenting it in innovative or simply ultra-lucid terms. Fire, in the hands of a Catholic poet, can never be just fire. It will always be the Holy Spirit. But by the time we reach Thomas Merton's "The Annunciation," the Spirit has become "sparks" that are scattering "seeds," and "blue things bud in Israel."[31] The reader's eyes are peeled.

Merton, of course, was a convert. It is noteworthy that more than a third of the poems in this book are written by converts. In a world where a proportion of Catholics do not believe in the Real Presence, where prayers can become so rote we cease to hear them, where the sacrifice at the altar can become habitual—even dull!—and Christ's wounds begin to seem like the ceramic representations we see in bad church art, we need truths given to us in arresting ways. This Ephrem did in his day, as did St. Francis, Dante Alighieri and Oscar Wilde, Claude McKay and George Mackay Brown.

---

30. Kathleen Raine, introduction to *The Collected Poems of Kathleen Raine* (Berkeley, CA: Counterpoint, 2001).

31. See page 410.

The Question of Shakespeare: Are All the Poets Here Catholic?

But all of these considerations of what makes a poem truly Catholic were enveloped by a deeper problem: Who truly counts as a Catholic poet? And does it finally matter? Perhaps the most controversial inclusion in this anthology of Catholic poems is the work of William Shakespeare. Whole books have been written about the identity of the greatest author in history. Joseph Pearce has argued unequivocally for the bard's Catholicism.[32] Clare Asquith has provided intriguing insights that suggest he was a secret Catholic.[33] There are many more pro arguments, and many counter. I am not a Shakespeare scholar nor researcher, only a lover. I only know that Shakespeare, more than any other writer, reaches all dimensions—emotional, psychological, historical, epic, lyrical, and spiritual. He had a disturbingly modern eye for what the world would look like without God: "Unaccommodated man is no more but such a poor, bare, forked animal as thou art," says Lear (which F.T. Prince quotes in these pages).[34] At the same time, the reach of Shakespeare is up to heaven and down to hell and through the realm of purgatory: "Confin'd to fast in fires / Till the foul crimes done in my days of nature / Are burnt and purged away," says Hamlet's father's ghost.[35] Yet I don't claim Shakespeare as Catholic primarily because of his writing on Catholic themes nor because of any special knowledge about his life. I include him here because the dynamism of the poetry is rooted in a Catholic mindset. His world is inhabited by the dead, spirits, the

32. Joseph Pearce, *The Quest for Shakespeare: The Bard of Avon and the Church of Rome* (San Francisco: Ignatius, 2008).

33. Clare Asquith, *Shadowplay: The Hidden Beliefs and Coded Politics of William Shakespeare* (New York: PublicAffairs, 2005).

34. *King Lear*, act 3, sc. 4. F.T. Prince, "Soldiers Bathing"; see page 349.

35. *Hamlet*, act 1, sc. 5.

perplexed living. Did any other writer, aside from Dante, have anxiety about the afterlife stamped through such a quantity of their lines? Did anyone explore so extensively the possibilities of human transformation and degradation through free will and the battling of supernatural powers (*Macbeth*, *Hamlet*—even *King Lear* in its pre-Christian doom)? Isn't this very Catholic? Even the fact that so many claim Shakespeare for their own says to me that he was all-embracing of human emotion, far-reaching—that is, catholic, and therefore, Catholic.

Even, or especially, non-Catholic writer and poet Ted Hughes located the formula for the "Tragic Equation" of Shakespeare's plays firmly in the context of a newly Puritan world where the Old Faith was being suffocated. Hughes recognized Shakespeare's engagement with a madness that, even unconsciously, bewailed the brutal eradication of the feminine (what Catholics would identify as Mary's unique role) from spiritual life.[36] But Hughes' argument sprang also from a pagan perspective. And every critic has their bias. Certainly the debate about Shakespeare's religion will not be solved within these pages. My inclusion of his work will be both opposed and applauded. But, for my cuts and keeps, there can be no doubt that Shakespeare's poetry beats with a Catholic heart.

The reader will also note that Oscar Wilde is with us, even though he did not convert until his deathbed. There is ample evidence, however, that the question of Catholic conversion was on his mind throughout his life, and even more importantly, his poems became Catholic before he himself did (Edith Sitwell falls into this category too). Spiritual awakening does not always run in tandem with acquisition of a certificate of Baptism. I would go so far as to say that "The Ballad of Reading Gaol" is

36. Ted Hughes, *Shakespeare and the Goddess of Complete Being* (London: Faber, 1992).

a poetic document of a man's conversion, and one of the most extraordinary and transformational poems in the Catholic canon: "How else but through a broken heart / May Lord Christ enter in?"[37] The same claim for Catholicism, in a curious, more mysterious sense, is made for Wallace Stevens' "To an Old Philosopher in Rome."[38] Like Wilde, Stevens' conversion was very late.

But otherwise, the reader will have the sense that every poet here knew what it was like to stand in line at the confessional, to hold a rosary, and to light a candle. None of these poems or poets are, as far as I am aware, ambivalent about the faith in the deepest sense. My modeler's knife had to shave off the poets who rejected the faith; those who did not want to be called Catholic; those who stated bluntly that their poetry was not Christian; and those whose great work was written before their conversion and was not, in essence, Catholic. Again, this meant pain and sacrifice.

Poet or "Narrator"

It is unfashionable of me to consider the heart or mindset of the poet. In an age where Roland Barthes heralded "the death of the author," the biography of the poet should not matter one jot to the text we are left with.[39] Most poets themselves are allergic to being given labels. The celebrated American poet Elizabeth Bishop reportedly refused to let her work be used in anthologies if she was only included because of her sex. I can't think of many professional poets who would care to be branded solely "Catholic" in their writing. Any prefix colors the readers'

37. Oscar Wilde, "The Ballad of Reading Gaol." See page 305.
38. See page 394.
39. Roland Barthes, "The Death of the Author," *Aspen*, no. 5–6 (1967).

interpretation of their work; it potentially closes off meaning. But the poet's faith, I concluded, *does* matter in a book that is made up of Catholic poems.

Poets will often moan that readers think their poems are true accounts of their lives. I've moaned on this count myself. By and large, we should never confuse the narrator of a work of literature with the author. Poets often adopt a persona, or they write in dramatic form. Still, poetry remains among the most personal of all the genres. It seems to spring directly from the heart and from heaven. It boils and seethes with the writer's purest obsessions. Geoffrey Chaucer and William Langland are examples of authorial distance and dramatization within these pages (though Langland, in particular, seems to be personally on fire at certain moments).[40] But throughout the centuries, from Clement of Alexandria to Elizabeth Jennings, what we see most is that poets are singing what touches them directly. The poetry here is urgent and relevant, precisely because it is those things to the writer. And when poets write on issues of faith, this seems to be magnified. There is no pretense. There is no posturing.

Bearing all this in mind, I've often taken the controversial step of speaking of the poet as the voice in the poem. Let's not be coy: we know that Oscar Wilde was in prison before he wrote "The Ballad of Reading Gaol," and that John Henry Newman was lost when he wrote "The Pillar of the Cloud." This poetry is real life.

It is also great.

---

40. See "The Monk" from *The Canterbury Tales*, page 153, and Passus 20 of *Piers Plowman*, page 148.

Great Catholic Poetry

As an adjective, *great* has an earth-shattering quality. Of course, we recognize the greatness of most of these poems, even out of a Catholic context. Much space in these pages has been devoted to Dante Alighieri's *Divine Comedy*, a poem that has been claimed as the greatest ever written.[41] It must certainly be seen as the greatest Catholic poem. No other poem transfuses so much blood into doctrine, so much drama into the unknown, so much flesh into the invisible. No other poem so expertly dramatizes the fundamental impetus of any sincere Catholic: to avoid hell and to see the face of God.

But standing there with my modeling knife, greatness was, perhaps, the most confusing quality to look for in a Catholic poem. Not many people, for example, would argue that Pope St. John Paul II was a great poet. Even fewer would make that claim for St. Thérèse of Lisieux. But the criteria for great Catholic poetry is, I discerned as I sculpted, subtly different than the claims made for great poetry in general.

A Poetry of Witness

During the Stalinist terror, the great Russian Orthodox poet Anna Akhmatova had to wait in line outside the prison in Leningrad to see her incarcerated son. She waited for months, standing in the cold with little hope. She stood with other mothers and wives, all freezing, all worn out by waiting and pain. One day she was recognized in the line by another woman, who asked the poet if she could write about what was happening. Akhmatova said that she could, and she would. And

41. See pages 103–142.

then a smile, Akhmatova wrote, passed over what had once been the woman's face.[42]

Part of the greatness of certain poems resides in their unflinching witness of historical events. This does not mean to say that any old lines written about a historic event will do, nor that Henry Walpole should be compared with Anna Akhmatova. But given that Walpole was splattered with blood as he witnessed a brother hanged, drawn, and quartered in the city of London (and given that he had a good degree of poetic talent), it is fitting that his poem about that event should be included with the Catholic greats.[43]

Spiritual Greats

But poetic greatness of the unconventional kind is not only found in historical accounts. When a man has a talent for writing and is a committed and gifted contemplative; when he is shot, and forgives his would-be assassin; when his prayer life is so evidently mystical that his insights seem to come directly from the divine—when that man writes poems, they are riveting witness to a place of transcendence that few have seen. I have no reservation whatsoever in calling much of John Paul II's poetry great.

In a similar vein, when a girl in a Carmelite convent becomes one of the greatest spiritual guides of our age; when she enters into the Catholic imagination with her poetry and adds to that imagination, carrying it into the next century—I feel that excluding her from the Catholic poetic canon would be unwise. Thérèse of Lisieux used poetry not as a sophisticated

---

42. Anna Akhmatova, "Instead of a Preface," introduction to *Requiem*.

43. "Upon the Death of M. Edmund Campion, One of the Society of the Holy Name of Jesus." See page 197.

worker of language but as a master of poetic ideas. Without her poetic vision, the canon would be diminished.

Greats in Translation

In any case, we are not lacking in poems that, by any standard in this world, would be called great. We have Shakespeare; we also have those trailblazers Chaucer and Hopkins, among many others who would be considered a part of the mainstream canon. But I was often frustrated by the knowledge that many great Catholic poems existed in other languages for which we lack even adequate translations.

It is only because of the endeavor and mastery of his translators that Dante's journey is accessible to most of us and can be happily included here. As I gathered my "soft clay" of contents, I had to be careful only to include poems in translation that truly rendered at least something of the greatness of the original. We are very fortunate to have resonant English-language versions not only of Dante but of Paul Claudel, Thomas Aquinas, and Mario Luzi, among others. Despite this being primarily an English-language volume, I'm glad to note that the poets come from twenty countries (and from the first century through the end of the twentieth).

The Minor and the Living

Any century will yield only a small number of great poems. It must be the biggest temptation for the editor of an anthology such as this to haul minor poets out of the dim past, dust them off, and claim them as great. I have striven, earnestly, not to do so. If a poet within these pages is minor, then the poem itself will have something of that linguistic compression and reach that indicates greatness.

A difficult but wise decision was made to exclude living poets. Greatness needs to stand some test of time; dust needs to settle on the fashions and predilections of the day to see what endures. But readers should be in no doubt that fine poetry that engages with the Catholic tradition is being written. More, it is flourishing, and will certainly yield more "greats" in the years to come.

The Female Voice

And the number of great female Catholic poets is set to grow in what has been sometimes rocky ground over the last centuries. "I would venture to guess that Anon, who wrote so many poems without signing them, was often a woman," asserted Virginia Woolf.[44] In the interests of balance in this anthology, it would be heartening to think so. The very feminine eighth-century "Donal Og" would seem to back this up. But in any case, the Church was, from medieval times on, a place where women could give poetic voice to their feelings and insights (not without risk; how much more quickly they were burnt at the stake for a fresh take on things would be for a historian to assess). The beguines Hadewijch and Mechthild of Magdeburg are evidence of enormous female poetic innovation and daring. By the Reformation, things were getting quieter for women. Poetry has been, historically, associated with authority. Its forms and allusions often required a classical education. Yet even as women became more generally educated, they tended to blossom (with notable exceptions) in the genre of the novel rather than poetry.

44. Virginia Woolf, *A Room of One's Own* (New York: Harcourt, 1989), 49.

The arrival of Modernism in the twentieth century changed this. Traditional poetic forms were often seen as narrow and stale. Traditional language was perceived as a way of keeping women down—and out of literature. While some women used formal poetry energetically, free-verse poets like Sylvia Plath and Adrienne Rich actively sought to tear down the old structures and to write the female perspective with authority. Such women would never have been Catholic! The Church was seen as perhaps the greatest Western ally of patriarchal suppression. Plath, who became a kind of high priestess of women's poetry after her suicide, killed off the specter of her own dead father in "Daddy" and ushered in an age not just of fatherlessness but Fatherlessness, for women who wanted full control over their minds and bodies. In the force of the first, second, and third feminist waves, the very essence of what it means to be a woman has been chewed over, subverted, redefined—and in the recent surge of gender theory, almost destroyed. It is perhaps only in the twenty-first century that Catholic women poets are fully understanding the freedom given to them by *having* a Father, and seeing that the Church, far from working against them, could potentially be their greatest defender.

Powerful women poets who kept the faith—like Edith Sitwell, Denise Levertov, and Elizabeth Jennings—have been, sadly, rarer than they should have been. My prediction for the twenty-first century is that we will see more greats of their kind "break[ing] / through earth and stone of the faithless world," to use Levertov's words, and from corners of the world less represented in this anthology.[45]

45. Denise Levertov, "Ikon: The Harrowing of Hell." See page 425.

In conclusion, and in handing the reader over to voices from across the millennia, I can only say that collecting these poems has been a kind of dream. Any misgiving anyone may harbor for the forceful shaping of those words *great Catholic poems* must melt in the face of what has emerged. For it is only when we cut that we see the true form of what we have been searching for. And she is beautiful: lyrical, sensual, didactic, historical, mystical, and epic. Every poem here has edified, enchanted, and sustained me, much as "Donal Og" did all those years ago. The process has convinced me even more that poetry is the sister of prayer, that it thins the veil between ourselves and God. I commend these poems to anyone seriously interested in beauty and our dance with the eternal.

A Word about Order and Poetic Terms

The poems are arranged in chronological order—though if poems were written or published very close together, I have on occasion arranged them thematically.

This anthology is aimed at those who want to know more about poetry but may feel bewildered by it, as well as those who read poetry regularly or write it and study it. On the whole, I'm of the belief that jargon can be unhelpful, but when I have used a literary term, I have mostly supplied an example from the poem or given an explanation. A simple glossary for relevant terms can also be found at the back of the book.

100 Great Catholic Poems

"The Magnificat"

(c. 85)

THE VIRGIN MARY, RECORDED BY LUKE

Our first poet is the Virgin Mary, the woman who magnifies God as any real poet tries to do, whether they are conscious of it or not. These verses of Luke 1:46–55 began as part of an oral tradition: the words were spoken spontaneously—or perhaps they were sung in an eruption of joy—when Mary visited her cousin Elizabeth with news of her miraculous pregnancy. Of course, there may be naysayers on this matter. There will be people who insist that this was a literary device of Luke's, albeit a divinely inspired one: that he put the words into Mary's mouth when he wrote his Gospel.

But it should not be hard to believe that these words came from Mary herself. We can imagine the excitement of any woman pregnant with her first child—the jubilation, the wonder, the fear, the love, the uncertainty. We might then *try* to imagine those feelings magnified in someone who knew that she had conceived the Messiah. She was pregnant with a nation's hope. She was so steeped in love for God that joy must have overshadowed every emotion. Of course she sings!

So much poetry is contained in that verb of the first line: to proclaim or "to magnify." It not only speaks of Mary's desire to glorify the Lord; it implies that she is immaculate, lucid as a pane of glass. In her song, Mary is magnifying patterns and connections in history and the world around her. Her theme is God's plan of salvation.

3

In these lines, we also hear Mary's deep familiarity with
Scripture. She would have known the language of the Psalms
and the exultations of women such as Hannah before her (see
1 Sam. 2:1–10). The linguistic patterns and images of those
Hebrew songs and Psalms would have come quickly to Mary's
tongue. The Magnificat is, in effect, Mary's own psalm. It
offers praise; it thanks God for his deeds and "reversals": the
poor being lifted up, the rich being taken down. She uses
the parallelism typical of the Psalms: one idea expressed or
developed in different ways over multiple lines. "My soul
proclaims the greatness of the Lord," she sings, and on the heels
of that thought, "my spirit rejoices in God my Savior." In the
similarity of the lines' structure, Mary offers a parallel between
soul and spirit, magnification and rejoicing. She is bubbling over
as a person does when she is in love and trying to find as many
ways as possible to express the way she feels.

The images of God and Israel contained within this poem
would have been second nature to Mary through her prayer
life—the strong arm of the Almighty, Israel as his servant—even
as she was physically forming the ultimate image of God in her
womb. Everything she says echoes both backward (to Abraham
and God's promises to him) and forward (to their fulfillment
in the coming of the Messiah). Mary, even more than Judith,
who also sang (see Jth. 16:1–17), is a woman of unsurpassable
instrumental importance—even necessity—for God's plan. She
is a woman stepping into a psalm and becoming the living proof
of its truth. She is a woman on fire; she is inspired. How could
the words belong to anyone but her?

"The Magnificat"

THE VIRGIN MARY, RECORDED BY LUKE

My soul proclaims the greatness of the Lord,
my spirit rejoices in God my Savior
for he has looked with favor on his lowly servant.

From this day all generations will call me blessed:
the Almighty has done great things for me,
and holy is his Name.

He has mercy on those who fear him
in every generation.

He has shown the strength of his arm,
he has scattered the proud in their conceit.

He has cast down the mighty from their thrones,
and has lifted up the lowly.

He has filled the hungry with good things,
and the rich he has sent away empty.

He has come to the help of his servant Israel
for he has remembered his promise of mercy,
the promise he made to our fathers,
to Abraham and his children for ever.

"A Hymn to Christ the Savior"

(198)

CLEMENT OF ALEXANDRIA

The author of this poem was born less than a century after
St. Luke recorded the Magnificat and as few as fifty years
after St. John penned his Gospel. Clement of Alexandria was a
convert who recognized the importance of Greek philosophy
in Christianity, and he left us tomes of writing on the faith.
His famous trilogy's middle book, *Paedagogus* ("The Teacher"
or "The Instructor"), is an almost inexhaustible disquisition
on Christ as guide in our lives. Clement proceeds to advise us
on matters such as eating, drinking, "how to conduct ourselves
at feasts," and even laughing and sleeping. At the end of his
discourse in prose, Clement slides seamlessly into prayer. But
even this was not enough. He had to write a poem.

The original Greek of these stanzas is wild and irregular. It
exclaims! It jolts in short lines. This is a hymn and an explosion.
It demonstrates that only poetry can give voice to the passion
within us that will not die. As St. Augustine would later say,
"Singing is for the one who loves."[1]

Writings about Christ (and his mother, as we will see later
on) have to break the bounds of ordinary language. Everyday
words cannot begin to describe or praise him. Clement does
dwell on the more usual descriptions of Jesus that characterize
his divinity: "Lord of all time and space," "Word eternal,"

---

1. Augustine, *Sermons* 336.1; PL 38:1472.

"Fount of mercy." But effective poems can never stop with this type of abstraction.

So the poet Clement plunges into a litany of metaphors for Christ as teacher, a list of visual images that we know from our lives and can therefore better understand. He draws from Scripture yet manages to be fresh and riotous. We are the "colts untamed" of the first line, and Christ is our bridle. We are the "unwandering birds," and he is our wing navigating us through choppy air. The metaphors continue: Christ is our shepherd, our rudder; he is our husbandman, bit, and fisherman; and, of course, he is our King.

In the third section, we see a mother, the "bride of grace," feeding her flock with the "milk of wisdom." Isaiah 49 speaks of God as a breastfeeding mother, and this image is picked up enthusiastically by Catholic poets through the centuries. But these lines also might suggest to us the Virgin Mary, who is the Church and who has also been identified with Wisdom.

The first and last stanzas are all about imploring God that the faithful be brought together to sing a passionate doxology—words that praise God—making this a poem that teaches, petitions, exults, and soars. In this English translation, the impetus is charged by an urgent beat of two, three, or four stresses a line and a riot of rhyme.

"A Hymn to Christ the Savior"

Translated from the Greek by Dr. William L. Alexander

CLEMENT OF ALEXANDRIA

I

    Bridle of colts untamed,
        Over our wills presiding;
    Wing of unwandering birds,
        Our flight securely guiding.
    Rudder of youth unbending,
    Firm against adverse shock;
    Shepherd, with wisdom tending
        Lambs of the royal flock:
    Thy simple children bring
    In one, that they may sing
    In solemn lays
    Their hymns of praise
With guileless lips to Christ their King.

II

    King of saints, almighty Word
    Of the Father highest Lord;
    Wisdom's head and chief;
    Assuagement of all grief;
    Lord of all time and space,
    Jesus, Savior of our race;
    Shepherd, who dost us keep;
        Husbandman, who tillest,
    Bit to restrain us, Rudder
        To guide us as Thou willest;
Of the all-holy flock celestial wing;
Fisher of men, whom Thou to life dost bring;

From evil sea of sin,
    And from the billowy strife,
Gathering pure fishes in,
    Caught with sweet bait of life:
Lead us, Shepherd of the sheep,
    Reason-gifted, holy One;
King of youths, whom Thou dost keep,
    So that they pollution shun:
Steps of Christ, celestial Way;
    Word eternal, Age unending;
Life that never can decay;
    Fount of mercy, virtue-sending;
Life august of those who raise
Unto God their hymn of praise,
        Jesus Christ!

III

Nourished by the milk of heaven,
To our tender palates given;
Milk of wisdom from the breast
Of that bride of grace exprest;
By a dewy spirit filled
From fair Reason's breast distilled;
Let us sucklings join to raise
With pure lips our hymns of praise
As our grateful offering,
Clean and pure, to Christ our King.
Let us with hearts undefiled,
Celebrate the mighty Child.
We, Christ-born, the choir of peace;
    We, the people of His love,
Let us sing, nor ever cease,
    To the God of peace above.

9

"Hymns on the Nativity of Christ in the Flesh" (Excerpt)

(Fourth century)

ST. EPHREM

The Eastern Catholic Church has always understood the importance of *wonder*: that essential awe that believers feel in the face of mystery. St. Ephrem's poetry works with this wonder. It marvels, it praises, and, crucially, it defends truth. The best poets and theologians know that poetry and theology are blood relatives. And for this future Doctor of the Church, explanations of the faith flowered easily into poetic form.

Ephrem the Syrian was born close to the fiery cradle of Christianity. Christ's word was alight and spreading. It had knocked Saul down to the ground and blinded him (see Acts 9:1–9); it made people refer to themselves for the first time as "Christian." As heresies cropped up like ragweed, they threatened a true understanding of Christ's two natures—both fully human and fully divine. Part of the way that Ephrem fought theological error like this was through poems that spoke the true nature of God's mystery. These were then set to popular folk tunes so that people could effortlessly memorize them.

Reading his "Hymns on the Nativity of Christ in the Flesh," we sometimes hear echoes of Mary's "Magnificat" (just as her words echoed the Old Testament). We're confronted with the same subversive ideas: the rich becoming poor, the high becoming lowly. But this time we're not talking about the fortunes of the populous, but about God himself! He is the rich

one entering the womb of his mother and coming out poor.
He is the "clother" of everything and everyone, who comes out
into the world "naked and bare." These Old Testament ideas of
reversal seem even more shocking when faced with this image of
God as a vulnerable baby. Here we see, in image and metaphor,
the core of the faith. The poem is disconcerting, and it's meant
to be.

Look at how the lines take the wind out of the heretics'
sails. The awe—the *wonder*—is embedded in the fact that Mary,
a human being, carried God; she fed God; she gave God milk
to drink. Just like Mary in her scriptural song, Ephrem uses
parallelism in the phrases: they are repetitive in structure and
meaning ("The Lord entered her . . . / The Word entered her");
they are easy to remember and internalize.

Further on, in the last stanza, Ephrem has Mary herself
speak. She is a harp, waiting to be played. If something so great
can become so small, if something so difficult can be made so
easy, then her "little mouth," too, she says in a further echo of
the Magnificat, can magnify his glory.

As you read, imagine how these lines would sound to ears
that deny Christ's humanity or his divinity and Mary's role
as the Mother of God. Listen to the unique stillness of the
first lines of the third stanza; it is like the quiet of the solitary
cave where Ephrem lived. We can almost hear the Incarnation
happening. This is poetry that penetrates and illuminates
Scripture. It sings with wonder.

Note:
The language of the translation has been updated here, and line breaks
created by the editor.

"Hymns on the Nativity of Christ in the Flesh" (Excerpt)

From the translation of the Armenian/Syriac by Rev. J.B. Morris
From Hymns VIII and X

ST. EPHREM

Mary gained in You, O Lord, the honors of all married women.
She conceived You within her without marriage.
There was milk in her breasts, not after the way of nature.
You made the thirsty land, suddenly, a fountain of milk.

If she carried You, Your mighty look made her burden light.
If she fed You it was because You were hungry;
if she gave You drink it was because You were thirsty;
when she embraced You, You, the coal of mercies,
did willingly keep her bosom safe.

Your Mother is a wonder.
The Lord entered her, and became a servant:
the Word entered her, and became silent within her;
thunder entered her, and His voice was still:
the Shepherd of all entered her; He became a Lamb in her,
and came forth, bleating.

The belly of Your Mother changed the order of things,
O You that orders everything!
The rich went in, He came out poor.
The high One went in, He came out lowly.
Brightness went into her and clothed himself
and came out a despised form.

The Mighty went in and clad himself with fear from the belly.
He that gives food to all went in to know hunger.
He that gives drink to all went in to know thirst.
The clother of all came forth from her naked and bare.

....

"And as the harp waits for its master,
my mouth waits for You. May the tongue of Your Mother
bring what pleases You;
and since I have learnt a new Conception by You,
let my mouth learn in You, O newborn Son,
a new song of praise.

And if hindrances are no hindrances to You
and since difficulties are easy to You
as a womb without marriage conceived You
and a belly without seed brought You forth
it is easy for a little mouth to multiply Your great glory!"

"Against the Burden of Sickness"
(Excerpt)

(382–390)

ST. GREGORY OF NAZIANZUS

The fourth-century author of this poem was, in some ways, a very modern man. When we hear of the travails of the early Church Fathers, or the stories of the saints suffering exile, stoning, or worse, it can be easy to imagine them as heroic or coolly courageous. Gregory of Nazianzus gives a subtly different impression. He went through a lot, he felt it keenly, and he liked to tell about it—especially in verse.

After a stormy sea crossing to Athens, Gregory had a dramatic conversion to the faith and went on to become a brilliant theologian and bishop. But there's no doubt that Gregory, like so many of the early theologians, had a poet's soul. He was certainly prolific in his poetry, writing thousands of lines in Greek. His title, "the Theologian," was given to him because he taught the truths of the faith through his verse (a *theologos* literally means "one who speaks God's word").

The poem below (which is taken from a longer sequence) lets us taste Gregory's complex rhetorical style in modern language—and to witness what, in some ways, would have been new frontiers in poetry. Gregory was one of the first Christian autobiographical poets. As moderns, we have become very used to poets baring their own lives—their illnesses, depressions, or loves—in their poems. It is easy to assume that this is new. But, in fact, Gregory was doing this just three hundred years after Christ.

As both a sensitive man who needed solitude but also had a desire to teach and a holy man who was very reluctant to take holy orders, Gregory cheerfully admitted to referring everything to himself. But rather than his poetry being self-absorbed, Gregory never failed to make Christ the touchstone and interpreter of his troubles and victories. In other words, through poetry, he elevated his own earthbound story of prevarication and suffering to something that was a part of the epic history of salvation.

In this poem, we are treated to the rare sound of a saint and future Doctor of the Church complaining. Gregory is also scared. Has Christ abandoned him? When Gregory was ill, he could not preach and take care of his flock—and what pain this caused! The image of his people as a baby attempting to feed from a dry breast is riveting. His longing to preach and to compose sermons is palpable. Later in the poem, he confronts the devil head on, then implores Christ to rescue him, casting himself as a character in Scripture, like Lazarus or the paralytic. The way that he laments and then practically commands Christ to help him is both disarmingly fresh and very ancient. Angst like this is easily found in the Psalms, and Gregory's depressive downs are matched by similarly Psalm-like praise that has wings. It is reassuring and touching to see that even the holiest can rave. The whole range of human emotion, Gregory seems to say, is fit for God to hear.

"Against the Burden of Sickness" (Excerpt)

Excerpted and adapted by the editor from a translation
from the Greek by Suzanne Abrams Rebillard

ST. GREGORY OF NAZIANZUS

I groan because I seem forgotten
by the quickening eye of glorious Christ.
    He cared for me so much, honored me,
even in the womb of my pure mother;
    he pulled me from sufferings and icy seas.

I groan because I've dropped the reins—
    I'm with the people, but they can't be with me.
I fed them sermons with the triple-
    light that issued from my tongue, but now,
as a weaning babe in his mother's arms

    pulls on a dry nipple with his thirsting lips,
so also from my tongue the people languish. . . .

. . . .

Mold covers my books, my homilies are left
    unwritten, and who will have the charity
to finish them? Everything has perished

while I live, and existence for me is feeble,
weaker than a ship cut loose from moorings.
    But even if you drag me, demon of deep groans,
never will my heart bend to you; rather,
    preserved, I will sink into mother-earth.

Let the worm have me as the serpent's price.
   You can take my skin; my soul remains intact.
What's stamped inside, God's image, I will hand to Christ,
   you slayer of men, you, who were beaten
even before you bound great Job, since through

   his troubles God crowned him with a holy victory
and doubled what you shattered. Such is the way
   of gentle Christ. But Lord, now command
that I be left unharmed; your word is my cure.
   I am a new Lazarus among the dead; but shout,

"Rise!" and let this corpse reanimate. Bedridden,
   I am a new paralytic, but shout, "You are of solid limb!"
and I will rise, lifting my bed high. I steal a cure
   with my own hands from your tasseled hem.
Swiftly check the flow of blood from my wasted flesh.

"Splendor Paternae Gloriae"

(Fourth century)

ST. AMBROSE

In how many Masses have the words "Light from Light" been
spoken to illustrate the consubstantial relationship between
God the Father and his Son? It is one of the most penetrating
and illuminating poetic images ever penned. And yet, the
human mind being what it is, even these words can become
dulled by familiarity. In this poem, which uses those very words,
we have a modern translation of an ancient morning hymn, and
it unspools the creedal image "Light from Light" as it turns to
Christ as light, asking for him to pour, in turn, upon us as we
contemplate the difficulties of the day to come.

The image of Christ as Light from Light, which St. Ambrose
draws on to such effect in the first two stanzas of this poem,
was vitally important to emphasize in the fourth century. This
Milanese priest became bishop in the swell of the heresy of
Arianism, which denied precisely that relationship between
Father and Son. Ambrose's poetry, like Ephrem's, was meant to
quash theological error—but also to do what only poetry can
do: to brand indelible images onto the mind and heart. Like
Ephrem's hymns, Ambrose's poem was set to music to make it
even more memorable.

In the twentieth century, the convert Thomas Merton
deliberately took away the element of song in this translation.
Merton's modern style involves using freer structures, working

against old forms and jolting readers into *seeing* images to which they may have become inured.

The result is a muscular poem of praise and petition to the Trinity. The first stanza is fairly metrically regular and full of delicious repetition (light/Light), just like the original—a dance of sounds and ideas. And then in the second stanza, Merton breaks his lines and brings us up short on purpose. Be aware that the last word of a line is often the most important; it has its own significance. Merton wants us to linger on "Sun." He wants us to register its double meaning (Sun/Son).

The Spirit should pour into our senses, says Ambrose, and Merton keeps this as a short line—"Flood our souls!"—so we have the space to soak that sensation up. Our blood, says Merton, should not be "chilled" by any betrayal of Truth— sticking closely to the sense of what Ambrose first wrote ("fraudis venena nesciat") but adding "chill" and "blood" to charge the words with physicality. "Blunt the teeth that hate our life": Merton's word choices could come from the Psalms; they demand as much as petition.

There is so much poetic and theological intertwining of ideas here that it can be hard to let every point soak in. The writer/petitioner sees his inner life reflected in the changing light of day: dawn as a clean conscience, noon as intense faith, and dusk as a challenge to spiritual clarity. The day also represents the consubstantial nature of the Father and the Son, and their outpouring in the Spirit.

In Merton's hands, this famous piece no longer has the feel of a musical hymn. It has recovered some of the freshness that it had when it was first scratched onto Ambrose's page. The short words and lines, and no less revolutionary images, shine.

"Splendor Paternae Gloriae"

Translated from the Latin by Thomas Merton

ST. AMBROSE

Thou splendor of the Father's glory,
Pouring upon us light drawn from Thy Light:
Thou art the Light of lights, the fount of brightness
And to our days the daylight-giving Day.

O Thou true Sun,
Shine down in everlasting glory,
And with the radiance of Thy Spirit
Flood our souls!

Cry we, then, in our prayers, to the Father,
Father of glory everlasting, and of mighty grace
To save us from the treachery of sin:

Confirm our souls in works of strength
And blunt the teeth that hate our life,
And contradict our evils into blessings
Giving us grace to do His will.

Govern our spirits, rule them Father!
Build in our chaste and unrebellious bodies
Fires of faith!
Nor let the poison of betrayal chill our blood.

And may Thy Christ our life-bread be,
His faith our drink:
Then slake we our glad spirits
Wisdom's mighty wine.

So may this day go by in joy,
And may our cleanness be like its clean dawn
Our faith like the high noon:
But let no evening shroud our minds in dusk.

But now the dawn begins to show:
O may true Day soon shine full upon us:
The Day which is the Father in the Son,
The Son in Him, His Word, entire.

And so, to God the Father, glory,
And to His only Son,
Together with the Spirit, the Paraclete,
Now and forever and ever.

Amen.

"Late Have I Loved Thee" from the *Confessions*

(c. 400)

ST. AUGUSTINE

Most people, religious or not, will at some point hear the words "Late have I loved thee." They were written by St. Augustine as part of his conversion story at the beginning of the fifth century in North Africa. Despite having a Christian mother (St. Monica), Augustine became a Manichean—a religious sect that saw the world as split between the goodness of spirit and the evil of matter. It took a penetrating experience of God to heal that worldview. We are fortunate in having these lines, which capture that experience. Though technically presented as prose, they are written in such wrought and exalted Latin that they defy and transcend the genre.[1] Even in translation, these lines have permeated the consciousness of humanity, crossing cultures and time. They do what only poetry can do: they compress an event full of philosophical, theological, and emotional ramifications into few words.

The structure of the first phrase, "Late have I loved thee," impresses itself on the mind: the stress falls on "late" and "loved," and those two words are also bound by the alliterative *l*. "Late" as the first word ushers in regret and longing—a sense of urgency. "Loved" then ushers in fulfillment and joy—a sense of peace. These same words are quickly repeated because the author's praise and love transports the lines from the simple

---

1. Line breaks added by the editor.

22

communicative act of prose; they make their own music. The acoustic repetitions are hypnotic: "late," "love," "I outside," "I sought thee outside." And the opposing concepts of the first two stanzas ("so ancient, so new"; "within me," "outside") swing the reader's emotions with the intensity of Augustine's own crashing, soaring epiphany as he recognizes that God is as loveable, and therefore as knowable, as all the things that he had been chasing in the world.

For despite love affairs and success in literary endeavors, despite friends and pleasures, the author of these lines experienced a certain restlessness. In his autobiography, Augustine recounts stealing a sack-load of pears from a tree as a teenager—not because the fruit was truly tempting but for the vivifying thrill of transgression. Even then, perhaps unconsciously, he was pulling at God's sleeve. But God waited until exactly the right moment to fill him with his presence.

These lines illustrate not only the beauty of the faith and the substance of our relationship with the divine, but also the essence of poetry itself—because God reaches us in the way of poetry. The bored boy who stole the pears had been deaf and blind to God. He had not noticed God's fragrance, nor tasted God, nor felt God touch him. But these lines chart the breaking open of every sense by God and to God, almost as if God were a ripe summer fruit. The former Manichean is understanding that God (despite being invisible) is both within the world and within himself, and that God can be known through love, in a tangible way. Like the blind man of Scripture, Augustine's sight is given to him. He also hears for the first time. God's breath, like Christ's breath on the Apostles, is in his mouth like the kiss of life. The touch of God has ignited his soul. Like great poetry, God, Augustine discovers, enters every sense.

Yet there is no complacency nor satisfaction here. The word "late" resounds like a deep bell throughout. He is left thirsting, panting. The poem is dynamic—the hunger, for Augustine, has only just begun, as for a man who smells food after a long fast and quickens his step.

"Late Have I Loved Thee"

Translated from the Latin by Francis J. Sheed

ST. AUGUSTINE

Late have I loved Thee,
O Beauty so ancient and so new;
late have I loved Thee!

For behold Thou were within me,
and I outside;
and I sought Thee outside

and in my unloveliness
fell upon those lovely things
that Thou hast made.

Thou were with me
and I was not with Thee.
I was kept from Thee by those things,

yet had they not been in Thee,
they would not have been at all.
Thou didst call and cry to me

and break open my deafness:
and Thou didst send forth
Thy beams and shine upon me

and chase away my blindness:
Thou didst breathe fragrance upon me,
and I drew in my breath

and do pant for Thee:
I tasted Thee, and now hunger
and thirst for Thee:

Thou didst touch me,
and I have burned for Thy peace.

"The Deer's Cry"
(St. Patrick's Breastplate)

(Fifth century / eighth century)

ST. PATRICK

Here is a poem that is also a prayer. Yet here is a prayer that, in its music and heightened language, is certainly a poem. And, as a poem, it has often been made into song. Attributed to St. Patrick, the fifth-century evangelizer of Ireland, it is thought to have been written in the eighth century. Both timelines are likely.

The story has it that, during his mission in Ireland, Patrick was journeying with fellow evangelists, aware of druids lying in wait to attack them along the road. As they walked, Patrick prayed this *lorica*, which means both "breastplate" and "prayer for protection." Legend maintains that as they passed the hidden druids, Patrick and his men appeared as a doe with her fawns and so were left unharmed. That is why the piece is known as "The Deer's Cry."

The poem is made up of plenty of repetition at the start of lines, which would work well to the beat of a long march down life's dark, unpredictable roads. The repetition also makes the piece easy to memorize: no doubt it was handed down orally until the point when it was more formally recorded—hence the two dates of composition.

In its initial pronouncement, the poem has the sound of a creedal declaration. It states, in its first four beefy lines, the essence of what Patrick would have been declaring to the

Irish: the existence of God who is three yet one. The rhyme of "threeness" with "oneness" and assonance of "Creator" and "Creation" hits us with the punch of truth. The words also let us know that this God, who is the Author of everything, is somehow infused into us. We rise stronger with him, as though he is the very marrow and sap of our bones.

Patrick then goes on, with hypnotic litany, to personally identify with the mysteries of Christ: how his baptism, burial, descent, and ascension are fused into us with the morning light. The lists come thick and fast: of the Communion of Saints, of the natural world—at which point the lines become what we might call Franciscan, although St. Francis himself was still some centuries off—of risks and perils, and of every which way that God can protect and guide us.

An author who certainly inspired Patrick was St. Paul, who wrote the first "Breastplate" in his Letter to the Ephesians: "Put on the whole armor of God" (Eph. 6:11). In all Patrick's inventories of heights and depths, there is a Pauline ring: "For I am convinced that neither death, nor life, nor angels, nor rulers, nor things present, nor things to come . . ." (Rom. 8:38). No stone of danger is left uncovered by this prayer-poem. It is a summoning of all the supernatural host. It is a fabulous example of how articulation of both fear and belief strengthens us: it is, in action, Paul's exhortation that we call on the name of Jesus (Rom. 10:13).

Patrick's famous "Christ with me, Christ before me" are lines that demonstrate poetry's role in clothing the invisible. Speak his name, Patrick says; locate him in every place. Recital of this piece is palpably fortifying. By naming and petitioning in such language, we are empowered in God.

"The Deer's Cry" (St. Patrick's Breastplate)

Translated from the Irish by Whitley Stokes,
John Strachan, and Kuno Meyer

ST. PATRICK

I arise today
Through a mighty strength, the invocation of the Trinity,
Through belief in the threeness,
Through confession of the oneness
Of the Creator of Creation.

I arise today
Through the strength of Christ's birth with His baptism,
Through the strength of His crucifixion with His burial,
Through the strength of His resurrection and His ascension,
Through the strength of His descent for the Judgement
    of Doom.

I arise today
Through the strength of the love of Cherubim,
In obedience of angels,
In the service of archangels,
In hope of resurrection to meet with reward,
In prayers of patriarchs,
In predictions of prophets,
In preachings of apostles,
In faiths of confessors,
In innocence of holy virgins,
In deeds of righteous men.

I arise today
Through the strength of heaven:
Light of sun,
Radiance of moon,
Splendour of fire,
Speed of lightning,
Swiftness of wind,
Depth of sea,
Stability of earth,
Firmness of rock.

I arise today
Through God's strength to pilot me:
God's might to uphold me,
God's wisdom to guide me,
God's eye to look before me,
God's ear to hear me,
God's word to speak for me,
God's hand to guard me,
God's way to lie before me,
God's shield to protect me,
God's host to save me
From snares of devils,
From temptations of vices,
From everyone who shall wish me ill,
Afar and anear,
Alone and in multitude.

I summon today all these powers between me and those evils,
Against every cruel and merciless power that may oppose
    my body and soul,
Against incantations of false prophets,
Against black laws of pagandom,
Against false laws of heretics,
Against craft of idolatry,
Against spells of women and smiths and wizards,
Against every knowledge that corrupts man's body and soul.

Christ to shield me today
Against poison, against burning,
Against drowning, against wounding,
So that there may come to me abundance of reward.
Christ with me, Christ before me, Christ behind me,
Christ in me, Christ beneath me, Christ above me,
Christ on my right, Christ on my left,
Christ when I lie down, Christ when I sit down,
    Christ when I arise.
Christ in the heart of every man who thinks of me,
Christ in the mouth of everyone who speaks of me,
Christ in every eye that sees me,
Christ in every ear that hears me.

I arise today
Through a mighty strength, the invocation of the Trinity,
Through belief in the threeness,
Through confession of the oneness
Of the Creator of Creation.

"Columcille Fecit" (Columba Made It)

(Sixth century)

ST. COLUMBA

St. Columba, one of the three patron saints of Ireland, is credited with writing this haunting poem of exile and acceptance—and his story of holiness through exile is certainly all over it. The name "Columba" means "dove" in Latin, and so does the Hebrew name "Jonah." It's hard not to see commonality between these two men, the Jonah of Scripture and Columba, both so bound by sea and circumstance, so in thrall to their passions and the waves. Both were called to places they did not want to be.

We know that Columba was forced out of his native land for causing bloodshed, though the exact circumstances of his exile are disputed. In any case, he was commanded never to set eyes on Ireland again. He did return (apparently to settle a dispute) but, legend has it, traveled blindfolded so as not to disobey his sentence.

Whatever wild stories abound, this poem has survived so many centuries because the issue of exile is central to the human condition. We are the "banished children of Eve," says the Salve Regina. "Life is your barque and not your home," said St. Thérèse of Lisieux.[1] This poem is embedded in that same sense of holy displacement and longing.

There are two distinct parts to the piece. The first has fourteen repetitions of "That . . ." at the start of the line, in

---

1. Thérèse of Lisieux, *Story of a Soul: The Autobiography of St. Thérèse of Lisieux*, trans. John Clarke (Park Ridge, IL: Word on Fire Classics, 2022), 89.

response to the wishful thinking of being back in Uchd Ailian (a place in Ulster). "That," as a stressed beat in "That I might," is wonderfully hypnotic to repeat. The listener cannot get lost in the scene; he is constantly pulled back to the fragility of the dream and to the strength of the narrator's wanting.

The sea is vividly personified here: it chants music to God. This tendency to ascribe praise and holiness to nature is a feature of religious poetry that we will see again. The waters are not neutral; as a part of creation, they are blessed. They are doing what they were always meant to do, and in this way they are like Mary: they are magnifying the Lord. The alliteration of "waves," "wide," and "world" through this first section, coupled with the sibilance of "sparkling strand" and "sorrow," conjure the wind's sounds and the glittering spray of those northerly islands. The sea's "roar by the side of the church" is so easy to hear. Through these observations, the saint arrives at wishing his "mystical name" to be "Cul ri Erin," or "back turned to Ireland." In other words, he desires his penance, and what he has lost, to be carved into his soul by a name.

The litany moves then to "at times," which alters the rhythm like a change in gear, as the saint spells out how he envisages a life of goodness—foraging, reading, singing the Psalms, fishing and giving food to the poor. God, we are told, in conclusion, has given him the best advice—but we're not told precisely what that might be! We can infer, however, that his heavenly Father is dealing with him in great nearness, honesty, and simplicity—a just reward for the honed-down life of the exile whose feet find stability only in God.

Notes:
Cul ri Erin: back turned to Ireland.
carcair: solitary cell.
duilisc: seaweed.

"Columcille Fecit" (Columba Made It)

Translated from the Irish by Michael O'Curry

ST. COLUMBA

Delightful would it be to me to be in Uchd Ailiun
    On the pinnacle of a rock,
That I might often see
    The face of the ocean;
That I might see its heaving waves
    Over the wide ocean,
When they chant music to their Father
    Upon the world's course;
That I might see its level sparkling strand,
    It would be no cause of sorrow;
That I might hear the song of the wonderful birds,
    Source of happiness;
That I might hear the thunder of the crowding waves
    Upon the rocks;
That I might hear the roar by the side of the church
    Of the surrounding sea;
That I might see its noble flocks
    Over the watery ocean;
That I might see the sea-monsters,
    The greatest of all wonders;
That I might see its ebb and flood
    In their career;
That my mystical name might be, I say,
    Cul ri Erin;
That contrition might come upon my heart
    Upon looking at her;

That I might bewail my evils all,
    Though it were difficult to compute them;
That I might bless the Lord
    Who conserves all,
Heaven with its countless bright orders,
    Land, strand and flood;
That I might search the books all,
    That would be good for my soul;
At times kneeling to beloved Heaven;
    At times psalm singing;
At times contemplating the King of Heaven,
    Holy the chief;
At times at work without compulsion,
    This would be delightful.
At times plucking duilisc from the rocks;
    At times at fishing;
At times giving food to the poor;
    At times in a carcair:
The best advice in the presence of God
    To me has been vouchsafed.
The King whose servant I am will not let
    Anything deceive me.

"Donal Og" (Young Donald)

(Eighth century)

ANONYMOUS

Although not overtly about spiritual matters, this poem beats, emphatically, with a Catholic heart: a heart that is also female, Irish—and broken by a man called Donal Og, or Young Donald. It tells the old story of abandonment, a tale of exquisitely reckless promises and a woman left undone.

In its structure and image the poem reminds us of both the opulence of the Song of Solomon and the music of the Psalms. "You promised me," laments the narrator at the beginning of the second stanza, and again at the start of the third and the fourth. "The voice of the LORD" says Psalm 29, and then again, "The voice of the LORD," and again and again, the lines begin this way. Repetition is hypnotic and builds emotion. We repeat both what we love, and what we cannot comprehend.

The narrator of this poem is detailing promises that are extravagant to the point of fairy-tale. The images of her despair when these promises are not fulfilled are plucked straight from the heart of Christianity—the lamb she is left to look on, the Well of Loneliness she goes to in her unquenchable thirst. The narrative climaxes at the sixth stanza, Palm Sunday—shortly after, we infer, the point at which she gave herself physically to young Donald. She is kneeling in church, reading the account of Christ's Passion and gazing at her human beloved. It can sound sacrilegious to compare one's own passion to the Passion of Christ. It can sound trivial, even, to say that she is mooning over some lad across the aisle as the most agonizing Scripture is read. But isn't this what human hearts are often about? She is distracted, consumed even, by her own passions as God is being led to his death.

Now the poem reflects the darkness that has come, the human promises that have been broken. Again, the narrator repeats, riffs, but this time on the darkness that has come over her. Just one image will not do. And what images! Her heart is as black "as the sole of a shoe left in white halls," she says, which is reminiscent of the "fine white court" he promised her—an image that makes us think, in turn, of the longing for the "courts of the LORD" in Psalm 84:2. Then begins the final repetition, the inventory of what he has taken from her. Is there any rendition in poetry that is as devastatingly accurate as this of a broken heart? Her bearings are gone—her west and her east, her sun and her moon—and the final line opens up the challenge of hope for every believer: she fears the loss of God.

Why? It has been theorized that the speaker is on the brink of suicide. It seems more likely that she has (unfounded) fears of being forever cut off from God because of her goings on with Donald. Society at that time would have been harsh in the extreme to young women in the narrator's position, and she may be seeing God in the same merciless light. But mostly, it seems to me, this line is about despair and darkness—a place we fall to where we can no longer easily perceive God at all. Donald's abandonment has brought her to the edge of nothing. It can be hard to realize that, in those circumstances, God is nearer than ever.

Translated by Lady Gregory, writer and patron of Irish theater in the early twentieth century, this version poignantly retains the lyrical flavor of the original eighth-century Irish, just as intended. The reader will note the strange change of tenses in the first two lines, from present to past (which seems to bring the hurting of last night into the "now"). Lady Gregory was occupied with teaching and reclaiming the Irish language. She would have been careful not to over-Anglicize or mistakenly "correct" the diction of the piece. What remains is one of the most hauntingly beautiful poems in Western literature.

"Donal Og" (Young Donald)

Translated from the Irish by Lady Augusta Gregory

ANONYMOUS

It is late last night the dog was speaking of you;
the snipe was speaking of you in her deep marsh.
It is you are the lonely bird through the woods;
and that you may be without a mate until you find me.

You promised me, and you said a lie to me,
that you would be before me where the sheep are flocked;
I gave a whistle and three hundred cries to you,
and I found nothing there but a bleating lamb.

You promised me a thing that was hard for you,
a ship of gold under a silver mast;
twelve towns with a market in all of them,
and a fine white court by the side of the sea.

You promised me a thing that is not possible,
that you would give me gloves of the skin of a fish;
that you would give me shoes of the skin of a bird;
and a suit of the dearest silk in Ireland.

When I go by myself to the Well of Loneliness,
I sit down and I go through my trouble;
when I see the world and do not see my boy,
he that has an amber shade in his hair.

It was on that Sunday I gave my love to you;
the Sunday that is last before Easter Sunday.
And myself on my knees reading the Passion;
and my two eyes giving love to you for ever.

My mother said to me not to be talking with you today,
or tomorrow, or on the Sunday;
it was a bad time she took for telling me that;
it was shutting the door after the house was robbed.

My heart is as black as the blackness of the sloe,
or as the black coal that is on the smith's forge;
or as the sole of a shoe left in white halls;
it was you put that darkness over my life.

You have taken the east from me; you have taken the
    west from me;
you have taken what is before me and what is behind me;
you have taken the moon, you have taken the sun
    from me;
and my fear is great that you have taken God from me!

"The Dream of the Rood" (Excerpt)

(Eighth century)

ANONYMOUS

In this remarkable dream-poem, one of the oldest works of English literature, the narrator hears the story of the Crucifixion, not from a bystander or human participant, but from the "rood," or cross, itself.

The entire text begins with the narrator describing a dream that he had of a shining cross bedecked with jewels and stained with ancient blood. The cross then takes up the tale (we begin our excerpt from this point) describing Good Friday from the unique point of view of a tree in a wood who is cut down by ruthless men and made to bear God on a hillside.

No one has told the tale quite this way. Even Jesus looks different within these lines. We are used to many different portrayals of Christ. Post-Renaissance representations of Jesus can make him seem almost effeminate. (Think of Batoni's famous Sacred Heart painting.) There is no such softness here. Writing in the tradition of Anglo-Saxon heroic poetry, this Christ is "bold" and rushes to climb upon the cross, underlining the free choice that he made in his death. In turn, the cross—who could, he says, have fallen down and "crushed them all"—responds to Christ's bravery by accepting its essential, excruciating role and staying straight.

The personification of this piece of wood is powerful and heartbreaking: "We were both reviled, we two together." In their intimacy and embrace, the cross and its bearer are like two lovers.

We are witness in this poem to Christ's death, the consequential darkness, the hands reaching to Jesus, and then the laying in the tomb. Our excerpt proceeds to recount how the cross was, from then on, revered and the power it has. At the end of the full text, the narrative returns to the dreamer, who tells of how his devotion to the cross is strengthened.

At the core of this remarkable writing is the recognition of the power of relics. Touch is powerful. The hem of Christ's robe was a channel of grace for the bleeding woman (Luke 8:43–48). Catholics use relics as a way of being near to God (by being near to those who are nearest to him). The cross, of all things, is closest to Jesus: it bore him up for the salvation of the world.

What a joy this poem is to read—not just in its depiction of Christ as a forceful hero, but in its robust Anglo-Saxon diction with its short, powerful words: "Standing bespattered with blood, driven through with spikes": the repetitive punch of the *b* and the *sp* impact the reader as a shadow of how Christ's agony impacted that wood. As ancient alliterative verse, this is one to read aloud, especially on Good Friday. You can practically hear the wood creak under the weight of Glory.

"The Dream of the Rood" (Excerpt)

Translated from the Old English by Burton Raffel

ANONYMOUS

"It was long ago (but I won't forget)
When they came to the forest and cut me down,
Pulled me out of the earth. Ruthless enemies took me
And made me a mocking show, forced me to hold their thieves.
They swung me up on their shoulders, planted me into a hill,
Set me deep and straight. I saw the Lord of the world
Boldly rushing to climb upon me
And I could neither bend, nor break
The word of God. I saw the ground
Trembling. I could have crushed them all,
And yet I kept myself erect.
 The young hero, God Himself, threw off His garments,
Determined and brave. Proud in the sight of men He mounted
The meanest gallows, to make men's souls eternally free.
I trembled as His arms went round me. And still I could
 not bend,
Crash to the earth, but had to bear the body of God.
I was reared as a cross. I raised the mighty
King of Heaven and could not bend.
They pierced me with vicious nails. I bear the scars
Of malicious gashes. But I dared not injure any of them.
We were both reviled, we two together. I was drenched with
 the blood that gushed
From the hero's side as His holy spirit swept to Heaven.
 Cruel things came to me there
On that hill. I saw the God of Hosts

Stretched on the rack. Clouds rolled
From the darkness to cover over the corpse,
The shining splendour; a livid shadow
Dropped from Heaven. The creation wept,
Bewailed His death. Christ was on the cross.
   From distant lands the eager ones came
To the hero. And I watched it all,
Wrapped as I was in sorrow I bent to their reaching hands,
Humble with courage. They carried away almighty God,
Raised Him out of His torment. I was abandoned of men,
Standing bespattered with blood, driven through with spikes.
They laid down the weary-limbed God, stood and watched
     at His head,
Beholding Heaven's King as He lay in quiet sleep,
Exhausted with hardship and pain. And they started to carve
     a sepulchre,
With His slayer watching. They chiselled the tomb of the
     brightest stone
And laid the Lord of victories there. And then they sang
A dirge, miserable in the dusk, and wearily began the journey
Home, leaving their mighty prince. He was left alone.
   Yet after His followers' voices drifted
Away, we crosses went on weeping,
Standing in place. The beautiful corpse
Grew cold. Then they came to cut us
Down. We shuddered with fear, and fell.
They buried us deep in a pit, but the faithful
Heard of my fate, and came, and dug me
Out, and adorned me with silver and gold.
   Only now can you hear, oh Heaven-blessed man,
How evil men have brought me pain
And sorrow. For now a season has come

When the men of all the world, and all creation,
Shall honor and worship me far and wide,
Pray to this symbol. The Son of God
Suffered on me, and made me glorious,
Towering on earth, so that every man
Who holds me in awe can be healed at my touch.
I was made to be a bitter punishment,
Loathed by men until I led them
To the road of life, and opened its gates."

"To Mary and Her Son" (Excerpt)

(Eighth century)

BLATHMAC, SON OF CÚ BRETTAN

Love poetry to the Virgin, seen as early as St. Ephrem, was developing in heartrending and theologically illuminating ways across the island of Ireland through the early centuries of the Irish Church. This text was discovered as recently as 1953, but thankfully all of its more than 259 stanzas have been translated into English, and here we have an excerpt addressed directly to Our Lady.

The original author, Blathmac, son of Cú Brettan, would have been a highly educated man, possibly a cleric, from a wealthy and powerful family. He evidently had a lively devotion to Mary. His love for her in the poem is spontaneous, familiar, and fresh. Like a father or a sweetheart, he calls her his "little white-necked one" and a "shining precious jewel."

Yet the poem is also testimony to certain aspects of Marian devotion that were evidently well-embedded in Ireland at that time. He wants Mary to go and "get" his petitions from her son. The words are illustrative of the chain of the faithful: Mary closest to Jesus, the poet close to Our Mother, and in turn the handing down of blessings and intercessions to anyone who recites the poem as prayer at bedtime and sunup. Furthermore, he prays that anyone who gives voice to it fasting on a Friday not go to hell, "provided only that it be [said] with full-flowing tears."

The nub of the poem is here with this reference to tears: the poet suggests that those who "keen," or "caoineadh," the death of Christ should be saved. Keening has a long tradition in Ireland. It was a passionate, barefoot wail of lament over the dead, eulogizing him or her and railing against what, or who, may have caused their demise. Though this wild emoting was usually women's work, the poet implies it is for everyone, and it seems as though there was a setpiece to be ritualistically rehearsed: "the full keen." Or perhaps by "full," the poet simply means that our hearts should be thoroughly grief-stricken and contrite. Simply put: he wants the world to keen enthusiastically with Mary and himself.

These stanzas demonstrate well Mary's unique vocation as chief keener for Christ's agony. When hearts are hardened, it is Mary who can show the faithful the undying grief particular to a mother. She leads us, the poet is saying, both in devotion to Christ and in sorrow. It behooves us to spend time talking with her, to "pity [her] heart's darling." She is the key that unlocks his love; she is the echo of his agony. Through her, we learn that most important empathy: compassion for the suffering God. Once we glimpse this suffering, we can begin to understand how we are loved.

This poem is also an example of the breathtaking multitude of songs, litanies, and praises written for Our Lady throughout the medieval period across Europe. Poetry was the most fitting expression of love for a woman with whom the ordinary person could identify, yet, at the same time, someone so elevated that being close to her meant having the ear of God.

"To Mary and Her Son" (Excerpt)

Translated from the Irish by James Carney

BLATHMAC, SON OF CÚ BRETTAN

May I have from you my three petitions,
beautiful Mary, little white-necked one;
get them, sun amongst women,
from your son who has them in his power.

That I may be in the world till old
serving the Lord who rules starry heaven,
and that then there be a welcome for me
into the eternal, ever-enduring kingdom.

That everyone who uses this as a vigil prayer
at lying down and at rising,
that it may protect him from blemish in the other world
like a breastplate and helmet.

Everyone of any sort who shall recite it
fasting on Friday night,
provided only that it be with full-flowing tears,
Mary, may he not be for hell.

When your son comes in anger
with his cross on his reddened back,
that then you will save
any friend who shall have keened him.

For you, beautiful Mary,
I shall go as guarantor:
anyone who says the full keen,
he shall have his reward.

I call you with true words,
Mary, beautiful queen,
that we may have talk together
to pity your heart's darling.

So that I may keen the bright Christ
with you in the most heartfelt way,
shining precious jewel,
mother of the great Lord.

Were I rich and honoured
ruling the people of the world to every sea,
they would all come with you and me
to keen your royal son.

There would be beating of hands
by women, children and men,
that they might keen on every hill-top
the king who made every star.

"The Song of Manchán the Hermit"

(Ninth century)

ANONYMOUS

This song—voiced for the monk St. Manchán—is written in the Irish tradition of nature poetry. It has its roots in that island's green hills and grey cliffs, and the sunset's sifting light. With disarming simplicity, the first couplet asks God for a simple dwelling place in this idyll.

The poet might not be the first Irish author, and is certainly not the last, to wish for such a thing. There is a sacred view of nature that runs through the poetic Irish tradition, whether formally religious or not. W.B. Yeats' famous "I will arise and go now, and go to Innisfree" expresses a yearning similar to Manchán's for solitude in nature.[1] Yeats would have been aware of the tradition in which he was writing. And, as a contemporary of Yeats, the translator of this poem, Eleanor Hull, would likely have read "Innisfree" before translating Manchán's first lines: "I wish . . . for a hidden hut in the wilderness." But there is a crucial difference between Manchán's dream and the pastoral ideal that so engaged Yeats in the nineteenth century.

First, let's look at how Hull makes Manchán's description of nature so appealing. Her mellifluous alliteration ("all-blithe lithe little lark"; "wide, wild woodland") prettifies the subject. She fashions the piece in a jaunty rhythm of seven stressed beats per line in rhyming couplets, and sprinkles assonance within

---

1. W.B. Yeats, "The Lake Isle of Innisfree."

the lines ("rich with gracious gifts"). The poem becomes a frolic with simple, joyous cadence.

But the core of the hermit's song is the eremitical life that germinated after the conversion of the country by St. Patrick. Christian history is bursting with accounts of hermits living in caves, in harsh conditions. Alongside those dank realities, this poem is witness to a vision of nature that sees every leaf and creature as a gift from God; that finds hope in the harmony of man and his environment. What makes this possible is a longing beyond even Yeats' mystical fantasy.

For the voice of this poem also has a decisive desire for the structures of the Church: "the hours," the Mass, the song. He is as nourished by prayers as he is by his spare meals and the keeping of hens and bees. God's position above and through everything is pivotal to his peace. The pool in Manchán's wilderness is the Spirit purifying the soul, and the birds are chanting psalms. His words are no less a glorification of the joys of country living, but they recognize humankind's need for sanctifying grace.

A yearning for the ascetic life is also a mark of the piece. Readers may recognize the elements of retreat described here: the need to pare down company (twelve "wise" men—the number of Christ's disciples), food, and clothing to what is good and necessary.

We cannot be certain about the identity of the original author of this poem. St. Manchán lived in the seventh century, but the text is dated at around the ninth. It may be that this is the expression of a holy dream by "Anon."

"The Song of Manchán the Hermit"

Translated from the Irish by Eleanor Hull

ANONYMOUS

I wish, O Son of the Living God, O Ancient Eternal King,
For a hidden hut in the wilderness, a simple secluded thing.

The all-blithe lithe little lark in his place, chanting his
    lightsome lay;
The calm, clear pool of the Spirit's grace, washing my sins away.

A wide, wild woodland on every side, its shades the nursery
Of glad-voiced songsters, who at day-dawn chant their sweet
    psalm for me.

A southern aspect to catch the sun, a brook across the floor,
A choice land, rich with gracious gifts, down-stretching from
    my door.

Few men and wise, these would I prize, men of content and
    power,
To raise Thy praise throughout the days at each canonical hour.

Four times three, three times four, fitted for every need,
To the King of the Sun praying each one, this were a grace,
    indeed.

Twelve in the church to chant the hours, kneeling there twain
    and twain;
And I before, near the chancel door, listening their low refrain.

A pleasant church with an Altar-cloth, where Christ sits at the
    board,
And a shining candle shedding its ray on the white words of
    the Lord.

Brief meals between, when prayer is done, our modest needs
    supply;
No greed in our share of the simple fare, no boasting or ribaldry.

This is the husbandry I choose, laborious, simple, free,
The fragrant leek about my door, the hen and the humble bee.

Rough raiment of tweed, enough for my need, this will my
    King allow;
And I to be sitting praying to God under every leafy bough.

"Pangur Bán"

(Ninth century)

AN IRISH MONK

This poem about a cat and a monk is commonly found in poetry anthologies of all kinds. The author was a ninth-century Irish religious studying in Germany, who wrote it among notes about St. Paul, angels, and other far loftier matters than his cat. At first glance, the piece appears to be a simple, whimsical distraction from study. The poet's subject is something most of us can identify with: the harmonious companionship of a pet. But, in fact, the verses reflect a sacred understanding of the world on the part of the monk; they signal that he is a soul anchored in his vocation.

Before we go deeper, let's consider the structure on which the ideas hang. Each of the eight stanzas of this wonderful translation is made up of two rhyming couplets, and each line has an unwavering count of four beats apiece, in the rolling rhythm of trochaic tetrameter (Dùm-da dùm-da dùm-da dùm-da—though, here, the last unstressed syllable is left off), which gives the air of a nursery rhyme. The two characters of the poem are, of course, the monk and Pangur Bán (or "White Pangur"), the cat. Early on, a kind of mirroring is set up between the two, which is emphasized by the repetition of words and syntax ("Hunting mice is his delight, / Hunting words I sit all night"). Mouse-hunting and word-catching are compared throughout the piece: the wall of the room, through which a mouse may pop its head, is compared to the wall of knowledge from where an epiphany may spring. Man and little beast are both practicing deeply satisfying arts.

Our relationship to animals can be both endearing and problematic. How much is the monk romanticizing, albeit humorously, this dear companion? How much do any of us project thoughts and motives onto the indecipherable consciousness of our pets? Animals do not have eternal souls nor intellect; perhaps we go too far in thinking that they are like us. Four hundred years before Thomas Aquinas wrote his *Summa* with its thoughts on the Ladder of Being, there seems little doubt that our Irish monk recognized the hierarchy that places Pangur above the trees that would have been growing outside his window, and himself above Pangur, and the angels that he was studying above himself, and God above them all. But this hierarchy connects and reveals likenesses as well as differences, and, as this poem shows, our Irish monk would have been very conscious of these similarities between creatures (similarities that poets are in the business of finding). "From the greatness and beauty of created things comes a corresponding perception of their Creator" (Wis. 13:5). Pope Francis uses this quotation in the introduction of his encyclical *Laudato Si'*, emphasizing the unbreakable bonds among all things that are made. Though animals may not be created in the image of God, they are still a part of the world that is groaning for renewal in Christ (Rom. 8:22). Nothing is left out of this renewal—not even Pangur (nor his mouse).

Pangur Bán is the monk's little echo, his small reflection. He makes the monk conscious of both his own greatness and his own smallness in the world. And, as the monk turns "darkness into light," he, in turn, is striving to reflect his maker.

"Pangur Bán"

Translated from the Irish by Robin Flower

AN IRISH MONK

I and Pangur Bán, my cat,
'Tis a like task we are at;
Hunting mice is his delight,
Hunting words I sit all night.

Better far than praise of men
'Tis to sit with book and pen;
Pangur bears me no ill-will,
He too plies his simple skill.

'Tis a merry thing to see
At our tasks how glad are we,
When at home we sit and find
Entertainment to our mind.

Oftentimes a mouse will stray
In the hero Pangur's way;
Oftentimes my keen thought set
Takes a meaning in its net.

'Gainst the wall he sets his eye
Full and fierce and sharp and sly;
'Gainst the wall of knowledge I
All my little wisdom try.

When a mouse darts from its den,
O how glad is Pangur then!
O what gladness do I prove
When I solve the doubts I love!

So in peace our tasks we ply,
Pangur Bán, my cat, and I;
In our arts we find our bliss,
I have mine and he has his.

Practice every day has made
Pangur perfect in his trade;
I get wisdom day and night
Turning darkness into light.

"The Seafarer" (Excerpt)

(Tenth century or earlier)

ANONYMOUS

"This tale is true, and mine." So begins this tenth-century
narrative in the voice of a sailor. They are compelling first
words—and ironic: literary critics have argued about the
authorship of this piece for centuries. Is it simply a sailor's
story, or is it a larger allegory about the human struggle? Or a
metaphor for Christian life? Was it written by one writer? Or
were the Christian thoughts at the end tacked on by someone
else? In the final analysis, we can only know this: the tale is true
and belongs to all of us.

Surely the poem leaks Christianity from every word and
wind-blown pore. It is a tale of suffering "in a hundred
ships, / In a thousand ports, and in me." These travails are,
at first, visited on the speaker: the sea *takes him*. And what
hardship! Cold, hail, ice, and hunger sear the page. No one
can read this poem and stay warm. But the lines speak of more
than the elements. They initially describe a "world blown clear
of love."

We know that Christianity is steeped in language of the
sea, a place both of great trouble and of rescue: "Your way was
through the sea, your path, through the mighty waters"
(Ps. 77:19). Jesus calmed the waters and walked on them. Like
Jonah, we fear perdition in "the heart of the seas" (Jon. 2:3)—a
place, potentially, of no sign nor bearing.

And yet, in the second part of this piece, there is a change of register. The sea becomes the sailor's choice; he has grown to love it. The poem then becomes a story of chosen asceticism, a purging of all worldly delights. He has decided to cast himself as much on God's providence as on the waters, "wondering what Fate has willed and will do." Fruits, birdsong, and women—all these the sailor renounces for the ocean and a certain longing.

By line fifty-eight ("And yet my heart wanders away"), the joys of God have become inextricable from the excitement of the sea. It seems the dicey voyage cuts pleasure to the bone, makes of it something eternal, something utterly dependent on God. The rest is all distraction. The saltwind has scrubbed clean the speaker's eyes; he sees the pith of life.

The last twenty-three lines have the ring of nuggets from Proverbs. Is this the same sailor who shivered and carped his way through the first section? He has taken on the almost supernatural calm of the Desert Fathers after fasting and solitude. He has lived an epic Lent. He knows exile and that the journey home is to God alone. Notably, the twentieth-century poet Ezra Pound produced a masterful version of this same poem, working the alliteration and robust, heightened sounds of the original Old English to great effect. But he rooted out the religious element. The result was a brilliant, raw meditation on mortality. But unlike this more faithful rendition, it was all fasting and no rejoicing. It offered no supernatural dimension and no way home.

"The Seafarer" (Excerpt)

Translated from the Old English by Burton Raffel

ANONYMOUS

This tale is true, and mine. It tells
How the sea took me, swept me back
And forth in sorrow and fear and pain,
Showed me suffering in a hundred ships,
In a thousand ports, and in me. It tells
Of smashing surf when I sweated in the cold
Of an anxious watch, perched in the bow
As it dashed under cliffs. My feet were cast
In icy bands, bound with frost,
With frozen chains, and hardship groaned
Around my heart. Hunger tore
At my sea-weary soul. No man sheltered
On the quiet fairness of earth can feel
How wretched I was, drifting through winter
On an ice-cold sea, whirled in sorrow,
Alone in a world blown clear of love,
Hung with icicles. The hailstorms flew.
The only sound was the roaring sea,
The freezing waves. The song of the swan
Might serve for pleasure, the cry of the sea-fowl,
The death-noise of birds instead of laughter,
The mewing of gulls instead of mead.
Storms beat on the rocky cliffs and were echoed
By icy-feathered terns and the eagle's screams;
No kinsman could offer comfort there,
To a soul left drowning in desolation.

And who could believe, knowing but
The passion of cities, swelled proud with wine
And no taste of misfortune, how often, how wearily,
I put myself back on the paths of the sea.
Night would blacken; it would snow from the north;
Frost bound the earth and hail would fall,
The coldest seeds. And how my heart
Would begin to beat, knowing once more
The salt waves tossing and the towering sea!
The time for journeys would come and my soul
Called me eagerly out, sent me over
The horizon, seeking foreigners' homes.
But there isn't a man on earth so proud,
So born to greatness, so bold with his youth,
Grown so brave, or so graced by God,
That he feels no fear as the sails unfurl,
Wondering what Fate has willed and will do.
No harps ring in his heart, no rewards,
No passion for women, no worldly pleasures,
Nothing, only the ocean's heave;
But longing wraps itself around him.
Orchards blossom, the towns bloom,
Fields grow lovely as the world springs fresh,
And all these admonish that willing mind
Leaping to journeys, always set
In thoughts traveling on a quickening tide.
So summer's sentinel, the cuckoo, sings
In his murmuring voice, and our hearts mourn
As he urges. Who could understand,
In ignorant ease, what we others suffer
As the paths of exile stretch endlessly on?

And yet my heart wanders away,
My soul roams with the sea, the whales'
Home, wandering to the widest corners
Of the world, returning ravenous with desire,
Flying solitary, screaming, exciting me
To the open ocean, breaking oaths
On the curve of a wave. Thus the joys of God
Are fervent with life, where life itself
Fades quickly into the earth.
....

We all fear God. He turns the earth,
He set it swinging firmly in space,
Gave life to the world and light to the sky.
Death leaps at the fools who forget their God.
He who lives humbly has angels from Heaven
To carry him courage and strength and belief.
A man must conquer pride, not kill it,
Be firm with his fellows, chaste for himself,
Treat all the world as the world deserves,
With love or with hate but never with harm,
Though an enemy seek to scorch him in hell,
Or set the flames of a funeral pyre
Under his lord. Fate is stronger
And God mightier than any man's mind.
Our thoughts should turn to where our home is,
Consider the ways of coming there,
Then strive for sure permission for us
To rise to that eternal joy,
That life born in the love of God
And the hope of Heaven. Praise the Holy
Grace of Him who honored us,
Eternal, unchanging creator of earth.
Amen.

"Prayer 88" of the
Book of Lamentations (Excerpt)

(c. 977)

ST. GREGORY OF NAREK

This poem from a tenth-century classic of mystical literature is more than a poem. It is a man. At least, that is what the poet wanted it to be. Gregory of Narek's *Lamentations* are meant to *embody* himself, and his message is meant to represent his very soul.[1] This notion of word-as-body began, of course, with the Word coming into the world through Jesus Christ. God, we might say, was the first to write the body. Catholic poets from Gregory to Vittoria Colonna have taken up this theme.

Gregory also wrote his *Lamentations* as a "life-giving salve for the sufferings of body and soul."[2] In Narek's native Armenia, the book became second only to the Bible and has been viewed as a cure for all kinds of sickness. Traditionally, sufferers sleep with a copy under their pillows. Like his forebear Gregory of Nazianzus, this Gregory was a sensitive man who suffered from periods of illness himself; in fact, he probably wrote many of the lamentations when he was ailing.

The ambition of this poem is, then, heady to say the least: it is a man; it is a medicine. It is also, as we shall see, a sacrifice. In this section, all of these aims are realized poetically as he

---

1. See Gregory of Narek, *Book of Lamentations* 54e, in *Speaking with God from the Depths of the Heart: The Armenian Prayer Book of St. Gregory of Narek*, trans. Thomas J. Samuelian (Yerevan, Armenia: Vem, 2002).

2. *Lamentations* 3e.

discusses what he hopes for from the existence of this book and its role in the confession of sins.

Language's powerful role in prayer is evident here. The "sighs and contrition" that Gregory writes of are inarticulate, but it is the poet's mission to give those feelings words and make them as monumental as stone. There is nothing like *saying* how you have sinned to better understand and confess it. There is nothing like opening the mouth in praise, to praise better and more wholeheartedly.

In the lines that follow, Gregory says, in effect, that he wants his book to be a record of himself and his most sublime praise ("may it rise as incense") and a vehicle of his preaching. This is the way the text becomes both sacrifice and man (or a record of the man, as the more prosaic might wish to put it). "May I be deemed to live / through the continued existence of this book": the pages immortalize Gregory.

Gregory recalls the ever-praying angels at the throne of God singing "Holy, holy, holy" as he envisions the text standing on the threshold between himself and God as a kind of advocate or fellow angel. This poetry not only represents Gregory; it *finds* him through his own words. It accuses him; it judges him. It, like Christ, shines a burning light on all that he is before God. It renders him naked. It is, if you like, the best examination of conscience ever. This is the way that the text is a medicine: through confession, the soul is healed.

God has no need of words. He knows Gregory. He can heal Gregory. But we need words. We need to praise, to confess, to implore, and to adore. Words act on and through us, strengthening belief, increasing knowledge, seducing with beauty. This poem is a baring of the soul and an appeal for salvation. The lamentations are a voice to speak through us.

"Prayer 88" of the *Book of Lamentations* (Excerpt)

Translated from the Armenian by Thomas J. Samuelian
Sections B–C

ST. GREGORY OF NAREK

Words unto God from the Depths of My Heart

And now, accept these prayers of sighs and contrition,
as you inhale the scent of this bloodless sacrifice of words,
    king of heaven.
Bless and sanctify the letters of this book of lamentation,
and fix your seal upon it,
as an eternal monument of
servanthood along with others pleasing to you.
May it stand before you forever,
and echo in your ears constantly.
May it be pronounced upon the lips of your chosen,
and may it be spoken by the mouths of your angels.
May it be spread before your throne,
and may it be offered in your sacred temples.
May it rise as incense in the houses of worship dedicated
to your name, and may it give fragrance at the
altar of your glory.
May it be kept among your treasures
preserved in your estate.
May it be recited to the ears of all generations,
and may it be preached to all peoples.
May it be inscribed on the doors of the mind
and imprinted on the threshold of the senses.

As if alive and in person, may it recount
the iniquities I have confessed.
And although I shall die in the way of all mortals,
may I be deemed to live
through the continued existence of this book.
May it by your will, Lord,
be protected from destruction,
that it might be for me, the condemned,
an ever watchful judge, fair accuser,
that reprimands with vigor and blames with rigor,
that relentlessly criticizes and sternly shames me,
that pitilessly hands me over to
the unbribable executioner from whom there is no escape
like a ruthless informant coldly exposing me to
the whole world.
May it loudly trumpet my faults in confession
without break or end.

This book will cry out in my place, with my voice,
as if it were me.
It will uncover what is covered up and
proclaim secrets.
It will lament what has been done and
extol what has been forgotten,
reveal the invisible and relate scandal,
preach about the depths of the soul
and tell of sins.
It will lay bare the unseen and display the shape of
what is hidden.
Through this book may traps be explored and
pitfalls be discovered.
May unspeakable faults be confronted and

the traces of evil wrung out.
May the life of your grace and mercy reign, O Christ.
May my dry bones be preserved in your treasury
so that at the time of eternal life,
at the dawn of that first spring light,
on the day of renewed splendor,
through your dew my soul might again stir,
with your immortal salvation
and according to the hope held out in your inspired
Scriptures, may I again become green and blossom,
and send up shoots of spiritual goodness
that will never dry out.

And to you, Savior, and to your Spirit,
of the same essence as the Father,
to your united lordship and your inexplicable Trinity,
all glory and adoration
with mystic praise
forever.
Amen.

"We Awaken in Christ's Body"

(c. 1009–1022)

ST. SYMEON THE NEW THEOLOGIAN

When Symeon the New Theologian was a young man in tenth-century Galatia, he had an experience of God that changed everything. After a day's work as a servant, he would pray, repeating "God, have mercy on me, a sinner." One such evening, the room became filled with so much divine light that it was all around him, even underneath him, so he could not be sure if he was walking on land—but he was not scared of falling. He seemed to almost *become* the light. He had no doubt that this was a manifestation of the divine.

Such full-on experiences of God's presence are rarely trouble-free. For the rest of his life, the monk Symeon insisted on the crucial importance of contemplation for true knowledge of God. Everyone, he maintained, could have experiences such as his. It's no surprise that he clashed with his superiors on this and other matters and was exiled for the last years of his life.

Yet what this poem shows us is that Symeon's burning closeness to God is healthily anchored in Scripture. Symeon would become known as the New Theologian (and be fully embraced by the Church). His theology was simply love, and contemplation was his way of being with the Beloved.

In this breathtaking translation of St. Symeon's fifteenth hymn, we have seven stanzas of the simplest language. The poem is almost devoid of the similes and metaphors that dazzle us in other verse (only at line ten does God appear as a "flash

68

of lightning"). It is as if the poet is telling us something so clear, yet so magnificent, that he can't risk fudging it with poetic acrobatics.

The poet is fully absorbed in that greater reality of Christ being in us and us in him. This concept is, of course, a biblical given: "Those who eat my flesh and drink my blood abide in me, and I in them," said Christ himself (John 6:56). This poem unpacks that line from John and shows it in a physical way. As it begins, the reader can imagine a man waking on a sunny morning and feeling life returning as he stretches each limb. But the "poor hand" that he stretches is Christ's hand; more, it is all of him, as Christ does not come to us in bits and pieces. Christ even enters his foot. As the narrator begins to move, the realization that Christ is in him saturates him. "Do my words seem blasphemous?" Symeon wonders. Yet the idea that we can all experience God like this is nothing other than perfectly true. We take him in on our tongues; he lives in us, and in turn we live in him.

But Symeon is not only talking about post-Communion prayer. He is telling us about the putting on of Christ (Rom. 13:14) and how this opening up to him at every moment casts light within our darkest places, how it purifies and heals us. Perhaps Christians are used to this kind of talk. What makes Symeon's poem so astonishing is his dwelling on each physical part. The importance of a foot, a hand! This is divinization seen at the anatomical level. And, in the deep joining of our bodies and souls, we know it to be true.

Perhaps what this poem describes is similar to what Symeon felt when that light washed over his room one evening: an awakening, an utter transformation of every part of his being.

"We Awaken in Christ's Body"

Translated from the Greek by Stephen Mitchell

ST. SYMEON THE NEW THEOLOGIAN

We awaken in Christ's body
as Christ awakens our bodies,
and my poor hand is Christ, He enters
my foot, and is infinitely me.

I move my hand, and wonderfully
my hand becomes Christ, becomes all of Him
(for God is indivisibly
whole, seamless in His Godhood).

I move my foot, and at once
He appears like a flash of lightning.
Do my words seem blasphemous?—Then
open your heart to Him

and let yourself receive the one
who is opening to you so deeply.
For if we genuinely love Him,
we wake up inside Christ's body

where all our body, all over,
every most hidden part of it,
is realized in joy as Him,
and He makes us, utterly, real,

and everything that is hurt, everything
that seemed to us dark, harsh, shameful,
maimed, ugly, irreparably
damaged, is in Him transformed

and recognized as whole, as lovely,
and radiant in His light
we awaken as the Beloved
in every last part of our body.

"The Crucifixion"

(Twelfth century)

AN IRISH MONK

This brief poem seems to rear up in grief like the cries of the bird and the Christ that it describes. It is an ancient song of lament that, in the first four lines, implicates the whole of nature in the Passion. This mysterious concept—of nature reacting to the death of God—is evident in Scripture (see Matt. 27:45). It also has the poetic logic of "pathetic fallacy": the use of nature in literature to reflect emotional states or events— storms breaking at the climax of stories, for example, or the sun shining on lovers. God's "poetry" at the death of Christ, however, is quite literal. There is no fiction or metaphor in the sky darkening at the death of Christ: the entire cosmos, every bird and tree, was shadowed and shaken. It is this reality with which the poem engages.

We know that Jesus was nailed to the cross at 9 a.m., long after the first cry of a bird at dawn. Yet here, in this poem, the first bird's cry heralds the Crucifixion. The poet is contrasting the day, with all of its happy noise, with the terrible night that the Crucifixion brings on. The cries of birds can only become, from that point on, a kind of keening.

"It was like the parting of day from night." This simple line holds so many truths and associations: at the death of Jesus, his soul is separated from his body; he will seem to be separated from the world. We recall the light pouring into the darkness in Genesis and how that light seemed, on this day, to withdraw.

Another striking aspect of the opening of the poem is the image of the dying Christ as a swan. Graceful, even regal, the swan has primitive associations in our unconscious with transformation and divinity. (In mythology, Zeus became such a bird.) Swans are often protected; for centuries, their meat was reserved for nobility. It is fitting, then, that the poet compares Christ to a swan.

At line six, this small but almost bottomless poem presents Jesus to us primarily as Mary's son. His greatest grief, this poem says, is the fact that she suffered so much for his suffering. This, of course, is the bind of love: to suffer more at the pain of the beloved than at our own.

And Mary's grief is the unwavering reminder of the human agony her son went through. She is the touchstone of its reality. In these lines, he is God-as-swan, but she reminds us that this is no pagan myth; it is a human happening, as well as divine, that she is tasked with navigating.

"The Crucifixion"

Translated from the Irish by Howard Mumford Jones

AN IRISH MONK

At the cry of the first bird
They began to crucify Thee, O Swan!
Never shall lament cease because of that.
It was like the parting of day from night.
Ah, sore was the suffering borne
By the body of Mary's Son,
But sorer still to Him was the grief
Which for His sake
Came upon His Mother.

"O Virga ac Diadema"

(Twelfth century)

ST. HILDEGARD OF BINGEN

Hildegard of Bingen did not only write poems. She also wrote music; she had visions; she wrote books about those visions and oversaw paintings of them; she preached; she was wise about plants and medicines; and she was abbess of a Benedictine monastery. It was the twelfth century, and Hildegard was the essence of an early Renaissance woman. She saw no boundary between the mystical visions that shook her soul from the age of five and an image; no firm demarcation between a poem and a piece of music, nor between a vision and a theological concept. Indeed, the poem below is also music, and also theology. "Invisible and eternal things are made known through visible and temporal things," she heard pronounced during a mystical experience.[1] Her writings, her music, and even her herbs and unguents were manifestations of the uncreated God.

A protagonist when women were rarely given space to speak, Hildegard places Mary and Eve at the center of humankind's great story in this piece, one of a series of lyrics dedicated to the Blessed Mother. The medievals were very much aware of the presence of the Virgin all the way through Scripture, and in the first stanza of this work, Hildegard represents her as both branch and crown. The image of a tree to denote the lineage of Jesus is used in Isaiah of course, and Mary is a central branch

---

1. Hildegard of Bingen, "The Cosmic Egg," from *Scivias* 1.3, in *Hildegard of Bingen: Selected Writings*, trans. and ed. Mark Atherton (London: Penguin Classics, 2001), 89–92.

of this tree. She is also a Queen, as spouse of the Holy Spirit. She is protected in her chamber—or, here, a "cloister"—like the "garden locked" in the Song of Solomon (4:12).

But in stanza four, Hildegard's poetics seem to take us to audacious heights when she writes of the creation of the Virgin. Mary, she says, came into being through "radiance divine." It sounds almost heretical. But Hildegard is working well within the bounds of metaphor: she uses the image of dew as what grows the rest of creation (as though, by implication, we are common grass), while, in comparison, divine light makes Mary flower on a high bough. Seven hundred years before the Church proclaimed the dogma of the Immaculate Conception, Mary's unique purity was already known and accepted as self-evident in medieval Europe. Mary is one of us; at the same time, by a unique grace flowing from her Son, she is raised up—grown on a higher bough, so to speak.

But there is more: the next stanza tells us that God foresaw her blossoming on the very first day of creation. How so? Of course, God always knew that Mary was the new Eve. He always knew that she would be an essential instrument in salvation. In other words, not only in poetic terms, but also in theological terms, Mary was always there, held in God's mind as an indispensable part of mankind's redemption.

The images continue, and how layered and laden they are! We have the ancient image of Eve being brought out of Adam's side conflated with Mary as the "golden matrix" coming from the Word. In other words, Mary's perfection was possible through her son and his future actions. He begot her as much as, or more than, she begot him. The following image of the female being a mirror of the male brings to mind another Marian metaphor that we come across in the Litany of Loreto: Mary as "Mirror of Justice." As a woman, Mary does not simply reflect man; she reflects God himself. That is to say, of all mankind, Mary bears the most similarity to Christ's perfection. "O Lady Savior" begins the last stanza—an exuberant title, even by the standards of medieval Marian devotion, and possibly one particular to Hildegard. What the poet shows us here is Mary's role in overturning what Eve let loose upon the world. This is indeed a love song. Hildegard was able to take in, with rare mystical perspicacity, God's redemptive plan. Her music and her lyrics seem to be pulled through a tear in the heavenly veil.

"O Virga ac Diadema"

Translated from the Latin by Nathaniel M. Campbell

ST. HILDEGARD OF BINGEN

O branch and diadem,
in royal purple clad, who in
your cloister strong
stand like a shield:

You burst forth blooming
but with buds
quite different than Adam's progeny—
th'entire human race.

Hail, O hail! For from your womb
came forth another life
that had been stripped by Adam from his sons.

O bloom, you did not spring
from dew nor from the drops of rain,
nor has the windy air flown over you; but radiance
divine has brought you forth upon
    that noblest bough.

O branch, your blossoming
God had foreseen within the first
day of his own creation.

And by his Word he made
of you a golden matrix,
O Virgin, worthy of our praise.

How great in strength
is that man's side,
from which God brought the form of woman forth,
a mirror made
of his own every ornament,
and an embrace
of his own every creature.

The heavens' symphony resounds,
And all the earth in wonder stares,
O Mary, worthy of our praise,
for God has loved you more than all.

O cry and weep!
How deep the woe!
What sorrow seeped with guilt
into our womanhood
because the serpent hissed his wicked plan!

That woman, whom God made to be
the mother of the world,
had pricked her womb
with the wounds of ignorance,
and offered to her offspring
the full inheritance of grief.

But, O dawn,
forth from your womb has come the sun anew;
the guilt of Eve he's washed away
and through you offered humankind a blessing
even greater than the harm that Eve bestowed.

O Lady Savior,
who offered to the human race a light
anew: together join the members of your Son
into the heavens' harmony.

"The Canticle of the Creatures"

(1225–1226)

ST. FRANCIS OF ASSISI

Perhaps the most shocking thing about this poem and its
radiant and revolutionary observations of the world is that
it was written at a time of intense suffering for its author. Ill,
almost blind, and wounded by the stigmata that he had received
from a seraph bearing the crucified Lord, Francis prayed, and
Christ reassured him of his place in the kingdom. It was Christ's
directive to rejoice in this assurance that inspired the canticle.
St. Francis even wrote music to accompany his words, although
they have no need of music: they come with their own.

The poem is deeply reminiscent of the song of the three
men in the furnace of Daniel: "Bless the Lord, all you works of
the Lord . . ." (Dan. 3:57). This Old Testament notion of water,
sun, moon, and stars actively blessing the Lord is as fresh as
Francis' characterizations of Brother Sun, Sister Moon, Brother
Wind, Sister Water, Brother Fire, Mother Earth, and Sister
Bodily Death. The sun, Francis says, has a likeness to God
himself. The personifications of some of the other elements are
endearing: fire is rambunctious; water sounds like a habited
nun; earth is nurturing.

The praise of God through these elements can sound
to us, these days, almost pagan or New Age. In fact, Francis'
preoccupation with them is in some ways reminiscent of the
creation account in Genesis. For all these things are from one
God, which is what the author of Genesis was emphasizing as

he noted every part, and this is what Francis is reinforcing now through rapturous song. There is no sun-god, but the sun is *of* God in a way that humanity tends to forget. The lightning flash of Francis' conversion made him see the gift of creation in a way that our fallen nature often twists, catastrophically. And this is the way that the popular image of Francis taming and communing with animals is true: the saint had an abiding love and respect for the creatures and elements of the world. He saw that they were his brothers and sisters—not made in God's image and likeness as we are, but nevertheless replete with their own essential mode of being in the world and, in their own particular way, imbued with the divine presence.

Stanzas eight and nine shift from praising God through the external world to extolling the virtues of forgiveness and peaceful endurance. The man who lives as God intended, we infer, is as stable and right in his place as the sun and the moon. Francis added on these lines in response to a conflict in Assisi between factions, hoping to inspire reconciliation. The last lines were added later still as the saint moved closer to "Sister Bodily Death."[1] Even in pain, even in his dying, Francis had the gift of recognizing the sanctity of every part of nature.

1. See Paul Murray, *God's Spies: Michelangelo, Shakespeare and Other Poets of Vision* (New York: T&T Clark, 2019) for information on the background to the writing of the Canticle.

"The Canticle of the Creatures"

Translated from the Italian by Paul Murray, OP

ST. FRANCIS OF ASSISI

Most high, all-powerful, good Lord,
yours are the praises,
the glory, the honour, and all blessing.
To you alone, Most High,
do they belong, and no human being
is worthy
to speak your name.

Be praised, my Lord, with all your creatures,
especially Sir Brother Sun
who is the day
and through whom you give us light,
and he is beautiful and radiant with great splendour
and bears a likeness of you, Most High.

Be praised, my Lord, for Sister Moon
and the stars.
In heaven you have formed them bright
and precious and beautiful.

Be praised, my Lord, for
Brother Wind,
and for the air, cloudy and serene,
and for all weather
through which you give sustenance
to your creatures.

Be praised, my Lord, for
Sister Water
who is most useful and humble and
precious and chaste.

Be praised, my Lord, for
Brother Fire
through whom you illumine the night,
and he is beautiful
and playful and robust and strong.

Be praised, my Lord, for our Sister
Mother Earth,
who sustains and governs us,
and produces diverse fruits with coloured flowers
and herbs.

Be praised, my Lord,
for those who forgive out of love for you,
and bear infirmity and tribulation.

Blessed are they
who endure in peace for, by you,
Most High,
they shall be crowned.

Be praised, my Lord, for our
Sister Bodily Death
from whom no living man can escape.

Woe to those who die in mortal sin.
Blessed are those
whom death will find in your most holy will,
for the second death shall do them
no harm.

Praise and bless my
Lord,
and give him thanks
and serve him with great humility.

"The Paradoxes of Love"

(Thirteenth century)

HADEWIJCH

An almost forgotten mystic of the thirteenth century, and
a woman of rare poetic talent and copious mystic vision,
Hadewijch came long before St. John of the Cross. But, hidden
in her own, particularly feminine dark night, she was a
contemplative sister to him.

As a beguine, Hadewijch would have been an educated
woman who wished to live an independent religious life of
poverty and contemplation. We deduce, from the writings
she left us, that she was centered on Christ, the Church, and
Scripture—and wholly and tempestuously in love with God.

Her poems are both startling and traditional. Most are
addressed to "Love," in the feminine, as God. Isaiah 49:15 also
likens God to a mother, and, a century after Hadewijch,
Mother Julian would write of the motherhood of Christ. But
Hadewijch is doing something more. Her "Love" seems, at
times, like a coquette! Writing at the time of courtly love poetry,
this mystic uses, to canny effect, the courtly dynamic of an
unobtainable woman (God as Love) being wooed by a knight
(Hadewijch). The poems are all longing, seduction, and sheer,
aching impossibility.

This is crucial to Hadewijch's poetic spirituality. God is
unobtainable in this life; the veil, even in deepest contemplative
union, cannot be torn. No one seems to have felt this more
acutely than Hadewijch.

As we read the declarations of this poem, the style of Solomon's commonsensical Proverbs comes to mind. But the paradoxes of tortured love listed here—"To languish for her sake is to be in good health"—also remind us of the upside-down world of Christ's Beatitudes: "Blessed are the meek, for they will inherit the earth" (Matt. 5:5). In the midst of the allegorical lover lamenting and praising the illogicality of his Love, we also hear the deep undertone of that Love crying, "Those who lose their life for my sake will find it" (Matt 16:25). In fact, Hadewijch's audacious paradoxes can sound almost shocking: "Her knowledge is error." St Paul provides an illuminating context for this point: "The wisdom of this world is foolishness with God" (1 Cor. 3:19).

In this courtly-scriptural dance, we also hear echoes of the language of the Psalms—"Her deepest abyss is her most beautiful form"—which foreshadows, too, St. John of the Cross, and says that where there is darkness and despair, there is also God singing in his absence like an empty wine glass touched by the sound of our calling. The more Love seems to run and hide, Hadewijch is saying, the closer he really is.

This is a layered trove of Catholic thinking. Every line demands a meditation. Every line reaches out to Scripture and the great web of mystical experience and tradition. It speaks of a mad method in a mystery that is unfathomable. But what person, in even the most cynical of secular cultures, could not help but be stunned by this depiction of Love, with its mind-blowing, life-changing reversals, its healing and wonders?

"The Paradoxes of Love"

Translated from the Middle Dutch by Mother Columba Hart, OSB

HADEWIJCH

What is sweetest in Love is her tempestuousness;
Her deepest abyss is her most beautiful form;
To lose one's way in her is to touch her close at hand;
To die of hunger for her is to feed and taste;
Her despair is assurance;
Her sorest wounding is all curing;
To waste away for her sake is to be in repose;
Her hiding is finding at all hours;
To languish for her sake is to be in good health;
Her concealment reveals what can be known of her;
Her retentions are her gifts;
Wordlessness is her most beautiful utterance;
Imprisonment by her is total release;
Her sorest blow is her sweetest consolation;
Her ruthless robbery is great profit;
Her withdrawal is approach;
Her deepest silence is her sublime song;
Her greatest wrath is her dearest thanks;
Her greatest threat is pure fidelity;
Her sadness is the alleviation of all pain.

   We can say yet more about Love:
Her wealth is her lack of everything;
Her truest fidelity brings about our fall;
Her highest being drowns us in the depths;
Her great wealth bestows pauperism;

Her largesse proves to be our bankruptcy;
Her tender care enlarges our wounds;
Association with her brings death over and over;
Her table is hunger; her knowledge is error;
Seduction is the custom of her school;
Encounters with her are cruel storms;
Rest in her is in the unreachable;
Her revelation is the total hiding of herself;
Her gifts, besides, are thieveries;
Her promises are all seductions;
Her adornments are all undressing;
Her truth is all deception;
To many her assurance appears to lie—
This is the witness that can be truly borne
At any moment by me and many others
To whom Love has often shown
Wonders by which we were mocked,
Imagining we possessed what she kept back for herself.
After she first played these tricks on me,
And I considered all her methods,
I went to work in a wholly different way:
By her threats and her promises
I was no longer deceived.

   I will belong to her, whatever she may be,
Gracious or merciless; to me it is all one!

"Adoro Te Devote"

(Thirteenth century)

ST. THOMAS AQUINAS

The great saint, philosopher, and theologian Thomas Aquinas wrote a series of hymns for the new feast of Corpus Christi in 1264. But public proclamation about the Real Presence of Christ in the Eucharist was not enough. At some point, he wrote this profound prayer-poem as a private devotion, perhaps to be recited after the consecration when he attended Mass as a noncelebrant.[1] Only much later were the words in English set to music and sung. These achingly personal lines are far different from the rollicking public confession of an Aquinas hymn such as "Pange Lingua." These words are intimate. This is a love poem.

Like Aquinas' hymns, this poem confesses the truth of the Presence of Christ in the Eucharist. It also petitions God that, one day, Aquinas will see him face to face. It is obviously a prayer. But it follows a meter and rhyme scheme that makes it poetry too. It seems that, on this occasion, the precise mind of Aquinas wanted to offer no less than poetry as prayer to God. "All things," he wrote, "are arranged according to various levels of beauty and excellence, and the more one draws near to God, so much the more these things are beautiful and excellent."[2] It

---

1. Paul Murray, *Aquinas at Prayer: The Bible, Mysticism and Poetry* (London: Bloomsbury, 2013), 241, referencing Robert Wielockx, 'La preghiera eucaristica di s.Tommaso: analisi testuale e testimonianza storica,' *Atti del convegno: l'anima eucaristica di san Tommaso d'Aquino*, in *Frontiere: Rivista di filosofia e teologia* 7 (January–December 2011): 333–334.

2. Thomas Aquinas, *Sermon-Conferences of St. Thomas Aquinas on the Apostles'*

makes sense, then, that a prayer for closeness to God would best be crafted as a poem, as poetry is the highest literary form.

This translation by the Victorian poet and Jesuit priest Gerard Manley Hopkins adds to the character of the poetry, while taking nothing away from the spirit of prayer. Aquinas' Latin is no doubt inimitable, and the reader feels at once the depth of contemplation in its lucidity. But, for English language readers, Hopkins' version is no lame substitute. In fact, his choices of words evoke wonderfully the veiled mystery. His use of "Godhead" as a first word immediately signifies the monumental sense of the Trinity. For, of course, when Christ is adored in the Blessed Sacrament, when he is received on tongues, God the Father and the Holy Spirit are also being adored and received. The immensity of all *this* is in hiding in a piece of bread: "Masked by . . . shadows."

The acoustics of "head," "here," "hiding," "shadows," and "shape" in the first two lines conjure nothing less than the hush of a church, the silence following the consecration of the Host. Hopkins offers us a lilting, most poignant music ("lost, all lost in wonder") that is never sentimental but seems to wound us with the truth of this Love—the ineffable and uncontainable present under the appearances of bread and wine.

Our senses, says the second stanza, are not much use to us in understanding this mystery. Where poetry often asks us to see, hear, taste, touch, and smell (see the visceral natural world in St. Columba and Manchán, for example), this poem confronts the failure of our senses at the last sublime hurdle of the altar. Only the faculty of hearing serves us, because we have heard the truth from Christ himself. But in terms of sight, we are blind two ways, the poet goes on to say: Christ did not show himself to be God on the cross, and here, in the Host, he

Creed, ed. Nicholas Ayo (Eugene, OR: Wipf and Stock, 1988), 37.

does not reveal himself to our eyes as man. The dynamic of the poem is therefore both immediate (we are before Christ) and blindly yearning (we cannot see him; this is all faith). Yet we are consoled by this Eucharistic bread made flesh, this fulfillment of poetry where the metaphor becomes reality.

There is a delightful medieval touch toward the end: Christ as pelican. It was thought that the pelican wounded herself with her long beak to feed her starving young with her blood. Artists seized on this as an image of Christ's self-sacrifice and our taking in of his Blood—"one drop of has the pow'r to win / All the world forgiveness of its world of sin."

"Adoro Te Devote"

Translated from the Latin by Gerard Manley Hopkins

ST. THOMAS AQUINAS

Godhead here in hiding whom I do adore
Masked by these bare shadows, shape and nothing more,
See, Lord at thy service low lies here a heart
Lost, all lost in wonder at the God thou art.

Seeing, touching, tasting are in thee deceived;
How says trusty hearing? That shall be believed;
What God's Son has told me, take for truth I do;
Truth himself speaks truly or there's nothing true.

On the cross thy godhead made no sign to men;
Here thy very manhood steals from human ken:
Both are my confession, both are my belief,
And I pray the prayer made by the dying thief.

I am not like Thomas, wounds I cannot see,
But I plainly call thee Lord and God as he:
This faith each day deeper be my holding of,
Daily make me harder hope and dearer love.

O thou, our reminder of the Crucified,
Living Bread, the life of us for whom he died,
Lend this life to me, then; feed and feast my mind,
There be thou the sweetness man was meant to find.

Like what tender tales tell of the Pelican,
Bathe me, Jesus Lord, in what thy bosom ran—
Blood that but one drop of has the pow'r to win
All the world forgiveness of its world of sin.

Jesus whom I look at shrouded here below,
I beseech thee, send me what I thirst for so,
Some day to gaze on thee face to face in light
And be blest forever with thy glory's sight.

"Ave Virgo Mater Christi" (Excerpt)

(Thirteenth century)

WALTER OF WIMBORNE

In the Middle Ages, devotion to Our Lady reached the headiest of poetic heights. With widespread use of prayers such as the Little Office of the Blessed Virgin Mary, the faithful were used to seeing the Virgin throughout the prophetic poetry of the Old Testament, and poets were contemplating how to describe such a woman. If Our Lord is the Word, what is his mother—someone so immaculate, so lush, so wise, and so lovely that she housed God himself? Walter of Wimborne would no doubt have said that she was best described with metaphor.

Reading this thirteenth-century Franciscan poet and schoolmaster, it is clear that he always has recourse to saying what Mary is like. Walter's Marian metaphors run, in the entirety of this poem, through 164 stanzas, and his praise is unvaryingly imaginative.

Mary is, he says, the "comment and gloss" of Scripture—the key to understanding so much in both the Old and New Testaments. Walter's list of metaphors crescendos: he uses terms we are familiar with such as "star of the sea" but becomes ever more inventive. She is also a ship, a gem, a medicine-chest, honey; she sews God with mud, using the needle of providence. This mixed metaphor draws from both Scripture and tradition: we are made "from the dust of the ground" (Gen. 2:7), and an apocryphal account has Mary weaving the temple veil. Walter reaches every which way to explain Mary's role and to praise her—and he is almost inexhaustible.

It was not just Walter who was driven to these heights of expression with regard to Mary. We only have to consider the Litany of Loreto ("Gate of heaven," "Mystical rose") to see that figurative language and the Mother of God have a very tight bond. So why does the Virgin, in particular, invite so much metaphor?

Firstly, when talking of Mary, ordinary language fails. Catholics have always recognized that the Virgin is, although entirely human, nearest to God, and as such lies beyond normal description. Imagine seeing a one-off eclipse of the moon. How would we describe it to a friend the next day? We would most certainly resort to metaphor: it was the color of blood, or cheese; it was the size of a hot air balloon or a penny. So it goes with Mary. But in using metaphors for Mary, we are not simply "resorting" to this language because we don't know how else to describe her. We are heaping praise. A lover will always compare the beloved to other things to illuminate the reach and depth of their love. Then, of course, Mary not only invites metaphors; she fulfills them. She is not *like* the New Eve; she *is* the New Eve. She is not *like* the ark of the covenant; she *is* the ark of the covenant. She is not *like* the Church; she *is* the Church.

Finally, she is, as any reader will conclude reading this poem, everything to us, precisely because she leads us to Everything.

"Ave Virgo Mater Christi" (Excerpt)

Translated from the Latin by Rachel Fulton Brown

WALTER OF WIMBORNE

Hail, virgin, mother of Christ,
you who by your modesty merited
to be called phoenix of virgins;
hail, virgin, whose fruit
gave to us the end of sorrow and
the limit of lamentation.

Hail, beautiful virgin,
for whose praise neither prose
nor meter suffices;
hail, virgin, turning-post of evil,
vein of life, through whom the death
of foul death is accomplished.

Hail, glorious virgin,
you who are the comment and gloss
of prophetic scripture,
whose gloss lays bare
that which is veiled
by the hard shell of the letter.

Hail, virgin, key of heaven,
hail, new ship weighed down
with novel wares,
through whom on full sails
is brought the full light from heaven
to the blind and wandering.

Hail, maidenly gem,
hail, bright star of the sea,
hail, treasure-chest of the divinity,
hail, torch and lantern
whom the supernal light sets light,
firebrand of eternal light.

Hail, virgin, whose womb,
diligently sealed,
swelled with a new growth;
without pain or torment,
the splendor and figure of the Father
wished to be born from you.

Hail, virgin, room of the Word,
chastely pregnant by chaste breath,
not impure seed;
to you worthily we offer odes,
you who knot God with mud,
and mother with virgin.

Hail, virgin, cell of the Word,
concealing the light-beam of divinity
under a cloud of flesh;
hail, virgin, medicine-chest of God,
through whom the clouded, bleary, blind
mind receives its salve.

Hail, virgin, abyss of honey,
you who drive far away the ancient gall
of death and sorrow,
you who with the needle of providence
joined God with mud
and the lowest with the highest.

Hail, virgin, saw of death,
whose womb is a casket
of celestial incense;
hail, virgin, whom the power
of the bountiful spirit made sacred,
fortunate, and fertile.

....

Virgin, medicine of the world,
clothing and sheath of the Word,
confidential servant of Christ,
confidant of the angelic assembly,
you who snatched us
from the ruin of vices.

Mingle your servant
drawn from the depths
with the happy company of heaven,
so that he may rejoice with them
and be fed on ambrosial feasts
forever. A-M-E-N

"I Cannot Dance, O Lord"

(Thirteenth century)

MECHTHILD OF MAGDEBURG

Whoever would think of *dancing* as something typically Catholic? And yet, as one holy medieval woman from Germany knew, dancing really is an ancient expression of Christian joy.

But Mechthild cannot dance. In fact, the title and first line of this short poem, taken alone, look as bleak as a party with no music. Yet there is a twist in the second line: she will only dance if God leads her.

Though we almost never think of dancing as being sacred, it is decisively present in Scripture: David danced before the ark in holy joy (2 Sam. 6:14); "You have turned my mourning into dancing," sings the Psalmist (Ps. 30:11). Dancing can be a manifestation of divine union, of forgetfulness of self, of trust, of joy. It is easy to imagine Adam and Eve dancing in their innocence in the Garden of Eden.

The fact that Mechthild urges God to lead her in such a dance is a sign that she wants *him* to be joyful too—and in this dynamic she is living the Catholic calling to love God like his bride (2 Cor. 11:2). Moreover, she wants her exuberance only to be a reflection of *his* glee. Like Mary, she wants to be a mirror of him. *He* needs to lead the dance.

From that intimate fiesta, she knows that love will grow; and from that love, knowledge will come; and from that knowledge, fruit will burgeon. She is rhapsodizing that her happiness can only come from him. For Mechthild, dancing is an outpouring of love; it is union.

Mechthild reminds us of Hildegard of Bingen and Hadewijch. A beguine (an independent holy woman), she was, like them, dazzlingly poetic, inventive, and female. She did not believe that, as a lay woman, she would be less privileged than men in having the ear of God. But in a world dangerously fearful of heresy, her exuberance discomfited the powers that be. By the end of her life, she had retreated into a Cistercian nunnery, blind.

As we read the boldness of her lines, we might imagine how she shocked the medieval establishment. Her last line speaks of sheer ecstasy (from the Greek *ekstasis*, to be outside of oneself); she is speaking of a state *beyond* human sense. Yet she says that this is where she "will stay." This is not a poem about a one-off state of rapture, but rather the ceaseless prayer and union with God that Mechthild was striving for, a state that requires steady trust and abandonment. It is about having the bravery to step into those flames of joy.

"I Cannot Dance, O Lord"

Translated from the Middle Low German by Jane Hirshfield

MECHTHILD OF MAGDEBURG

I cannot dance, O Lord,
Unless You lead me.
If You wish me to leap joyfully,
Let me see You dance and sing—

Then I will leap into Love—
And from Love into Knowledge,
And from Knowledge into the Harvest,
The sweetest Fruit beyond human sense.

There I will stay with You, whirling.

Preface to
the *Divine Comedy*

Now to that greatest of Catholic poems, the *Divine Comedy*, a work so steeped in theology and the urgent pilgrimage that runs through every serious Catholic's life that Pope Paul VI declared, "Dante is ours."[1]

Written in exile from Florence, where Dante had been caught up in power struggles, the *Commedia* takes us on a skin-tingling tour of hell, purgatory, and heaven. At the start of this epic work, Dante is famously "Nel mezzo del cammin di nostra vita" (In the middle of life's journey). He is ripe for self-appraisal, for conversion—at the psychological and spiritual crux.

Split into three parts (or *cantiche*), each made up of thirty-three cantos (except for *Inferno*, which has thirty-four), the original *Commedia* in Italian is written in terza rima, which rhymes in groups of three: ABA BCB CDC etc. The number three is stamped throughout the work, in both structure and image, reflecting the Trinity and in turn the great hope of the poem: to behold the face of God.

If we take each canto as a separate poem, we can excerpt two each from *Inferno*, *Purgatory*, and *Paradise* and get a good glimpse of Dante's vision. And it is *Dante's* vision. The theological truths of much of the *Commedia* are, in many ways, sound. But let's not forget that Dante does the writer's job of clothing the invisible or ineffable with his own images and fancy

1. Paul VI, *Altissimi Cantus*, motu proprio, December 7, 1965.

(and, often, his own agenda). Wise readers will bear in mind that no one knows who is in hell, nor what it looks like. Yet there is a compelling sense of veracity throughout Dante's journey—particularly heaven—and that is why the poetry is great.

The *Comedy*'s greatness also lies in the fact that this pilgrimage relates, on another level, directly to our time here on earth: occasionally in our spiritual lives we might feel something like an intimation of the winds of hell or the warmth of heaven. We might become hyper-aware of our faults or, at other times, feel closer to God. That's also why Dante's journey is relatable. The hairs on our skin rise for a reason.

For our digested journey, we have three excellent translations for the three regions of the afterlife. Each translator has made his own decisions about how much to mirror Dante's terza rima, or not. Anthony Esolen writes in blank verse, John Ciardi in modified terza rima, and Dorothy L. Sayers and Barbara Reynolds (who completed Sayers' translation after her death) in full terza rima.

Canto I of *Inferno* (Excerpt)

(c. 1308–1321)

DANTE ALIGHIERI

It is 1300, at the break of dawn on Good Friday, and the poet Dante finds himself in the middle of his life, in a dark wilderness. We know that, in reality, the author was in exile from his home when he wrote his masterpiece. From this opening canto we also learn that he "had wandered from the straight and true." The original Italian speaks of a lost *via*, or "way," which echoes Christ's declaration in John 14:6 : "I am the way." Spiritually, then, Dante is astray. The way to heaven seems inaccessible.

This place of wilderness is obviously an allegory. When the poet says he can't remember how exactly he got there, we are put in mind of the somnambulant progress of the sinner who drifts, almost imperceptibly, from God day by day, until getting back on the right path requires a supernatural intervention. This might be Dante's spiritual crisis; but, from the beginning, his journey never lacks a sense of the presence of that necessary grace. The rays of sun that he spies are the "light of Heaven." He only has to find a way to get there.

As with any pilgrim, what blocks the poet are his own sins; but for Dante, in this scene, sins are embodied as animals. First of all, a leopard springs in front of him, almost making him turn back. Significantly, it is the light of the new sun and stars that reminds him of the great Creator and spurs him on. (We will meet those stars again at the very end of our journey.) Then an angry lion blocks his path, and then a wolf pushes him back toward the wilderness. Medieval symbolism would suggest that these animals (also mentioned in Jeremiah 5:6) represent lust, pride, and avarice. The reader can be in no doubt of the poet's bewilderment and fear. How on earth can he get through? While allegory and symbolism can often be a little two-dimensional in literature, Dante's beasts are a masterstroke. Far from being symbolic cardboard cutouts, they are "flashy," "hot," and "scrawny." They physically bar the way—as sins will tend to on the way to sanctity.

What saves Dante from the beasts and being pushed back into the wilderness is the appearance of a man (or "shade," spirit) before him. This is the classical poet Virgil, who will guide Dante through the regions of hell and nearly all of purgatory. Virgil, though pre-Christian, has written his own description of the underworld in his *Aeneid*, and Dante regards him as a master poet and father figure. Now that the two poets have met, Dante's formational journey (in the right direction) is assured. He will be handed to other guides through the hours ahead. Between them, they will bring him through the grotesquerie of the inferno and the painful hopes of purgatory, until the summit of heaven. No more could be asked of a conversion experience. We are at the nadir of a man's life. The revelations ahead will change him utterly.

Canto 1 of *Inferno* (Excerpt)

Translated from the Italian by Anthony Esolen

DANTE ALIGHIERI

Midway upon the journey of our life
   I found myself in a dark wilderness,
   for I had wandered from the straight and true.
How hard a thing it is to tell about,
   that wilderness so savage, dense, and harsh,
   even to think of it renews my fear!
It is so bitter, death is hardly more—
   but to reveal the good that came to me,
   I shall relate the other things I saw.
How I had entered, I can't bring to mind,
   I was so full of sleep just at that point
   when I first left the way of truth behind.
But when I reached the foot of a high hill,
   right where the valley opened to its end—
   the valley that had pierced my heart with fear—
I raised my eyes and saw its shoulders robed
   with the rays of that wandering light of Heaven
   that leads all men aright on every road.
That quieted a bit the dread that stirred
   trembling within the waters of my heart
   all through that night of misery I endured.
And as a man with labored breathing drags
   his legs out of the water and, ashore,
   fixes his eyes upon the dangerous sea,

So too my mind, while still a fugitive,
    turned back to gaze again upon that pass
    which never let a man escape alive.
When I had given my weary body rest,
    I struck again over the desert slope,
    ever the firmer foot the one below,
And look! just where the steeper rise began,
    a leopard light of foot and quick to lunge,
    all covered in a pelt of flecks and spots,
Who stood before my face and would not leave,
    but did so check me in the path I trod,
    I often turned to go the way I came.
The hour was morning at the break of dawn:
    the sun was mounting higher with those stars
    that shone beside him when the Love Divine
In the beginning made their beauty move,
    and so they were a cause of hope for me
    to get free of that beast of flashy hide—
The waking hour and that sweet time of year;
    but hope was not so strong that I could stand
    bold when a lion stepped before my eyes!
This one seemed to be coming straight for me,
    his head held high, his hunger hot with wrath—
    seemed to strike tremors in the very air!
Then a she-wolf, whose scrawniness seemed stuffed
    with all men's cravings, sluggish with desires,
    who had made many live in wretchedness—
So heavily she weighed my spirit down,
    pressing me by the terror of her glance,
    I lost all hope to gain the mountaintop.

And as a gambler, winning with a will,
    happening on the time when he must lose,
    turns all his thoughts to weeping and despair,
So I by that relentless beast, who came
    against me step by step, and drove me back
    to where the sun is silent evermore.
Now while I stumbled to the deepest wood,
    before my eyes appeared the form of one
    who seemed hoarse, having held his words so long.
And when I saw him in that endless waste,
    "Mercy upon me, mercy!" I cried out,
    "whatever you are, a shade, or man in truth!"

Canto 5 of *Inferno* (Excerpt)

(c. 1308–1321)

DANTE ALIGHIERI

As we take our first step into the inferno with Dante and Virgil, it is useful to know that the structure of this hell is cone-shaped: in effect, it is a massive crater in the earth caused by Lucifer plummeting from heaven. The truths manifested in its shape are theologically convincing. The famous "circles of hell" are divided into categories of sins. The worst, like fraud and treachery, are deeper into the earth and nearer to Satan. The lesser though still serious sins, such as promiscuity, are higher and nearer to purgatory. Crucially, and correctly, all those in hell have not repented; their place in hell is predicated on their own free choice. Their punishments reflect or contrast the nature of their sin, a mechanism called *contrapasso*. We see this type of poetic punishment even in the natural order: if we fill our stomachs too full of good things, we get a stomachache. Every torture lingeringly described in Dante's hell illustrates what we, in some sense, bring upon ourselves.

But as we tiptoe through these perilous regions, let's be clear that in writing his masterpiece Dante had many personal irons in the fire and scores to settle publicly. On the one hand, he is relatively enlightened and progressive: he sets pre-Christian and non-Christian thinkers like Plato and the Islamic philosopher Averroes in limbo where the "only" pain they know is their exclusion from heaven. But in the ninth circle of hell, where the treacherous are condemned, Dante sticks Ugolino della

Gherardesca, who, in real life, was imprisoned with his children for acts of political betrayal. His sons eventually starved to death, and—some say—were then eaten by their ravenous father. In hell, Dante has Ugolino gnawing on the skull of Archbishop Ruggieri, the man who (also treacherously) locked them up in the first place—thus neatly and aptly meting out punishment to both. The inferno is full of such dazzling and bespoke cruelty.

But it is the wind of passion with which we are concerned in this extract. We enter into a land of howling gales—these are the gusts of lust that throw us around as though we had no volition. Dante's attention is caught by a particular pair of "shades" (dead) buffeted along in infinite motion and asks if he can speak to them. They are the lovers Paolo and Francesca, who in real life were killed by Giovanni Malatesta, the latter's husband and the former's brother. Dante's prayer to hear their tale is enough to sweep them in his direction. They separate from a group of similarly afflicted lovers, "Dido's flock." (Dido was a queen of Carthage who killed herself when her lover, Aeneas, abandoned her.) The wind then ceases long enough for Paolo and Francesca's story to be told. Love is to blame, says Francesca, and this wind that caught them up in life, and holds them now, is the living metaphor of their passion. Their killer, the wronged husband, is destined for a lower circle of hell, the realm of Cain. Dante feels pity for the lovers, as he cannot for those condemned for greater crimes. It was a book, Francesca confides, that was their undoing (and Dante is no doubt conscious of the author's responsibility in these matters). Now they will be swept together in that flux for all eternity. What they once longed for (to be together forever) is now their damnation.

Most of us have been slave to those winds of passion. But although Francesca emphasizes the lack of control behind her sins, Dante was well aware of the Christian doctrine of free will. They chose their actions. Yet, even so, their murder gave them no time to repent. As though on the edge of a vertiginous and ever-controversial precipice (a place where no author can know the mind of God), Dante swoons in grief.

Canto 5 of *Inferno* (Excerpt)

Translated from the Italian by Anthony Esolen

DANTE ALIGHIERI

And "Poet," I began, "I greatly long
    to speak to those two shades who fly as one
    and seem so lightly carried on the wind."
And he responded: "You shall see them when
    they sail nearer to us; then beg them by
    the love that drives them on, and they will come."
Soon as the wind had swerved their flight our way,
    I cried, "O weary spirits, if Another
    does not forbid it, come and speak with us!"
As turtledoves who heed the loving call—
    with firm and lifted wings they shear the air
    and fly to the sweet dovecote, swift of will—
So did they veer away from Dido's flock
    and come to us through that malignant air,
    such force had the affection of my cry.
"O living spirit, courteous and good,
    traveling the black night to visit us
    who left the world dyed purple with our blood,
Were He who rules the universe our friend,
    we would entreat him, praying for your peace,
    for you have pitied us our twisted fate.
All that you please to hear and speak about
    we two will hear and speak with you, as long
    as the wind falls in silence. Where the Po

Rushes with all its tributaries down
    to its sea harbor, that it may have peace,
    in that place lies the town where I was born.
Love that flames soonest in the gentle heart
    seized him for that sweet body which was snatched
    from me—and how it happened hurts me still.
Love that allows no loved one not to love,
    seized me with such a strong delight in him
    that, as you see, it will not leave me yet.
Love led us to one death. The realm of Cain
    waits for the man who quenched us of our lives."
    Such were the words they offered. And I bowed
My head to hear the story of those souls
    and what they suffered, bowed so low, at last
    the poet said, "What are you thinking of?"
When I could speak I thus began, "Alas,
    what great desire, what sweet and tender thoughts
    have led these lovers to this woeful pass!"
Turning to them once more, I spoke again.
    "Francesca," I began, "your torments move
    my heart to weep in pity for your pain.
But tell me, in the season of sweet sighs,
    how did it happen, what made Love give way
    that you should know the truth of your desires?"
And she to me: "There is no greater grief
    than to recall a time of happiness
    while plunged in misery—as your Teacher knows.
But if so great a longing urges you
    to know about the first root of our love,
    then I will tell you, speaking through my tears.

One day we two were reading for delight
    about how love had mastered Lancelot;
    we were alone and innocent and felt
No cause to fear. And as we read, at times
    we went pale, as we caught each other's glance,
    but we were conquered by one point alone.
For when we read that the much-longed-for smile
    accepted such a gentle lover's kiss,
    this man, whom nothing will divide from me,
Trembled to place his lips upon my mouth.
    A pander was that author, and his book!
    That day we did not read another page."
And all the while one spirit told their tale,
    the other wept so sadly that I fell
    for pity of it to a deathlike faint—
and I dropped like a body stricken dead.

Canto 10 of *Purgatorio* (Excerpt)

(c. 1308–1321)

DANTE ALIGHIERI

Before dawn on Easter Sunday, Dante exits hell with Virgil, and they find themselves on the shore of purgatory, "that second kingdom given / the soul of man wherein to purge its guilt / and so grow worthy to ascend to Heaven."[1]

Many images from purgatory will be familiar to lovers of mythology. A boatman brings the souls in; at the end of his stay here, Dante will be washed in the forgetfulness of the river Lethe. Purgatory is as tightly structured as hell, but though it can be miserably terrifying, there are angels to be seen, fragments of praise to be heard; ultimately, the divine rumble of heaven approaches.

We focus here, though, on a painful corner, one that is particularly illustrative of Dante's brilliance in showing the consequence of sin. We come face to face (or face to back of the head) with the proud. Having accessed a tight passage via the Gate of Purgatory, Dante and his guide have beheld three divine and living sculptures on a cliffside. They depict the Annunciation, King David dancing before the ark of the Lord, and the emperor Trajan interrupting a campaign to promise justice to a bereaved mother. What do all three of these scenes have in common? Three people—the Virgin Mary, King David, and the emperor Trajan—all with the greatest reasons to be proud, are in these sculptures endlessly casting aside self-importance and expressing God-loving humility.

1. *Purgatorio*, canto 1, lines 4–6.

Then, at the point at which we pick up the vision, Dante and Virgil witness the fate of the proud: those who, in life, stood for the opposite of such humility. The envious, wrathful, slothful, avaricious, gluttonous, and lustful are above, progressively nearer to heaven for the relative lightness of their sins. But the torments suffered by the proud are so shockingly weighty that Dante has to caution the reader not to dwell on them, but to focus on what will follow. After all, unlike the citizens of hell, these people are on course for paradise. (Later, Dante will meet a shade who goes so far as to call his pain a "gift of grace."[2]) For now, Dante sees people—though he can barely recognize them as such—carrying rocks upon their backs so heavy that they are crushed into the earth. He asks us to think of "corbels," those supports for shelves or ceilings sometimes carved to look like doubled-over men. This is what he beholds crawling along like bugs. The greater the pride in life, the heavier the rock to carry now.

Why is pride such a heinous sin? Pride makes men believe that they can act as gods, that they can control and dominate rather than serve. Dante beautifully downsizes man's place in the supernatural hierarchy by likening us to grubs—albeit grubs destined to become celestial butterflies. Reading Dante, we can fall into the trap of seeing his vision of God as one of an inventive sadist. But what Dante presents us with is poetic truth—that is, truth so freshly and sharply realized that it stings. The passage to the place of this excerpt is called the "Needle's Eye," and for good reason: he is simply showing us, in new terms, how small (compressed, as though by a rock!) we need to be to get through the narrow gate (see Matt. 7:14).

Despite the abject grimness of what we are shown here, the wings of grace are ready to bear us on.

2. *Purgatorio*, canto 23, line 72.

Canto 10 of *Purgatorio* (Excerpt)

Translated from the Italian by John Ciardi

DANTE ALIGHIERI

The poet said: "Look there: they seem to crawl
   but those are people coming on our left:
   they can tell us where to climb the wall."

My eyes, always intent to look ahead
   to some new thing, finding delight in learning,
   lost little time in doing as he said.

Reader, I would not have you be afraid,
   nor turn from your intention to repent
   through hearing how God wills the debt be paid.

Do not think of the torments: think, I say,
   of what comes after them: think that at worst
   they cannot last beyond the Judgment Day.

"Master," I said, "those do not seem to me
   people approaching us; nor do I know—
   they so confuse my sight—what they may be."

And he to me: "Their painful circumstance
   doubles them to the very earth: my own eyes
   debated what they saw there at first glance.

Look hard and you will see the people pressed
   under the moving boulders there. Already
   you can make out how each one beats his breast."

O you proud Christians, wretched souls and small,
   who by the dim lights of your twisted minds
   believe you prosper even as you fall—

can you not see that we are worms, each one
   born to become the Angelic butterfly
   that flies defenseless to the Judgment Throne?

What have your souls to boast of and be proud?
   You are no more than insects, incomplete
   as any grub until it burst the shroud.

Sometimes at roof and ceiling-beam one sees
   a human figure set there as a corbel,
   carved with its chest crushed in by its own knees,

so cramped that what one sees imagined there
   makes his bones ache in fact—just such a sense
   grew on me as I watched those souls with care.

True, those who crawled along that painful track
   were more or less distorted, each one bent
   according to the burden on his back;

yet even the most patient, wracked and sore,
seemed to be groaning: "I can bear more!"

Canto 11 of *Purgatorio* (Excerpt)

(c. 1308–1321)

DANTE ALIGHIERI

> Ah, what a difference between these trails
> and those of Hell: here every entrance fills
> with joyous song, and there with savage wails![1]

So the poet will exclaim further on in purgatory, highlighting
one of the fundamental differences between the inferno and
this place of transformation. For Dante's purgatory is, above all,
hopeful. Perhaps it is his vision that has helped the faithful see
this stop-off in the afterlife as an anteroom to heaven rather
than a locked dungeon of torment.

The greatest mark of this hope is the ubiquity of prayer
within the canticle. Souls who are piloted by the Angel of God
to shore in canto 2 sing *in exitu Israel de Aegypto* (Ps. 114). At
sundown, in a wondrously beautiful glade in purgatory, the
Salve Regina rises from the very grasses (canto 7). Throughout
this part of the journey, prayers arise, are caught on the air.
Everyone here knows where they are going, and what they suffer
is assuaged by this knowledge.

Immediately after being so struck by the sight of the
prideful crushed by their boulders of sin (in our last poem), we
now hear what these penitents are saying as they crawl toward
Dante and his guide. Astonishingly perhaps, what they utter is a

---

1. *Purgatorio*, canto 12, lines 112–114.

prayer of love, supplication, and praise—a poetic explication of the Lord's Prayer.

We might wonder whether the words of Jesus Christ need a spin! Yet, in reality, writing such as this is fruit of meditation.

Of course, the very fact that Dante chooses *this* prayer for the proud has to be revealing. It is the first ever Catholic prayer. (The angelic greeting and the Magnificat came to be used as prayers years after they were spoken.) What the poet does is unpack its call to humility.

And, for the proud, every part is deeply concerned with this essential virtue. In the very first lines, God is described as being in heaven, which the reader will be familiar with. But this celestial address, Dante specifies, is not arrived at by constraint of some geographical boundary, but rather because the world is fallen. Now, of course, God is here on earth too: we abide in him and he in us (John 15:4). Yet at the same time we are very distant from him; we are traveling toward him on our pilgrimage. The souls in purgatory are at the sharp end of this situation. They are at the last desperate stretch and sense acutely how we feel more of God's love the nearer we grow to him. The *first works* that line three speaks of are the heavens, where those closest to God, the angels and saints, reside. That is where the proud with their cumbersome burdens are longing to be.

The proud are also now rightly conscious of God as cause of their life and the lives of every creature, and how those lives should be spent acknowledging and praising this "quickening" in them by the Almighty. All the lines of the prayer are soaked with this obeisance, the fundamental recognition that we cannot reach heaven by our own efforts—our talents, our prestige or work—a mistaken idea that the proud often have. They realize now that their wills must be offered to God, as the angels do theirs, and the manna that we need to go forward (the "daily bread") cannot be earned.

By contrast, the last lines are a prayer for those on earth. Despite their pains, the souls in purgatory are privileged in being beyond the temptation of the devil ("the Adversary"). While the purgatorial souls pray for the living, Dante is clear that, in their fraught yet beauteous voyage, our prayers, in turn, can lend them godspeed.

Canto II of *Purgatorio* (Excerpt)

Translated from the Italian by John Ciardi

DANTE ALIGHIERI

Our Father in Heaven, not by Heaven bounded
  but there indwelling for the greater love
  Thou bear'st Thy first works in the realm first-founded,

hallowed be Thy name, hallowed Thy Power
  by every creature as its nature grants it
  to praise Thy quickening breath in its brief hour.

Let come to us the sweet peace of Thy reign,
  for if it come not we cannot ourselves
  attain to it however much we strain.

And as Thine Angels kneeling at the throne
  offer their wills to Thee, singing Hosannah,
  so teach all men to offer up their own.

Give us this day Thy manna, Lord we pray,
  for if he have it not, though man most strive
  through these harsh wastes, his speed is his delay.

As we forgive our trespassers the ill
  we have endured, do Thou forgive, not weighing
  our merits, but the mercy of Thy will.

Our strength is as a reed bent to the ground:
  do not Thou test us with the Adversary,
  but deliver us from him who sets us round.

This last petition, Lord, with grateful mind,
  we pray not for ourselves who have no need,
  but for the souls of those we left behind.

—So praying godspeed for themselves and us,
  those souls were crawling by under such burdens
  as we at times may dream of. Laden thus,

unequally tormented, weary, bent,
  they circled the First Cornice round and round,
  purging away the world's foul sediment.

If they forever speak our good above,
  what can be done for their good here below
  by those whose will is rooted in God's love?

Surely we should help those souls grow clear
  of time's deep stain, that each at last may issue
  spotless and weightless to his starry sphere.

Canto 31 of *Paradiso* (Excerpt)

(c. 1308–1321)

DANTE ALIGHIERI

Now we are blessed with a partial view of heaven.

The poet and his guide have initially proceeded through paradise by way of different planets, but now they lead us high into the Empyrean realm. At the start of this canto, we see the ranks of the blessed grouped together as a spotless rose. This overwhelming sight, this spouse of Christ, is vast and complex (of "countless leaves") yet perfectly ordered in its structure (row on row). We can imagine the pixels of this huge bloom as the faces of the blessed. (Any visitor to Notre Dame in Paris will have seen an artistic representation of this image in the south rose window.) This army of saints is tended to by another army: winged angels with glowing faces and whitest garments who, like bees, minister to the celestial flower with peace and love. Dante's awe accelerates as he describes the divine light that bathes this whole vision from above. This is a taste of what he will come to see at the end of his journey. A preparation.

We are edging toward a joy that is indescribable. But the poet here is still grasping at earthly comparisons to make us understand how much loftier, how much greater, this beauty truly is. He refers us to the barbarians (who lived under a sky where the constellation of Helicè, the Great Bear, shines year-round, with the Little Bear, her son) and their first sight of the Lateran (the papal palace in Rome in Dante's time). These people were floored by the sight of that earthly majesty. It stands to reason that Dante the Florentine is (almost) struck dumb by this sight! He looks around for his guide.

As a pre-Christian philosopher, Virgil is barred from entering paradise and has, by this point, long gone. Beatrice—who, in real life, Dante adored from afar in Florence and who died at the age of twenty-five—is the woman whose intervention initiated this journey, and, toward the end of purgatory, she takes over from Virgil as guide. Throughout the *Commedia* the reader is struck by descriptions of Beatrice. Listen to Virgil describing her to Dante: "Her eyes were flashing brighter than the stars, / and she addressed me with an angel's voice."[1] Beatrice's beauty and holiness in the *Commedia* transform her from an attractive Florentine woman to someone who more resembles the Virgin Mary herself! And, in fact, Beatrice here can be said to be a "type" of Mary. She is transformed by the light of God and prays for Dante's soul. She is queenly and wise. Her untimely death, she scolds him in purgatory (canto 31), should have turned his attention to heaven, not to earthly pleasures. From Beatrice's arrival, it sometimes feels as though Dante is mesmerized by an old crush rather than heavenly things—and, in some ways, he is. But God also works through the human chain of holiness, and it is Beatrice who brings the poet to the Virgin, who will then hand him to her Son. His old desire for the girl who captivated his heart in Florence transforms into a pure longing for the paradise she has made her home.

Now, as he turns to Beatrice, his darling, she is gone back to her place in the rose.

She has handed the poet over to his last guide: Bernard of Clairvaux. The saint points upward to Beatrice in her glory. She is further than the thunderous sky if it were "plunged in

1. *Inferno* (trans. Anthony Esolen), canto 2, lines 55–56.

the deepest ocean"; he can only see her by supernatural means. At this point, Dante offers a prayer to his beloved, thanking her for coming down to hell (to give Virgil his commission as guide) and praising her for her influence on him. Once again, his words make us wonder if he really is talking to Mary: "O thou in whom my hopes securely dwell . . ." In fact, this prayer is touching witness to what true love means: willing the good of the other. Beatrice's love has drawn him to Love.

The reader's skin by now should be tingling. After such hellish mud and blood and purgatorial pain, Dante is on his way to the Mother of God—and then, eventually, the Trinity. In his imaginative feat, Dante strikes at some aching vein. Whatever the external trapping of descriptions he may now use, we know he speaks the truth; we feel its light in our hearts.

Canto 31 of *Paradiso* (Excerpt)

Translated from the Italian by Dorothy L. Sayers
and Barbara Reynolds

DANTE ALIGHIERI

So now, displayed before me as a rose
   Of snow-white purity, the sacred might
   I saw, whom with His blood Christ made His spouse.

But the other, winging ever in His sight,
   Chants praises to the glory it adores,
   Its Maker's good extolling in delight.

As bees ply back and forth, now in the flowers
   Busying themselves, and now intent to wend
   Where all their toil is turned to sweetest stores,

So did the host of Angels now descend
   Amid the Flower of the countless leaves,
   Now rise to where their love dwells without end.

Their glowing faces were as fire that gives
   Forth flame, golden their wings; the purest snow
   The whiteness of their raiment ne'er achieves.

Down floating to the Flower, from row to row,
   Each ministered the peace and burning love
   They gathered in their waftings to and fro.

Between the Flower and that which blazed above
    The volant concourse interposed no screen
    To dim the splendour and the sight thereof;

For God's rays penetrate with shafts so keen
    Through all the universe, in due degree,
    There's naught can parry them or intervene.

Drawn from the new age and antiquity,
    This realm of saints, whose joy no dangers mar,
    Gazed on one sign in love and unity.

O trinal light, which shining as one star
    It fills them with delight to gaze on there,
    Looks down on us, storm-driven as we are!

If the barbarians from regions where
    The sky by Helicè is daily crowned,
    Rotating with her son she holds so dear,

By Rome and all the wonders therein found
    Were moved to stupor when the Lateran
    Above all works of mortals was renowned,

I, coming to holiness from the profane,
    To the eternal from the temporal,
    From Florence to a people just and sane,

Into what stupor, then, must I needs fall!
    Truly, 'twixt it and joy I then preferred
    No sound to hear, no word to speak at all.

As when a pilgrim, to new life restored,
   Beholds a shrine, and hopes within him rise
   That of its wonders he may take home word,

So I amid the living light mine eyes
   Directed, gazing upon every row
   Now upwards and now down, now circle-wise.

To charity their faces sweetly woo,
   Made beauteous in our Maker's light and smile,
   And gracious dignity their gestures show.

Already now the general form and style
   Of Paradise my glance had taken in,
   But on no part had lingered yet a while.

And, with new-kindled eagerness to win
   My Lady's guidance, unto her once more I
   Turned me, to hear her speak of what I'd seen.

One thing I meant, another is my story:
   Not Beatrice, an elder there I saw,
   Clad in the raiment of the saints in glory.

A joyfulness benign his features wore;
   Such gentle kindliness his air implied
   As ever tender-hearted father bore.

"And she, where is she?" instantly I cried.
   "'Tis Beatrice who sends me unto thee
   For thy desire's fulfilment," he replied.

"Lift up thine eyes, yonder thy Lady see
    In the third circle from the highest place,
    Enthroned where merit destined her to be."

Without a word I lifted up my gaze,
    And there I saw her in her glory crowned,
    Reflecting from herself the eternal rays.

The greatest height whence thunderings resound
    Less distant is from mortal vision, though
    Plunged in the deepest ocean it were found,

Than was my sight from Beatrice, and lo!
    By no material means made visible,
    Distinct her image came to me below.

"O thou in whom my hopes securely dwell,
    And who, to bring my soul to Paradise,
    Didst leave the imprint of thy steps in Hell,

Of all that I have looked on with these eyes
    Thy goodness and thy power have fitted me
    The holiness and grace to recognize.

Thou hast led me, a slave, to liberty,
    By every path, and using every means
    Which to fulfil this task were granted thee.

Keep turned towards me with thy munificence
    So that my soul which thou hast remedied
    May please thee when it quits the bonds of sense."

Canto 33 of *Paradiso*

(c. 1308–1321)

DANTE ALIGHIERI

Now we are gifted with the beatific vision.

Or one man's imagining of seeing the face of God. For what has been so concrete and mappable, so anecdotal and imaginatively wild in hell and purgatory, so paintable with his celestial rose, will now become something quite other. Already, in canto 1 of *Paradiso*, Dante speaks of being *transhumanized*; in other words, this celestial trek changes him radically—his way of seeing and, ultimately, his mode of expression.

Dante's tour of the ten heavens with Beatrice and then Bernard of Clairvaux takes him into terrain undocumented and ineffable. Of course, no one knows what hell and purgatory are like either. Yet Dante seems to intuit that our choices, our very fallen selves, would play a large part in the shape of reality there. Human faults and virtues play their part in heaven too. But as we go further even than the Celestial Rose, the poet is stripped of landmarks and associations. Here, for a poet, metaphors may be doomed to fail. Dante has, before these lines, given us some advance visions of Christ and the Virgin Mary; we have seen the ranks of the blessed in our last excerpt. But when Dante reaches the face of God, he is before the reason and source of all existence—the beginning and end of poetry.

Before he (or we) can contemplate this sight, Bernard—the saint famous for his ardent Marian devotion—does the necessary: he prays to the Virgin, praising her and encapsulating something of her unique status in our life of prayer: "The seeker after grace who shuns thy knee / May aim his prayer, but fails to wing the flight." In other words, loving Mary brings us closer to God; devotion to her privileges our petitions.

Bernard proceeds then to his specific requests: Mary's intercession is needed to enable Dante to reach these heights, and to have the spiritual capacity and purity to apprehend what awaits him there.

Mary's eyes disclose how much joy this prayer gives her: "Unto the eternal light she raised them then . . ." Pause at that stanza: we are witnessing how Mary sees God with more penetration and concentration than any other creature.

When Dante looks up too, he is, of course, at a loss. Speech and memory are not up to the job of describing what he sees. Like the prophet Sybil's wisdom that was written on leaves that the wind took, his impressions are ungraspable, and yet they are sweetly instilled within him.

Like Bernard, the poet must have recourse to prayer that he will have the strength and inspiration to convey "one single spark" of all he sees, because *witness* is so deeply important. And yet, this is fantasy, isn't it? One man's guess. But, as he apprehends God as light, Dante is swimming in the earliest divinely inspired writings of St. John the Evangelist and the Nicene Creed. All the details of this canto pound with theology. And it could well be that the poet, having contemplated so long, is really doing (to some degree) what all poets try to do: he is glimpsing God's truth.

As St. John of the Cross will come to know centuries later, blindness is necessary for this to happen. But here, so very close to God, blindness will only come if Dante *looks away*. ("The piercing brightness of the living ray / Which I endured, my vision had undone, / I think, if I had turned my eyes away.") In fact, his vision is expanded and "consumed" as he continues to look. And what does he see?

What Dante does *not* do at this point is fulfill popular expectations by having Jesus stroll up to meet him. He does not even give us the scriptural image of the Son of Man sitting on a throne at the right hand of the Father. There will be readers who will be disappointed by this. Dante's own tongue, he admits, is clumsy as a babe's as he attempts his description. But bear with him; what he shows us is convincing, not least because of its impact on *himself*, and his struggle to tell it.

His first "vision," then, is the universe as windblown pages of a book collated by Love. "Substance, accident, and mode unite"—the essence of everything, everything else about it, and how it relates to everything else, is held as one in this Love. But the vastness of this sight is impossible for him to properly contain in his memory: stunned into lethargy, he immediately remembers less of it than humanity does of the first boat, the Argo, when it sailed over the bedazzled Neptune's head twenty-five centuries before.

Then the light changes the poet: there is nothing else, now, that he desires. And everything he has ever begun is "made perfect." The light he is in does not change (God never changes), but *he* is changed, and with this change, his understanding is deepened; he has more capacity to see. ("The transformation which in me took place / Transformed the single changeless form for me.") *Here* is the "realism" of Dante's heaven. Gone are mankind's naïve and individualistic notions of the afterlife as a reunion party or an eternal holiday. Here Dante's truth stands tall.

As he beholds the beatific vision, he sees three interlocking spheres. The first two (Father and Son) reflect one another, and the third is breathed equally from them both (demonstrating the *filioque*: the Spirit proceeding from the Father and the Son). This vision, which defies ordinary sight, is the family of the Trinity, a constant exchange of love and knowing. Again, as Dante's eyes adjust, he sees more: the image of man is visible within. This mystery—of our image and likeness of God, and the Incarnation of God—lies at the heart and stands at the summit of the whole *Commedia*. There is no formula, Dante says, to understand nor express it. Divine comprehension flares only momentarily within him. By now, though, his will and desire coincide with God's and become tiny cogs in the great machine of transcendent love.

What are we to make of this last word, of Truth's finale as shapes and light? It is the greatest poetic asceticism. Purgation of any literary flourish. A dart that strikes at the beating heart of everything.

Canto 33 of *Paradiso*

Translated from the Italian by Dorothy L. Sayers
and Barbara Reynolds

DANTE ALIGHIERI

"O Virgin Mother, Daughter of thy Son,
   Lowliest and loftiest of created stature,
   Fixed goal to which the eternal counsels run,

Thou art that She by whom our human nature
   Was so ennobled that it might become
   The Creator to create Himself His creature.

Thy sides were made a shelter to relume
   The Love whose warmth within the timeless peace
   Quickened the seed of this immortal bloom;

High noon of charity to those in bliss,
   And upon earth, to men in mortal plight,
   A living spring of hope, thy presence is.

Lady, so great thou art and such thy might,
   The seeker after grace who shuns thy knee
   May aim his prayer, but fails to wing the flight.

Not only does thy succour flow out free
   To him who asks, but many a time the aid
   Fore-runs the prayer, such largesse is in thee.

All ruth, all mercy are in thee displayed,
    And all munificence; in thee is knit
    Together all that's good in all that's made.

This man, who witnessed from the deepest pit
    Of all the universe, up to this height,
    The souls' lives one by one, doth now entreat

That thou, by grace, may grant to him such might
    That higher yet in vision he may rise
    Towards the final source of bliss and light.

And I who never burned for my own eyes
    More than I burn for his, with all my prayers
    Now pray to thee, and pray they may suffice,

That of all mortal clouding which impairs,
    Thine own prayers may possess the power to clean
    His sight, till in the highest bliss it shares.

And further do I pray thee, heavenly Queen,
    Who canst all that thou wilt, keep his heart pure
    And meet, when such great vision he has seen.

With thy protection render him secure
    From human impulse; for this boon the saints,
    With Beatrice, thronging fold hands and implore."

The eyes which God doth love and reverence,
    Gazing on him who prayed, to us made plain
    How prayers, devoutly prayed, her joy enhance.

Unto the eternal light she raised them then:
    No eye of living creature could aspire
    To penetrate so fixedly therein.

And I, who now was drawing ever nigher
    Towards the end of yearning, as was due,
    Quenched in my soul the burning of desire.

Bernard conveyed to me what I should do
    By sign and smile; already on my own
    I had looked upwards, as he wished me to.

For now my sight, clear and yet clearer grown,
    Pierced through the ray of that exalted light,
    Wherein, as in itself, the truth is known.

Henceforth my vision mounted to a height
    Where speech is vanquished and must lag behind,
    And memory surrenders in such plight.

As from a dream one may awake to find
    Its passion yet imprinted on the heart,
    Although all else is cancelled from the mind,

So of my vision now but little part
    Remains, yet in my inmost soul I know
    The sweet instilling which it did impart.

So the sun melts the imprint on the snow,
    Even so the Sibyl's wisdom that was penned
    On light leaves vanished on the winds that blow.

O Light supreme, by mortal thought unscanned,
   Grant that Thy former aspect may return,
   Once more a little of Thyself relend.

Make strong my tongue that in its words may burn
   One single spark of all Thy glory's light
   For future generations to discern.

For if my memory but glimpse the sight
   Whereof these lines would now a little say,
   Men may better estimate Thy might.

The piercing brightness of the living ray
   Which I endured, my vision had undone,
   I think, if I had turned my eyes away.

And I recall this further led me on,
   Wherefore my gaze more boldness yet assumed
   Till to the Infinite Good it last had won.

O grace abounding, whereby I presumed
   So deep the eternal light to search and sound
   That my whole vision was therein consumed!

In that abyss I saw how love held bound
   Into one volume all the leaves whose flight
   Is scattered through the universe around;

How substance, accident, and mode unite
   Fused, so to speak, together, in such wise
   That this I tell of is one simple light.

Yea, of this complex I believe mine eyes
    Beheld the universal form—in me,
    Even as I speak, I feel such joy arise.

One moment brings me deeper lethargy
    Than twenty-five centuries brought the quest that dazed
    Neptune when Argo's shadow crossed the sea.

And so my mind, bedazzled and amazed,
    Stood fixed in wonder, motionless, intent,
    And still my wonder kindled as I gazed.

That light doth so transform a man's whole bent
    That never to another sight or thought
    Would he surrender, with his own consent;

For everything the will has ever sought
    Is gathered there, and there is every quest
    Made perfect, which apart from it falls short.

Now, even what I recall will be exprest
    More feebly than if I could wield no more
    Than a babe's tongue, yet milky from the breast;

Not that the living light I looked on wore
    More semblances than one, which cannot be,
    For it is always what it was before;

But as my sight by seeing learned to see,
    The transformation which in me took place
    Transformed the single changeless form for me.

That light supreme, within its fathomless
    Clear substance, showed to me three spheres, which bare
    Three hues distinct, and occupied one space;

The first mirrored the next, as though it were
    Rainbow from rainbow, and the third seemed flame
    Breathed equally from each of the first pair.

How weak are words, and how unfit to frame
    My concept—which lags after what was shown
    So far, 'twould flatter it to call it lame!

Eternal light, that in Thyself alone
    Dwelling, alone dost know Thyself, and smile
    On Thy self-love, so knowing and so known!

The sphering thus begot, perceptible
    In Thee like mirrored light, now to my view—
    When I had looked on it a little while—

Seemed in itself, and in its own self-hue,
    Limned with our image; for which cause mine eyes
    Were altogether drawn and held thereto.

As the geometer his mind applies
    To square the circle, nor for all his wit
    Finds the right formula, howe'er he tries,

So strove I with that wonder—how to fit
    The image to the sphere; so sought to see
    How it maintained the point of rest in it.

Thither my own wings could not carry me,
    But that a flash my understanding clove,
    Whence its desire came to it suddenly.

High phantasy lost power and here broke off;
    Yet, as a wheel moves smoothly, free from jars,
    My will and my desire were turned by love,

The love that moves the sun and the other stars.

"Pearl" (Excerpt)

(Fourteenth century)

GAWAIN POET

This is a story of the worst kind of grief, and a vision of heaven. The narrator begins his tale in a garden where he lost the pearl of his life: his daughter. She died before the age of two, and he is stricken. We cannot know if this is fiction, but it seems unlikely. The poem is too raw for make-believe; despite it being exquisitely formed, a timeless hurt resounds in every line.

"Pearl" has a very distinctive structure. The original Middle English text (penned, it is thought, by the same author who wrote "Sir Gawain and the Green Knight") uses alliteration, rhyme, and a method (used in this translation) of echoing a word or phrase in the first and last lines of stanzas; in this excerpt, the poet uses "delight" and "prince" with/or "pleasing/ pleasure." It is no accident that each stanza has twelve lines, making a total of 1212 lines through the whole poem, recalling the structures of the heavenly Jerusalem as described in Revelation 21:15–21.

Contained within this ornate form, the narrator falls asleep in the garden where he lost his "pearl" and has a vivid dream that he sees the child, now a grown woman, across a stream that he cannot cross. His daughter is radiantly attired in pearl-sewn garments, with one pearl of unparalleled supernatural beauty at her breast. She is blissfully happy; she is a bride of Christ.

The father's shock that she should occupy such an elevated position, and his own struggle with grief, inspire an elegant and

calming catechesis from his daughter. She tells the parable of
the workers in the vineyard (Matt 20:1–16) and places herself as
the little one who snuck in at dusk and yet was rewarded as a
queen to live in bliss. Her father is confused; surely the Virgin
Mary is Queen? The grown child's responses are beautiful and
correct: all the elect are queenly, but Mary is the Queen of
them all. The daughter goes on to lead her father to a hillside
where he can see the heavenly Jerusalem and Christ with the
blessed, with his daughter in their ranks. In some ways, the
poem is reminiscent of scenes from Dante's *Divine Comedy*: the
young girl as guide is as calm and beatific as Dante's Beatrice.
But the details of what this narrator witnesses and how he
describes the jewels of heaven are almost irrelevant (although
they are breathtaking). What is more important is his sense
of amazement when he sees the heavenly Jerusalem. His grief
(which will not die) is coupled with awe and love for Christ.

The stanzas we have here begin at this point: the father sees
the splendid and wounded Christ and his daughter with him.
Agonizingly, unable to contain himself further, he tries to cross
the stream to reach his "pearl." Of course, he cannot.

Nonetheless, this has to be one of the most consoling pieces
of literature for bereaved parents of faith. References to pearls
and gems are common in Scripture, but perhaps the most
pertinent quotation for this poem is "For where your treasure is,
there your heart will be also" (Matt. 6:21). The narrator's pearl is
with Jesus.

"Pearl" (Excerpt)

Translated from the Middle English by Simon Armitage
Stanzas 95–101

GAWAIN POET

My delight in gazing at the Lamb in His glory
caused much amazement and wonder in my mind.
He was perfect, unimpaired, and more worthy of praise
than any tongue could ever tell of.
The clothes He wore were wonderfully white,
His looks graceful, His demeanour gracious.
But an open wound, wide and weeping
could be seen by His heart where the skin was skewered,
and blood poured from His punctured side.
Alas, I thought; who inflicted such injury?
Any heart would sooner be scorched by sorrow
than take delight from so dark a deed.

No one doubted the Lamb's delight;
although He was hurt by that heinous wound
He suffered in silence, displayed no pain.
In all His glances He was wonderfully glad.
And the faces of all His glorious followers
were alive with life, lit by love.
Then looking, I saw there my little queen,
who I thought was standing on the shore of this stream.
Lord, how happy and at peace she appeared,
so pure and content among her companions.
And instantly I wanted to wade that water,
longing for her, the delight of my life.

Delight deluged my eyes and ears
till my mortal mind was dizzied by madness.
Nothing mattered more than being near her.
I wanted to join her over the water
and no one would halt me, hold me back
or stop me summoning every morsel of strength
and swimming that stream. I would cross the current
or die trying and drown in its depths.
But suddenly that notion was snatched away;
as the brook beckoned and I bounded forward
my bold intent was abruptly blocked:
my plan was not to the Prince's pleasing.

My Prince was displeased that I had approached
that teeming flood in a state of frenzy.
Rashly I had rushed towards the river
but suddenly felt a restraining force,
and just as I leapt from land to stream
my stunt startled me out of my dream.
I woke in the same green garden again
with my head laid on the little hill
where my priceless pearl had disappeared.
Roused from sleep all my sadness resumed,
and sinking in sorrow I said to myself,
"Let this be pleasing to my Prince's pleasure."

It deprived me of pleasure and caused me pain
to be cast so quickly from that fair country,
exiled from all its exquisite sights.
My heart laboured with a heavy longing
and I cried out loud in mournful lament:
"Oh pearl," I said, "so high in honour.

To hear your voice in that hallowed vision
meant more to me than anything on earth.
If all that tripped from your tongue holds true
and you walk in whiteness wearing the crown
then I'll happily dwell in this dungeon, knowing
what part you play in pleasing the Prince."

Had I put His pleasure before my own,
and yearned only for what was yielded,
and acted only with honest intent,
and done as my perfect pearl had pleaded,
then I might have lingered longer in His presence
and witnessed more of His mystery and wonder.
But a fellow will always seek further fortune;
I reached for more than was mine by right,
and that glimpse of life in the land everlasting
was shattered in a moment and the gates slammed shut.
Lord, they are mad who meddle with your laws
or propose to spoil a Prince's pleasure.

To please the Prince and join Him in peace
is the simple choice for His faithful flock,
for day and night He has never been less
than a God, a Lord, and a loving friend.
Here on this mound this happened to me:
at first I pined for my fallen pearl,
then gave her up to go to her God,
with my blessing, and also the blessing of Christ,
who the priests prove to us time after time,
His body as bread, His blood as wine.
May we live both as His lowly servants
and beautiful pearls, pleasing to Him. Amen. Amen.

Passus 20 of
Piers Plowman (Excerpt)

(1372–c. 1389)

WILLIAM LANGLAND

Imagine if sins, virtues, and abstractions were people you ran
into through the day. Would you rather spend an afternoon
with Envy, or a night with Gluttony? Would you dine with Peace
or work with Truth? Back in the fourteenth century, poetry was
flexing muscles strange to modern readers: it was discerning
moral issues, exhorting the faithful, stirring revolt—and
entertaining with outrageous stories. Its "characters" were often
personifications of concepts such as these that served to edify as
much as entertain.

Piers Plowman was written at a bleak time for England. The
first wave of the Black Death had wiped out around half of the
population; the Hundred Years' War meant more death, taxes,
and poverty; the Peasants' Revolt was brewing; the Western
schism of the Church was underway. Through all strata of
society, confusion, corruption, and fear were rife.

William Langland was deeply concerned with the soul—
both individual souls and the souls of Church and state. In this
searching allegorical dream-story, "Will" has a vision of the "fair
field full of folk" (humanity)—some doing well, many behaving
appallingly and fleecing the poor.[1] He goes on to meet a vivid
cast of characters, including Holy Mother Church, Lady Meed
(payment), False Faithless, Reason, Peace, the Seven Deadly

1. *Piers Plowman*, Prologue, line 19.

Sins—and a host of other aspects of individuals and society. He passes through instructive visions, seeking the best way to salvation. The titular Piers Plowman is both just a plowman and a representative of Christ, and the *passus* (or steps) that we are led through are a pantomime of debates, spats, and sermons. At times it reads like a cross between *Alice and Wonderland* and *The Pilgrim's Progress*.

At heart, the poem stirs the muddied waters of goodness and religion gone badly awry. Like Dante before him, and like his contemporary Chaucer, Langland was appalled by corruption in the Church, and many of his characters speak of the kinds of clerical sin that paved the way for the Reformation. But truth in *Piers Plowman* is firmly allied with Holy Mother Church. Christ, too, is present, and the text—even and especially today—reads like a good shake of the shoulders to the faithful who forget the necessity of moral integrity, of setting conscience over pride, and of seeking Christ in all things.

The excerpt here is from the ending of Will's dream of the Harrowing of Hell. Christ is leading out hordes of the dead—leaving behind Satan and his minions. Peace, Love, Truth, and Righteousness are reconciled (illuminating the fact that any one of those things divorced from the others is dysfunctional). The alliterative lines are punctuated by quotations from Psalms and hymns until, at the very end, Will wakes up.

In Scripture, dreams are often prophetic (think of both Josephs' dreams in the Old and New Testaments). In poetry, the same applies. Through the jumble of argument and quest, this dream near the end of the book brings the narrator to the cross as the lynchpin of truth and right reason—and the only channel through which goodness and truth can cohere. We are reminded of the earlier "Dream of the Rood" in Will's vision of the cross as being like a jewel. He has understood what will save his soul.

Notes:

Flesh sins, flesh clears, flesh of God reigns as God: From a hymn sung on
Ascension Day.

***After darkest clouds, the sun will shine bright; / And love shine brighter after every
fight***: Proverbial, though the Latin wording in the poem fairly closely follows that
of a poem by Alan of Lille.

per secula seculorum: "forever and ever." Formula for ending a prayer.

Mercy and truth have met each other; justice and peace have kissed: From
Psalm 85:10.

Te Deum laudamus: "We praise thee God." A famous hymn sung at matins
every Sunday.

Behold how good and pleasant it is: From Psalm 133:1, which continues "when
kindred live together in unity."

Passus 20 of *Piers Plowman* (Excerpt)

From the C Version
Translated from the Middle English by George Economou

WILLIAM LANGLAND

"Thus by law," said our Lord, "I will lead out of here
The people I love and who believe in my coming.
But for the lies that you lied, Lucifer, to Eve
You shall bitterly abide," God said, and bound him with chains.
Ashtoreth and company hid in nooks and crannies,
They dared not look on our Lord, the least of them all,
But let him lead forth those he liked and leave behind
      whomever he pleased.
   Many hundreds of angels then harped and sang,
Flesh sins, flesh clears, flesh of God reigns as God.
Then Peace piped a note of poetry:
After darkest clouds, the sun will shine bright;
And love shine brighter after every fight.
"After sharpest showers," said Peace, "brightest is the sun;
There is no warmer weather than after watery clouds,
Nor any love dearer, nor dearer friends,
Than after war and wreckage when love and peace are masters.
There was never a war in this world nor wickeder envy
That Love, if he wanted to, could turn it to laughter,
And Peace through patience stop all perils."
   "Truce," said Truth, "You tell us the truth, by Jesus!
Let us kiss each other and clutch in covenant!"
   "And let no people," said Peace, "perceive that we squabbled,
For nothing's impossible to him who is almighty."

"That's the truth," said Righteousness and kissed Peace
    reverently,
And Peace her, *per secula seculorum.*
  *Mercy and truth have met each other; justice and peace have
    kissed.*
Truth trumpeted then and sang *Te Deum laudamus,*
And then Love strummed a loud note on the lute,
  Behold how good and pleasant it is, etc.
  Till dawn the next day these damoiselles caroled
On which men rang bells for the resurrection, and right with
    that I awoke
And called Kit my wife and my daughter Calote:
"Arise, and go reverence God's resurrection,
And creep on your knees to the cross and kiss it as a jewel
And most rightfully as a relic, none richer on earth.
For it bore God's blessed body for our good,
And it terrified the Fiend, for such is its might
No grisly ghost may glide in its shadow!"

"The Monk"
from the General Prologue to
The Canterbury Tales

(1387–1400)

GEOFFREY CHAUCER

As we walk through a large art gallery, we might suddenly
notice the pale, wooden faces of medieval portraits blossoming.
Shadows gather under eyes and cheekbones, fabric falls in lit
folds, flesh and muscle hold luscious tones. Similarly, entering
Geoffrey Chaucer's fourteenth-century tavern in Southwark, we
are conscious of being among fleshed-out people—"the smell of
the sheep."[1] Gone are the personified abstractions of Langland's
Piers Plowman. Chaucer's poetry is the first flowering of literary
Realism in English—the kind we love to read in Jane Austen
and see in films, where characters are complex and layered, like
anyone we know. We can hear the people of the *Tales*; we can see
them draining their ale and smell the horses idling outside by
the river. Chaucer's work was, similarly to Langland's, set in the
chaos of post-plague, post-revolt, post-schism world. It was also
profoundly Catholic.

The pilgrims of *The Canterbury Tales* are conducting a
storytelling competition en route. They are a mixed bag:
Prioress, Friar, Miller, Plowman, Knight, Wife, Summoner, to
name a few. If some of the religious—like the Pardoner, who
nurses a bag of pig bones to sell as relics—are corrupt, others,

---

1. See Francis, Holy Chrism Mass homily, April 2, 2015, vatican.va.

like the Parson, are endearingly holy. The dainty nun is
worldly. The Miller is a brute, the Wife is a bully, the Knight is a
gentleman. The religious population, both lay and consecrated,
was so vast at that time that, on pilgrimage, all life was there.
Here we have the Monk from the General Prologue (where
each character is presented in what could be a masterclass of
characterization for novelists or screenwriters).

You will be struck by how smoothly the writing goes:
though this is a translation from the Middle English, it reflects
Chaucer's original "heroic couplets" (rhyming couplets in iambic
pentameter). The rhymes are not too clunky but exact enough to
provoke a chuckle. Chaucer is tongue-in-cheek about the Monk,
this "manly man'" who has a lot of fine horses and a bridle that
chimes as loud as the chapel bell. The monk rejects ideas of
religious brothers living an austere or cloistered life, and the
narrator (ostensibly) agrees: St. Augustine can keep his pious
studying for himself.

But the consequence of the Monk's laxity can be seen in the
second half of this extract: though a religious, he is, most of all,
a fantastic horseman with all the fancy gear. The description of
his outer appearance (fur-trimmed cuffs, a gold pin in a love-
knot, supple boots) pointedly includes his popping eyes, which
seem to be on fire. Any doctor could tell us how much the eye
reveals about a person's inner workings—particularly when they
feast on swan. And, of course, "The eye is the lamp of the body"
(Matt. 6:22). Through the Monk's eye, Chaucer is telling us that
his soul is not in order.

Yet there is affection in this description. A preachy hatchet
job on any of the pilgrims would have meant a thin and two-
dimensional tale. Even the clearly immoral or unpleasant in
these stories is handled with careful observation and wit. Like
some of the best modern writers, Chaucer merely shines an

omniscient, sometimes ironical, authorial light on his cast of merry men and women.

Notes:

palfrey: horse.

Saint Benet: St. Benedict.

Saint Maur: St. Maurice.

Saint Austin: St. Augustine of Canterbury.

"The Monk"
from the General Prologue to
The Canterbury Tales

Translated from the Middle English by Nevill Coghill

GEOFFREY CHAUCER

A *Monk* there was, one of the finest sort
Who rode the country; hunting was his sport.
A manly man, to be an Abbot able;
Many a dainty horse he had in stable.
His bridle, when he rode, a man might hear
Jingling in a whistling wind as clear,
Aye, and as loud as does the chapel bell
Where my lord Monk was Prior of the cell.
The Rule of good St Benet or St Maur
As old and strict he tended to ignore;
He let go by the things of yesterday
And took the modern world's more spacious way.
He did not rate that text at a plucked hen
Which says that hunters are not holy men
And that a monk uncloistered is a mere
Fish out of water, flapping on the pier,
That is to say a monk out of his cloister.
That was a text he held not worth an oyster;
And I agreed and said his views were sound;
Was he to study till his head went round
Poring over books in cloisters? Must he toil
As Austin bade and till the very soil?
Was he to leave the world upon the shelf?
Let Austin have his labour to himself.

This Monk was therefore a good man to horse;
Greyhounds he had, as swift as birds, to course.
Hunting a hare or riding at a fence
Was all his fun, he spared for no expense.
I saw his sleeves were garnished at the hand
With fine grey fur, the finest in the land,
And on his hood, to fasten it at his chin
He had a wrought-gold cunningly fashioned pin;
Into a lover's knot it seemed to pass.
His head was bald and shone like looking-glass;
So did his face, as if it had been greased.
He was a fat and personable priest;
His prominent eyeballs never seemed to settle.
They glittered like the flames beneath a kettle;
Supple his boots, his horse in fine condition.
He was a prelate fit for exhibition,
He was not pale like a tormented soul.
He liked a fat swan best, and roasted whole.
His palfrey was as brown as is a berry.

"There Is No Rose of Such Virtue"

(Fifteenth century)

ANONYMOUS

This deceptively simple little poem, written in a mixture of Middle English and Latin,[1] is heavy on theology—but its knowledge is neatly packed and brilliantly clear. At the time of its writing, Mass, the Divine Office, and Scripture would have all been in Latin. We can't know for certain who wrote the piece, but the mix of languages gives it both a secular and ecclesiastical feel; it is common and complex.

The rose has long been associated with the Virgin Mary. "I am a rose of Sharon, a lily of the valleys," says the lover in the Song of Solomon, a text in which Mary has often been identified as the female speaker (Song of Sol. 2:1). By the Middle Ages, the rose was often used as a metaphor for the Blessed Mother—St. Bernard of Clairvaux likened her to a rose, and St. John Henry Newman later called her "Rosa Mystica."[2] Catholic happenings bleed into this poetic tradition, which then feeds back into reality. When Juan Diego opened his *tilma* in Guadalupe in 1531, it was of course a cascade of roses that poured out. Still today, stories of the surprising scent of roses mean that Our Lady is around. And, of course, the Rosary, her prayer, is named for a garland of roses.

---

1. Spelling updated by the editor.

2. John Henry Newman, "Rosa Mystica (The Mystical Rose)," in *Meditations and Devotions of the Late Cardinal Newman* (New York: Longmans, Green, and Co., 1893), 66–67. The term was previously used in the sixteenth-century Litany of Loreto.

In this poem, Mary is once again compared to a rose, this time of virtue. But the medieval meaning of *vertu* was far more loaded than the modern. *Vertu* also signified moral excellence, spiritual power, and physical stamina. It would also have had, among other things, connotations of a plant-based medicine and a pledge. In short: Mary is not a fragile flower. *Alleluia*!

The next stanza makes her power abundantly clear: this one small rose holds heaven and earth. There is an *akathist* hymn in the Byzantine tradition that hails the Virgin as "Container of the uncontainable." One woman's flesh and bone held the sum total of reality. This is not the pallid Mary of so much sentimental art; this is a walking miracle. *Res miranda*—something to be marveled at!

Through Mary we are able to experience God as man. She has an intimate and unique relationship with each person of the Trinity, and each is equally important: Father, Son, and Spirit. Like the petals of a rose, these relationships are distinct but whole, making *pari forma* (equal form).

Now we are singing with the shepherds and angels, *Gloria in excelsis Deo* (Glory to God in the highest!), and so let us rejoice—*Gaudeamus*! And now, *transeamus*—let us pass from the insubstantial world and set our gaze on heaven.

This text was written at the end of the fifteenth century and was set to music as a carol. Its popularity endures; the most famous modern recording of it is by Sting. And so poetry, like so many arts, continues to carry Mary into every corner of the world.

"There Is No Rose of Such Virtue"

ANONYMOUS

There is no rose of such virtue
As is the rose that bore Jesu;
Alleluia.

For in this rose containéd was
Heaven and earth in little space;
Res miranda.

By that rose we may well see
That He is God in persons three;
Pari forma.

The angels sung the shepherds to:
Gloria in excelsis Deo:
Gaudeamus.

Now leave we all this worldly mirth
And follow we this joyful birth;
Transeamus.

"O Rosary that Recalled My Tear"

(c. 1470)

AITHBHREAC INGHEAN CORCADAIL

Catholics have always known the emotional power of objects.
They know how a fragment of clothing can bring a saint close
to us in prayer. But perhaps there is no more personal object
for a Catholic than her rosary. This stunning Scots Gaelic
poem is addressed to the rosary of the poet's dead husband. As
she twines the beads through her fingers, a tear is "recalled"
(provoked), thinking of the hands, now dead, that once held
them. This is a highly structured and public poem. At the same
time, it is an intimate expression of grief.

For the Irish and Scots, poetry has, historically, been the
voice of the people. The bard's role was to be society's memory
and its representative. He was also the appraiser, the praiser,
and the blamer. Bardic poetry recounted battles, memorialized
disputes, and made and broke reputations. While Aithbhreac
Inghean Corcadail may not have been a professional bard, in
this poem she is fulfilling the role by providing an elegy for
her dead husband Niall Og (Young Niall). For Corcadail is not
only giving poignant form to her own grief; she is recording his
eloquence, his recitation skills, and his keen appreciation and
patronage of the arts. The poem is, in a sense, his obituary.

But it is more. Young Niall is likened to a bird, a fish,
and a dragon. The very soil is in mourning. The dead man,
whose presence is so tangibly recalled by his rosary, is now in
everything. Everywhere the widow looks, she sees his goodness.

Death has broken down the constraining lines of his person and written him large on the world and in every lovely thing. We are reminded of the twelfth-century "The Crucifixion" in nature's expression of human and divine sorrow. In this manifestation of man's death writ on nature, we hear also Joseph Mary Plunkett's witness to Christ's Passion ("I See His Blood upon the Rose"). In the poem's ability to channel emotion to a rosary in the hand, we feel the pulse of Catholicism.

There is a plaintive music to the piece that has no remission. There is no remedy nor resolution for the woman's sorrow, which we might expect from other poetic forms such as the sonnet. Rather, the comfort comes from Christ, to whom she turns toward the end of the poem, and her invocation of the Mother of God through the rosary.

Lines two and four rhyme simply and cleanly in this translation. This kind of disciplined yet simple structure vastly aids memorization of the piece, and no doubt the original Scots Gaelic was written in similar fashion. Aithbhreac's aim was to immortalize her dead husband, and this meant that the piece would have been recited around many a fire, particularly by the descendants of Niall Og, who no doubt held his rosary even as they spoke the words.

"O Rosary that Recalled My Tear"

Translated from the Scots Gaelic by Derick Thomson

AITHBHREAC INGHEAN CORCADAIL

O rosary that recalled my tear,
dear was the finger in my sight,
that touched you once, beloved the heart
of him who owned you till tonight.

I grieve the death of him whose hand
you did entwine each hour of prayer;
my grief that it is lifeless now
and I no longer see it there.

My heart is sick, the day has reached
its end for us two, brief the span
that I was given to enjoy
the converse of this goodly man.

Lips whose speech made pleasant sound,
in every land beguiling all,
hawk of Islay of smooth plains,
lion of Mull of the white wall.

His memory for songs was keen,
no poet left him without fee,
nobly generous, courteous, calm,
of princely character was he.

Poets came from Dun an Óir,
and from the Boyne, to him whose hair
was all in curls, drawn by his fame;
to each he gave a generous share.

Slim handsome hawk of Sliabh Gaoil,
who satisfied the clergy's hopes,
salmon of Sanas of quiet stream,
dragon of Lewis of sun-drenched slopes.

Bereft of this man, all alone
I live, and take no part in play,
enjoy no kindly talk, nor mirth,
now that his smiles have gone away.

Niall Og is dead; none of his clan
can hold my interest for long;
the ladies droop, their mirth is stilled,
I cannot hope for joy in song.

Gigha of smooth soil is bereft,
no need of music Dun Suibhne feels,
the grass grows green round the heroes' fort;
they know the sorrow of the MacNeills.

The fort that brought us mirth, each time
we made our way there; now the sight
of it is more than I can bear
as I look on it from each height.

If Thou, Son of the living God,
hast breached the cluster on the tree,
Thou has taken from us our choicest nut,
and plucked the greatest of the three.

The topmost nut of the branch is plucked,
Clan Neill has newly lost its head:
often the best of the generous men
descends to the MacNeills' last bed.

His death, the finest of them all,
has sapped my strength, and cost me dear,
taking away my darling spouse,
O rosary that recalled my tear.

My heart is broken in my breast,
and will not heal till death, I fear,
now that the dark-eyed one is dead,
O rosary that recalled my tear.

May Mary Mother, the King's nurse,
guard each path I follow here,
and may her Son watch over me,
O rosary that recalled my tear.

"Quia Amore Langueo" (Excerpt)

(Fifteenth century)

ANONYMOUS

In the richness of the medieval Catholic imagination, Christ
is seen as lover, parent, brother, healer, feeder, husband, and
protector—and all of these facets are played out in this haunting
love poem, spoken, from the third stanza, in the voice of Christ.

"Quia Amore Langueo" was a hit in the fifteenth century,
and several versions have survived. Its Latin title and refrain
are taken from the Vulgate translation of the Song of Solomon,
which in the NRSV reads "for I am faint with love" (Song of Sol.
2:5). Christ as the Beloved and the faithful as his Bride is the
dominant theme of the poem. But the poet plays adroitly with
this scenario, and pricks our lazy familiarity with God in ways
that modern readers might view as strange.

The setting is this: Jesus sits on a hillside, crowned with
thorns. On his hands are a pair of bloody gloves. His sides are
bleeding. He is lamenting the faithlessness and neglect of his
lover (mankind). This idea of humanity being akin to a cheating
woman is used in the Old Testament to demonstrate God's
dealings with Israel (as in Jeremiah 3:1: "You have played the
whore with many lovers"). This poem brings the historical fact
of the killing of Christ into this allegory. In other words, Christ
steps into biblical metaphors to express the pain of his betrayal,
the fierceness of his loyalty, and the perfection of his divine
patience as the husband to humanity.

Medieval attention to man's innate sadism is well spelled
out: our choices bloody his gloves and hobble him; he cannot
move because of the ferocity with which we nailed him down.
Much of the imagery here is redolent of the cult of the Sacred
Heart and earlier devotions to Christ's wounds. Jesus takes
his brood into the bloody shelter of his body, where he feeds,
cleans, and clothes—like a mother, in mystical and poetic terms.
This idea was not new. "Our precious mother Jesus," Julian of
Norwich wrote, "may feed us with himself."[1]

And yet, despite being all and everything, despite a chamber
being prepared for the beloved (reminding us of John 14:2: "I
go to prepare a place for you"), despite an all-consuming and
infinitely faceted love, when the lover is finally ensconced in the
house of Jesus, things are still not quite as they should be. The
lover cannot, somehow, accept what Christ has to give.

In a sense, what we witness here in this poem is removed
from the real Christ of the Gospels—his walking, his eating, his
teaching, his anger, his rationality. This is a Christ of a certain
type of Catholic imagination. This is Christ stepping into his
own parables: the king planning a wedding feast for ungrateful
guests (Matt 22:1–14), the bridegroom coming to the foolish
bridesmaids with no oil (Matt 25:1–13), the abandoned Father
who longs for his son's return (Luke 15:11–32). Through this
poem, we are asked to step into them too.

1. Julian of Norwich, *Revelations of Divine Love* 60.

"Quia Amore Langueo" (Excerpt)

Translated from the Middle English by the editor

ANONYMOUS

In a valley of this restless mind,
I sought in mountain and in mead,
Trusting a true-love to find.
Upon a hill I then took heed,
Drawing near to a voice I heard
That lamented in great sorrow,
"See, dear soul, how my sides bleed,
Quia amore langueo."

Upon this hill I found a tree,
Under the tree a man was sitting,
He was wounded head to feet,
His heart's blood, I saw, was letting.
A man who looked much like a king,
A gracious face to look into.
I asked him why he was lamenting.
He said, "*Quia amore langueo.*"

"I am True-Love, and false was never.
My sister, man's soul, I loved her thus:
The two of us cannot be severed:
I left my kingdom glorious,
prepared for her a palace precious.
She flees; I follow. I love her so,
I suffer this pain piteous,
Quia amore langueo.

My fair spouse and my love bright,
I saved her from beating; she had me beat!
I clothed her in grace and heavenly light,
This bloody shirt she put on me!
For longing of love I would not cease
Such sweet strokes as these are—lo!
I've loved her ever, as I repeat,
Quia amore langueo.

Man, don't marvel I sit so still:
love has shod me wondrous tight,
My feet are buckled by her will
With these sharp nails. You know alright
My love's no taint of any lie.
I opened myself to her as whole;
By my Body she is enticed,
Quia amore langueo.

I made in my side a comely nest.
Look in: how wide the wound is there!
This is her chamber. Here shall she rest,
That she and I may sleep so paired.
Here she can wash if she is smeared.
Here is a place for all her woe.
Come when she will, she shall have cheer,
Quia amore langueo.

I will abide till she is ready,
I will seek her if she says no,
If she is reckless, I will entreat
If she disdains, I will implore,
If she cries, I cannot ignore—
My arms well-spread to clasp her so.
Now soul, try me! Cry once, I'm yours!
Quia amore langueo.

My love's in her chamber. Hold your peace!
Make no noise, but let her sleep.
My babe, she mustn't know disease;
I cannot hear my dear child weep.
With my pap I shall her keep.
Don't marvel that I tend her so
My side-wound would not be so deep,
But *Quia amore langueo.*

Wax not weary, my own wife.
What good is it to live appeased?
My reign goes further in hard strife,
Is better than in days of peace.
I will support you in woe and weal!
From me, dear soul, please do not go.
Your prize is settled at life's close,
Quia amore langueo.

"Done Is a Battle
on the Dragon Black"

(Sixteenth century)

WILLIAM DUNBAR

William Dunbar, priest and one of the grandfathers of the
Scottish poetic tradition, was a "makar" or bard of the court
of King James IV. This role of makar (which has recently been
resurrected in Scotland) involves the poet in question writing
verse for events of national significance—in essence, being a
poetic voice of the people. In that same spirit, Dunbar wrote
many poems for royal occasions, including the marriage of
Margaret of England to King James of Scotland in 1503. But his
poems were also humorous. He petitioned for work through
his versifying, and even excused himself due to a headache.
His oeuvre is a good example of how poetry, in those days, was
used as a communicative act and not just a high-brow artform.
Devotional pieces such as this were also a feature of his poetic
output. And from this poem, it is easy to see how very good
Dunbar was with painting a picture in words.

The forceful music of this poem is incomparable. In its
original Middle Scots it is even punchier—though every attempt
has been made to retain as much of its punch as possible
in translation. The stress on the first syllable encapsulates
everything of this triumphal Easter poem: "Done!" The ensuing
line with its alliterative *d* and *b* and assonance of "dragon" and
"black" ensure that these words are never forgotten. With four
strong beats to a line, this is the poetry of memorization, the

kind of verses to return to the reader through the day and in the
dead of night.

The dragon, of course, is Satan. Interestingly, the original
"serpent" in Genesis may have been something more akin to a
dragon. In Revelation 12:9, John tells us that "the great dragon
was thrown down, that ancient serpent, who is called the Devil
and Satan." In medieval art, dragons-as-devils abound. St.
George, of course, rousted a dragon, and so, logically enough,
Christ here is a knight. As we have already seen, the image of
Christ in our consciousness is always clothed by our needs,
our history, our moment in time. In "The Dream of the Rood,"
seven hundred years earlier, Christ was a burly Anglo-Saxon
warrior. Here he is a dragon-slaying knight—but no courtly lute
could gently strum this story. "Done!" Dunbar exclaims, giving
masculine weight to Jesus in the heft of the stressed beat. The
rhymes, as they occur, emphasize this event of good upturning
bad: "black" of the devil goes "crack" in the gates of hell.
Ransom is "paid" as Christ rises from the "grave."

In the second stanza, the devil becomes not just a dragon
but a serpent and a tiger, and in the third, Christ turns
from lamb to lion. Perhaps bizarrely to a modern reader, the
ascending Christ is also compared to Apollo in the next stanza:
Greek god of truth, prophecy, and light, among a multitude of
other things. This analogy stresses not only Christ's divinity but
also his sheer machismo. Finally, we have the image of a cleared
battlefield and an empty jail (evoking Christ's promise from
Isaiah in Luke 4:18–19). This classic Easter poem, which builds
on repeated iterations of the Resurrection, is a joy in its forceful
triumph.

"Done Is a Battle on the Dragon Black"

Translated and updated from the Middle Scots and Latin
by the editor

WILLIAM DUNBAR

Done is a battle on the dragon black,
Our champion Christ has crushed his force;
The gates of hell broke with a crack,
The sign is raised of the triumphal cross,
The devils keen with hideous voice,
The souls are saved and to bliss can go,
With blood, our ransom Christ has paid:
The Lord has risen from the grave.

Defeated is Lucifer, that deadly dragon,
The cruel serpent with the mortal sting;
The keen old tiger, with his teeth all bared,
Has lain in wait for us so long,
Thinking to grip us in his claws strong;
The merciful Lord willed it not so,
Regarding that prey he made him fail.
The Lord is risen from the grave.

He for our sake that suffered to be slain,
And like a lamb in sacrifice was gi'en,
Is like a lion risen up again,
And like a giant raises on high;
Aurora blooms, radiant and bright,
Aloft the glorious Apollo ascends,

From night departs the blissful day:
The Lord is risen from the grave.

The great victor is risen high again,
That for us to death was wounded;
The sun that waxed all pale shines bright,
And, darkness cleared, our faith's re-found;
The knell of mercy from heaven sounds,
Christians are delivered of their woe,
All error is of now put straight:
The Lord is risen from the grave.

The foe is chased, the battle is done,
The prison broken, jailors all fled;
The war is gone, confirmed is the peace,
The fetters loosed and dungeon emptied,
The ransom made, the prisoners redeemed;
The field is won, o'ercome is the foe,
Despoiled of the treasure that he stole:
The Lord is risen from the grave.

"Too Long My Chaste Love"

(1546)

VITTORIA COLONNA

It was the greatest regret of Michelangelo that he kissed the hand, not the cheek, of the dying Vittoria Colonna. She was the first woman to publish a book of poetry in the country that would come to be Italy, and hers are emotionally charged poems. This sonnet uses a vivid vocabulary. Its currency, though spiritual, is of the body: she is intimately involved with Jesus as the living flesh of God. But this piece of writing is no conventional form of praise. She wants to bring Christ into the world in a particular way.

At the beginning of her poetic endeavors, Colonna wrote simply and solely to vent her pain at the death of her husband, the Marquis of Pescara, whose death inspired years of extravagant mourning. Prohibited from her desire as a widow to become a nun, at a certain point this wealthy, very well-connected woman seems to have made a conscious decision to give God her writing and, in that, her very self.[1] She shook off her grief, and from that point on worked for Christ through her art and life. It was from that decisive spark that she began to blaze.

Her mission was artistic and spiritual. She wrote poems for Michelangelo and inspired him to draw and write. She was intimate friends with Cardinal Reginald Pole of England (to

1. My knowledge of Colonna comes mostly from online talks by Ramie Targoff, author of *Renaissance Woman: The Life of Vittoria Colonna* (New York: Farrar, Straus and Giroux, 2018).

whom she said she owed the salvation of her soul) and a host of other great minds of the Renaissance.

In this decisive sonnet, we hear Colonna realizing the past weight of her worldly ambition. In our next poem, by Michelangelo, we will see a similar, though more full-blown, artistic crisis. And Gerard Manley Hopkins and Thomas Merton in the centuries to come will also come near to turning their back on writing for fear that the single-minded pursuit of it might mean putting art before God.

Colonna's solution to this dilemma is to vow that all of her writing, from now on, will be for Christ. But her relationship with him is more than poet and muse. She vows to use the nails of the cross as her pens, his blood as her ink, and his flesh as her parchment. For a writer, can there be any more intimate involvement with Jesus? She seeks to enter into his very being and to sing for him from within the body of his Passion.

Spurning pagan places of cult, Parnassus and Delos, Colonna is intent, instead, on supernatural Christian pastures where she seeks light and the water of eternal life. Like Thérèse of Lisieux, whose sister lined up glasses of water of various sizes to show how people are capable of receiving different quantities of love, Colonna knows that the greater her thirst, or love, the more God can give her.[2]

This poem of letting go is the sound of a heart expanding.

---

2. Thérèse of Lisieux, *Story of a Soul: The Autobiography of St. Thérèse of Lisieux*, trans. John Clarke (Park Ridge, IL: Word on Fire Classics, 2022), 46–47.

"Too Long My Chaste Love"

Translated from the Italian by the editor

VITTORIA COLONNA

Too long my chaste love kept hunger for fame
Alive that birthed a serpent in my breast,
But now I turn in pain to God, intent
On sole solution: now the holy nails

Will be my pens, my ink will be his precious
Blood, his lifeless sacred skin my page
On which I'll write all he sustained.
No need to call on Delos, Parnassus.

I aspire to other waters, other mountains,
Where human feet alone can't tread nor climb.
That Sun that lights the elements and skies,
I pray he opens to me his clearest fount

And that he gives me so much of himself
That this thirst of mine is quenched.

"Arrived from Across a Stormy Sea," after Sonnet 285

(1552–1554)

MICHELANGELO

On the wall of the Sistine Chapel, the figures of the Last Judgment greet us in glorious turmoil. Men and women are being both lifted up and pulled down. At the center of all that honed flesh is Christ: utterly godly and resplendent in his manly form. Michelangelo controversially painted a great deal of nude flesh in the scene, and, in the years that followed, swaths of fabric were slathered on for modesty. But this naked explosion of divinity meeting humanity might tell us something about Michelangelo—and the stanzas here.

"Il Divino," as he was dubbed, left us over three hundred poems, and in this raw piece, written only a few years before his death, anxiety regarding his own mortality is laid very bare. He is approaching that last wall of human bodies ascending and descending. He is contemplating the "two deaths": one physical, and one to be feared at the Last Judgment.

And what do we find in the center of the poem? Regret—and it tears at us almost as much as it does him. Could he really have believed that his lifelong dedication to art was an error?

The poem begins with the well-worn image of a boat coming into port as a metaphor for life coming to an end. The place to which he has been journeying is a place of account and reckoning. In this delicate context, he speaks directly of art, saying that he made of it "an idol and a monarch"—that is, he placed it above God. How much truth is there in this?

It must, in some sense, be true that art consumed Michelangelo's life. To be twisted up a ladder painting *that* chapel would, alone, have taken every atom of physical and creative strength. Yet now, in this poem, he speaks of "amorous thoughts" that are "vain and giddy" (that last adjective bringing deliciously to mind the painter standing at the top of his ladder in the Sistine Chapel). At the end of his life, as he approaches the great Artist, God himself, it seems that his accomplishments burn up to nothing in his own mind. He is left wondering if too much time has been spent adoring art (and, perhaps even more pointedly, the naked human form in his art that shocked so many), when there is plainly only one thing to work for, only one thing to adore: Christ's embrace from the cross.

Yet there can be no doubt that Michelangelo's art is infused with what John Paul II called "a spark" of divine wisdom.[1] He must have known that by entering so intensely into his own creation, he would closely echo God's creation. In other words, Michelangelo's vocation was about recognizing and imitating God's natural beauty. To *truly* see the human form, he had to contemplate it with uncensorious love. *That* is what lifts those muscular saints in the Sistine Chapel to the point of graceful flight. Those bodies are not simply daringly realistic; they are shown in naked and direct relation to their Maker. If he felt that this was a waste of his time, that his art was too earthly, or that he cared about it too much, surely he was mistaken.

Michelangelo's original poem in Italian is a lucid sonnet. I have chosen a translation by Paul Murray, OP, with shorter lines to convey the piece's innate austerity, its spare and bleak assessment. The rhymes and music fall naturally: in the final stanza, "crave" and "save" are a perfect fit, evoking the believer's close dance with Christ, of needing and completion.

1. John Paul II, "Letter to Artists" I, April 4, 1999.

"Arrived from Across a Stormy Sea," after Sonnet 285

Translated from the Italian by Paul Murray, OP

MICHELANGELO

Arrived from across
a stormy sea in a frail boat, the course
of my life has at length
brought me to that common port
where all must render
account, and give reasons for every
deed, miserable or good.

Now I see just how
loaded with errors was that fond
imagining of mine,
that fantasy, which made of art
an idol and a monarch,
and which, to our common cost,
we humans still aspire.

What will
become now of my amorous
thoughts,
once vain and giddy,
now that two deaths
draw near, one that menaces,
the other certain?

For neither
painting nor sculpture
can any longer
bring the peace I crave. And so, to
Love Divine I turn
who, from the Cross, extends
his arms to save.

"About Those Words, 'My Beloved Is Mine'"

(Sixteenth century)

ST. TERESA OF AVILA

Visitors to Rome might see a startling and unsurprisingly famous statue by Gian Lorenzo Bernini. In marble, the sculptor has captured Teresa of Avila in sheer ecstasy, with an angel brandishing a spear above her heart. We have a record of the vision that might have inspired this piece of art: the angel, according to Teresa, was short and beautiful, and the tip of the spear he is sporting in the statue went on to pierce her heart deeply, right through to the entrails.[1] The pain—both spiritual and physical—was intense and sweet. The sheer eroticism of the sculpture, and of Teresa's description, is inescapable. But the reality of God's love, this encounter seems to say, is that it is all-encompassing—and quite literally visceral.

This poem would also seem to have been inspired by that angelic encounter.

Born into the perils of the Spanish Inquisition and reform, Teresa became a nun and went on to found the Discalced Carmelite Order with St. John of the Cross. As well as being a supreme organizer, Teresa wrote poetry that sprang directly from mystical inspiration. When describing the "third water" of prayer in her autobiography, she writes of a "glorious bewilderment," a "heavenly madness," and goes on to say

---

1. The vision of the spear-wielding angel, which resembles the imagery of this poem, is recorded in chapter 29 of Teresa's life, completed in 1565. See *The Life of Saint Teresa of Avila by Herself*, trans. J.M. Cohen (London: Penguin Books, 1957), chap. 29.

that she knew of someone (herself) who, despite not being a poet, wrote fluidly stanzas that expressed the sweet agony of experiences with God.[2]

In this short piece, God (rather than his messenger) is characterized as a spear-wielding hunter. He throws the malleable and wounded Teresa into the arms of love. The language of our relationship with God has been, from the Song of Solomon, that of lovers, and the refrain here—"My love belongs to me, and I belong to him"—is taken from that canticle (see Song of Sol. 2:16). We are the receivers; we are called upon to give ourselves entirely to him. This is the language of the marriage bed.

Of course, hunters and arrows belong to another world, and God-as-hunter may seem an extreme analogy. But Teresa is attuned to the death of herself (her attachments, her sins) as she draws close to her Creator. Crucially, the arrow in this poem has been "smeared" the way that hunters' arrows would be dipped in poison so that, once hit, the deer would collapse before it could run off. This "poison" is infused into Teresa's bloodstream. The substance of it is God's love, which then circulates in her body, mind, and heart. What this means is that she, in turn, can love him in his own unsurpassable currency. In the exchange, she loses everything but gains everything. She is transformed.

2. Teresa of Avila, *The Life of Saint Teresa*, chap. 16.

"About Those Words, 'My Beloved Is Mine'"

Translated from the Spanish by Dana Delibovi

ST. TERESA OF AVILA

I gave it all, relinquished all,
and in this way, I bartered:
my Love belongs to me,
and I belong to Him.

When the sweet Hunter
shot me and left me wounded,
when my soul lay panting
in those tender arms,

to balance out the cost
of a new life, I took this trade:
my Love belongs to me,
and I belong to Him.

He pierced me with an arrow
smeared with the poison of love,
and my soul succumbed,
to be one with its Creator.

Now, I don't want another—
to my God, I have surrendered:
my Love belongs to me,
and I belong to Him.

"Seek Yourself in Me"

(c. 1576)

ST. TERESA OF AVILA

"Seek yourself in me": these words were heard by St. Teresa of Avila in prayer. She found them thought-provoking enough for a letter to be sent to several friends, including St. John of the Cross, asking what they made of them. Once she had received their replies, she then wrote back, in Teresian fashion, lightly mocking them or disagreeing somewhat disdainfully. In his letter (now lost), John of the Cross must have stated the necessity of being dead to the world in order to find Christ, for Teresa countered, smartly, that Mary Magdalene (to whom Teresa had a deep devotion) was far from dead to the world when she found him.

As we have seen in our last poem, Teresa's writings bear witness to an intense and visionary prayer life. But she was candid about her faults, and she was clearly indignant at the suggestion that absolute purity was a prerequisite for unity with Jesus. There can be no doubt that she was best placed to comment on the words that Christ spoke to her. And she wrote this poem so that he speaks them to us too.

"Abide in me as I abide in you" (John 15:4): this poem, like the verses by St. Symeon, is a simple yet wondrous illustration of those words. In effect, the text illuminates the conundrums that any serious believer will have had: How can I both abide in him and have him simultaneously abiding in me? What if I'm not perfect—how, then, can Christ make his home in me?

How can I possibly be in him, imperfect as I am? This piece is
a simple answer to these questions, but at the same time it is
a highly structured piece of poetry. The rhyme scheme of the
translation is the perfect medium for the clear (yet in some ways
incomprehensible) message that Jesus aims at each of us: though
still a work in progress, you are beautiful; you are written on
my heart. So, you are in him. To find your true self, you need to
plunge into his heart.

The second stanza also makes it clear that he is in us—we
are his dwelling and his home. Lines 8–10 conjure the famous
painting *The Light of the World* by William Holman Hunt, which
shows Jesus outside a door with no handle. The importance
of this idea in the spiritual life cannot be overstated: God will
enter us even if we are sinful—but only if we let him. The
important thing in prayer is to remain porous. All else falls,
somehow, into place. And finding him (last stanza) is only a
matter of saying his name.

The way that Scripture easily comes to mind as we read the
poem shows us that this is a true fruit of prayer. Teresa, a great
saint, knew that she was not perfect. And yet Christ embraced
her. This poem of hope is just what we might expect from one of
the most privileged and sensitive prayers in history.[1]

---

1. This translation of "Seek Yourself in Me" (Extract from Poem 8) by Paul Murray,
OP, is based on the translation by E. Allison Peers in *The Complete Works of St Teresa of
Jesus* (London: Sheed and Ward, 1978), 287–288.

"Seek Yourself in Me"

Translated from the Italian by Paul Murray, OP,
based on the translation by E. Allison Peers

ST. TERESA OF AVILA

It was by love that you were made,
Lovely and beautiful to be.
So, though it's true that you have strayed,
Upon my heart you are portrayed—
Soul, seek yourself in me.

In you, dear Soul, I am confined.
You are my dwelling and my home.
And, even if one day I find
Closed-fast the portals of your mind,
I'll beg for entrance when I come.

O Search for me not far away
For, if you would attain to me,
You only need my name to say
And I am there without delay.
Soul, seek yourself in me.

"The Dark Night"

(1577–1578)

ST. JOHN OF THE CROSS

The phrase "dark night of the soul" has passed into modern parlance as a term for depression or existential angst. Yet though it springs from a harrowing period in history and one man's life, the poem that created an ocean of comment and cultural reference is one of the most incandescently *joyful* pieces of great literature.

In 1577, John of the Cross (who, with Teresa of Avila, was intent on reforming the Carmelite order) was seized by a group of Carmelites, held hostage in a tiny room for months, starved, and beaten regularly. Strangely—almost incredibly—John composed poems of extraordinary light in that dark and suffocating cell.

Reams of commentary by the poet accompany this poem.[1] The piece itself is a summary of the three-stage spiritual journey: purgation (deprivation of sensual and spiritual consolation, purification from sin), illumination (acceptance of worldly losses and moving toward God), and union with God (consciousness of God's presence at all times and complete conformity to his will). But this poem is far from an academic treatise. Because John uses the trope of God's relationship with man as being like a love affair, even nonbelievers can identify with this poem. It is deliciously seductive and conveys the

1. John of the Cross, *The Dark Night*, in *John of the Cross: Selected Writings*, ed. Kieran Kavanaugh (New York: Paulist, 1987).

overwhelming sensation of being in love like no other. But here, the Lover happens to be the Creator.

The "house," we are told in the first stanza, is hushed. For John, this dwelling place is the body, the ticking mind, the insistent memory, the chattering monologue we so often carry between our ears. All of this is now asleep. This is the "sensory purgation" necessary to begin the journey. The pilgrim-lover is becoming detached from sin and worldly consolations. In the second stanza, John writes in his commentary that we should also consider the necessary "spiritual purgation," which might involve dryness in prayer and no sense of God's presence. Both of these purifications are terrible, says the saint. This is the "dark night." But in truth, the darkness, says John, protects and delivers the soul from anything that is not God. The night is a time of preparation.

Key to reaching the Beloved in this darkness is the "secret ladder" of stanza two, which the speaker accesses "disguised." Why so much secrecy? Why the flavor of a clandestine tryst? In his commentary, John writes that "secret wisdom" will be infused into the soul through love, and this can only happen in the dark. But from what or whom is the lover hiding? Memory, rationality, suspicion, guesswork, presumption, even intellectual understanding—all of these can impede the soul's unity with God. The lover is hiding from the busyness of the outside world, and also from himself. The ladder, says John, is living faith. In the Old Testament, we read of Jacob's vision of a ladder and angels ascending and descending (Gen. 28:10–22). The ladder connects heaven and earth; it is the vertical path for the questing lover to reach his Beloved.

By stanza three, the protagonist (the soul) has no light but his burning heart. This is the illuminative stage of his journey. The pilgrim-lover's eyes are set entirely on God.

Now we are heading to the point at which the soul is united with the Beloved. In the unitive phase, the pilgrim-lover's will is entirely in accordance with God's will. (This is what Dante writes of at the very end of the *Divine Comedy* in our second extract from *Paradiso*.) Here God and pilgrim are described as two mortal lovers, senses stilled, entirely focused on each other's physical and spiritual presence. Anyone who has been in love will know the sensation of the world melting and time slowing to a standstill while they are in their lover's arms. This is the best way, says God through the Song of Solomon, and also by way of St. John, of understanding this final stage of the journey.

This translation from the Spanish does not retain John's rhyme scheme, but it does keep his incantatory repetitions ("Ah, the sheer grace!") and lucidity. The final image of divine love has to be, excepting those of the Song of Solomon, the most sublime ever written. In this version, the last unstressed syllable of "lilies" captures so well the fading of all worldly things.

"The Dark Night"

Translated by Kieran Kavanaugh and Otilio Rodriguez

ST. JOHN OF THE CROSS

One dark night,
Fired with love's urgent longings
—Ah, the sheer grace!—
I went out unseen,
My house being now all stilled;

In darkness and secure,
By the secret ladder, disguised,
—Ah, the sheer grace!—
In darkness and concealment,
My house being now all stilled;

On that glad night,
In secret, for no one saw me,
Nor did I look at anything,
With no other light or guide
Than the one that burned in my heart;

This guided me
More surely than the light of noon
To where he waited for me
—him I knew so well—
In a place where no one appeared.

O guiding night!
O night more lovely than the dawn!
O night that has united
The lover with his beloved,
Transforming the beloved in her lover.

Upon my flowering breast
Which I kept wholly for him alone,
There he lay sleeping,
And I caressing him
There in a breeze from the fanning cedars.

When the breeze blew from the turret
Parting his hair,
He wounded my neck
With his gentle hand,
Suspending all my senses.

I abandoned and forgot myself
Laying my face on my beloved;
All things ceased; I went out from myself,
Leaving my cares
Forgotten among the lilies.

"Although by Night"

(1577–1578)

ST. JOHN OF THE CROSS

In the months of his brutal captivity, St. John of the Cross
was denied the Mass, sufficient food, and light, excepting the
daylight that broke through a small window. Yet, perhaps
surprisingly, his sense of and need for God seems to have
become exquisitely heightened.

Like light and food, thirst runs right through Scripture as a
metaphor of our yearning for God, and his desire for us. We are
the deer panting for streams of water (Ps. 42:1). "I am thirsty,"
says Christ on the cross (John 19:28). In his dank cell, when
prayer could well have been dry, and God could have seemed an
arid eternity away, even nonexistent, John knew his presence
like a spring in the darkness or the sound of the nearby river
through the small window. Imagine the sound of running water
in all that cooped-up silence—the message of depth and length
that it would carry in its music, its glints of light.

Through this poem, John extends this metaphor of
God-as-water, bringing to mind the ever-encompassing stream
that flowed from the temple in Ezekiel 47. This infinite
presence penetrates every prison—even that of our own misery
and dryness.

In these lines, we cannot know the stream's source (God
has no source); this poetic stream (like God) is not created, yet
it nourishes everything. It is fathomless, unsurpassable, and
waters all nations. We have seen this conflation of water with

193

light ("its radiance is never clouded") in Vittoria Colonna's sonnet too. The mix of these two metaphors points to their common properties of giving and sustaining life in all things. Their shifting reference suggests endless transformation.

In the ninth stanza, the metaphor surges on to encompass the Trinity: another stream proceeds from two streams, yet neither of the original takes precedence in this birthing of the Spirit. By the end, we find that this "living fountain-head" of God is also, of course, the Eucharist. Like Thomas Aquinas in "Adoro Te Devote," St. John sees that recognizing God within the "living bread" is done "by night" (i.e., in faith).

As you read, pause a moment at the epigraph: "Song of the soul that delights in knowing God by faith." Reading some of the other poems in this anthology, we can become used to hearing about visions, locutions, and glorious experiences of prayer. St. John of the Cross reminds us that faith is ultimately about not being able to see. He shows us that when we are stripped of every consolation, the presence of God sustains us in every room or situation in which we might find ourselves, buried and constant as a beating heart—or a hidden spring.

The reader cannot fail to be seduced by the rhythm of John's words and his refrain (in the original, "aunque es de noche"). The rhyming couplets before the refrains are effortless and seem to lull as though we are rocked in a boat. The music of this translation by Lynda Nicholson cleaves blissfully well to the original.

"Although by Night"

Translated from the Spanish by Lynda Nicholson

ST. JOHN OF THE CROSS

Song of the soul that delights in knowing God by faith

How well I know the spring that brims and flows,
  Although by night.

This eternal spring is hidden deep,
How well I know the course its waters keep,
  Although by night.

Its source I do not know because it has none
And yet from this, I know, all sources come,
  Although by night.

I know that no created thing could be so fair
And that both earth and heaven drink from there,
  Although by night.

I know its depths possess no bed to fathom
And that none may ford across or sound them,
  Although by night.

Its radiance is never clouded and in this
I know that all light has its genesis,
  Although by night.

I know its currents carry such abundance
They water hell and heaven and all nations,
  Although by night.

The current welling from this fountain's source
I know to be as mighty in its force,
  Although by night.

And from these two proceeds another stream.
I know that neither over this one reigns supreme,
  Although by night.

This eternal fountain is concealed from sight
Within this living bread to give us life,
  Although by night.

And here is calling out to all the creatures.
These waters quench their thirst, although by darkness,
  Because they lie in night.

I long for this, the living fountain-head.
I see it here within the living bread,
  Although by night.

"Upon the Death of M. Edmund Campion, One of the Society of the Holy Name of Jesus"

(1581–1582)

ST. HENRY WALPOLE

This poem describes a particularly horrific sixteenth-century form of execution: being dragged through the streets on a pallet tied to a horse-drawn cart, hanged by the neck until *almost* dead, then disemboweled and cut up into four pieces (quartered). But the diabolical imagining of the torturers is undone in this poem by the poetic imagining of the poet, who subverts the execution's horrific machinations to rally the faithful and champion the Creed.

In 1581, the young Jesuit priest Edward Campion was hanged, drawn, and quartered at Tyburn in London. Like many others, he had left Protestant England for Rome, become ordained as a Catholic priest, and returned home on a dangerous mission. While ministering to English Catholics, Campion prepared ten theological "challenges" to the Anglican authorities, and he was eventually captured. Between being tortured on the rack, he was granted time to debate these points with Anglican theologians. When he was, finally, sentenced to death, he sang the *Te Deum*.

It is believed that the author of these stanzas was Henry Walpole, who was present at Campion's execution and was spattered by his blood during the butchering. Walpole also went on to became a Jesuit and would also be tortured and executed at Tyburn.

The stanzas here are from a longer poem, which the author describes early on as "low and homely verse."[1] In fact, what ensues is smooth iambic pentameter in regular rhyme, which passes from the poet's initial awkwardness to the point where our excerpt begins, with the rallying cry: "England look up, thy soil is stained with blood"—a line worthy of a Shakespearean king.

The image of this grotesque killing doing good in the English faithful is worked to great effect. Christ's parable of the sowing is evoked: seeds that fall into soil wet with this martyr's blood will surely "take," and the spread of Campion's wisdom will grow too, to the benefit of the English: "If thou hast grace their deaths will do thee good."

Of course, the martyr, now in heaven, is unkillable. But even at the material level, death cannot silence writers. The poet can't help goading the authorities that Campion's ten challenges (on, among other points, the Real Presence) gained *more* traction following his death—though the initial publisher reportedly lost his ears for his trouble.

But the brilliance of the piece is in envisioning Campion's quartered body as joining "with joy again" and how this dismembering will create more unity and constancy in the Body of Christ. It is painful to think that Christians of any stripe could be intent on such dismembering violence against a member of the Body of Christ, when St. Paul so clearly described the unity of that Body and how the pain of one is the pain of all. Campion's hurdle (this was the implement he would have been

1. Henry Walpole, "Upon the Death of M. Edmund Campion, one of the Society of the Holy Name of Jesus," in *Firmly I Believe and Truly: The Spiritual Tradition of Catholic England*, ed. John Saward, John Morrill, and Michael Tomko (Oxford: Oxford University Press, 2011), 120.

strapped to as he was drawn through the streets) "draws us with him to the cross." The message is clear: what is done to one is done to all.

This is blood-soaked history in rhyme, and it is sobering to know that there were also many Anglican martyrs in the reign of this queen's sister. We might reflect, through this poem, on the nonsensical tragedy of the countless Christians who have tortured and killed each other in Christ's name.

"Upon the Death of M. Edmund Campion, One of the Society of the Holy Name of Jesus"

ST. HENRY WALPOLE

....

England look up, thy soil is stained with blood,
Thou hast made martyrs many of thine own,
If thou hast grace their deaths will do thee good,
The seed will take which in such blood is sown,
And Campion's learning fertile so before,
Thus watered too, must needs of force be more.

....

The tower saith the truth he did defend;
The bar bears witness of his guiltless mind;
Tyburn doth tell he made a patient end,
On every gate his martyrdom we find;
In vain you wrought that would obscure his name,
For Heaven and earth will still record the same.

....

His prison now the city of the king,
His rack and torture joys and heavenly bliss,
For men's reproach with angels he doth sing
A sacred song which everlasting is
For shame but short and loss of small renown,
He purchase hath an ever during crown.

His quartered limbs shall join with joy again,
And rise a body brighter than the sun,
Your blinded malice tortured him in vain,
For every wrench some glory hath him won,
And every drop of blood which he did spend,
Hath reaped a joy which never shall have end.

Can dreary death then daunt our faith, or pain?
Is't lingering life we fear to lose, or ease?
No, no, such death procureth life again,
Tis only God we tremble to displease,
Who kills but once, and ever still we die,
Whose hot revenge torments eternally.

We cannot fear a mortal torment, we
This Martyr's blood hath moistened all our hearts,
Whose parted quarters when we chance to see,
We learn to play the constant Christian's parts,
His head doth speak, and heavenly precepts give,
How we that look should frame ourselves to live.

His youth instructs us how to spend our days,
His flying bids us how to vanish sin,
His straight profession shows the narrow ways
Which they must walk that look to enter in.
His home return by danger and distress,
Emboldens us our conscience to profess.

His hurdle draws us with him to the cross,
His speeches there provoke us for to die,
His death doth say this life is but a loss,
His martyred blood from Heaven to us doth cry,
His first and last, and all conspire in this,
To show the way that leadeth unto bliss.

Blessed be God which lent him so much grace,
Thanked be Christ which blest his martyr so,
Happy is he which sees his Master's face,
Cursed are they that thought to work him woe,
Bounden be we to give eternal praise,
To Jesus' name which such a man did raise.
Amen.

"The Burning Babe"

(1595)

ST. ROBERT SOUTHWELL

This most famous poem by Robert Southwell is a machine in the way that the heart is a machine: it beats, blazes, and powers a world of sense and emotion. The poem is about brightness in a dark world. It is a vision of a weeping baby Jesus "burning" on a snowy night.

Best first read aloud, the poem is written in "fourteeners" (fourteen-syllable lines, with seven stresses) and dazzling rhyming couplets. Southwell heightens the contrast between heat and cold with alliteration ("hoary"/"heat"/"heart") and ups the impact of the images in the same way ("Babe"/"burning"/"bright"). This dense music creates a poetic boilerhouse of Catholic ideas.

Distressingly, the baby Jesus is born in "fiery heats" and laments that no one goes to him to warm themselves. What this "furnace" consists of is deliberately layered and complex. In one important sense, the fire represents the Passion: it causes the baby pain, and the crown of thorns fuels the blaze. But, at the same time, the baby himself says that his "faultless breast" is the furnace and "love is the fire."

Southwell goes on to expand this metaphor, saying that the smoke is sighs, the fuel is justice, and the air, to feed the purifying flames, is mercy. This kind of elaborate "conceit" (a metaphor that germinates and runs throughout a poem) is typical of metaphysical poetry and can be seen in the work of poets who followed Southwell, like John Donne.

The metaphor of a furnace is elaborated in true
metaphysical fashion. Southwell compares men's souls to
metal that is melted down in Christ's heart (bringing to mind 1
Corinthians 3:15: "The builder will be saved, but only as through
fire"). The baby also melts, toward the end, into a bath of
cleansing blood.

There is no resolution as to whether the fire is good or
bad, and nor can there be. The poet is engaging with the
inextricable relationship between pain and love in Christ's
mission. The cross, the symbol of agony, has become the
greatest symbol of love. The poem burns with this paradox.
It also collapses time; uncomfortably, we are presented
with the baby Jesus in the flames of his Passion in a graphic
foreshadowing of what is to come.

Southwell wrote the piece while in hiding from the English
Protestant regime. On his return to England from Rome, he had
taken refuge in the house of Anne Howard and there carried out
his ministry and composed some of the most celebrated poems
in the English language. This forbidden way of life couldn't
continue. A trap was set: he was caught, tortured unspeakably,
and eventually hanged, drawn, and quartered at Tyburn.

This Christmas poem is testimony to the blazing love that
gave him his courage. We can well picture the recusant priest
taking a breath of air in snow at midnight, with this image, in
all its wholeness and complexity, coming to him as a gift.

"The Burning Babe"

ST. ROBERT SOUTHWELL

As I in hoary Winter's night stood shivering in the snow,
Surprised I was with sudden heat which made my heart to glow;
And lifting up a fearful eye, to view what fire was near,
A pretty Babe all burning bright did in the air appear;
Who, scorched with excessive heat, such floods of tears did shed,
As though his floods should quench his flames, which with his
      tears were fed:
"Alas!" (quoth he) "but newly born, in fiery heats I fry,
Yet none approach to warm their hearts or feel my fire but I!
My faultless breast the furnace is, the fuel wounding thorns:
Love is the fire, and sighs the smoke, the ashes, shame and
      scorns;
The fuel Justice layeth on, and Mercy blows the coals,
The metal in this furnace wrought are men's defiled souls:
For which, as now on fire I am to work them to their good,
   So will I melt into a bath, to wash them in my blood."
   With this he vanished out of sight and swiftly shrunk away,
   And straight I called unto mind, that it was Christmas day.

"Saint Peter's Complaint" (Excerpt)

(1595)

ST. ROBERT SOUTHWELL

During the six years of his hidden ministry during the English Reformation, Robert Southwell produced prose tracts on living a good Christian life and more great poetry. He had spent some years in Italy during his youth and was influenced by the ornate design of Italian verse. One poem in particular, "Le Lagrime di San Pietro" by Luigi Tansillo, inspired Southwell to write 132 stanzas about the remorse of St. Peter for his betrayal of Christ.

Inventive in its self-castigation and contrition, the poem is bathed in both tears and seawater. Through the piece as a whole, Peter compares himself and his tears to Moses, David, Hannah, Cain, and Adam, among others. The metaphors, as well as the references, are very scriptural. As a fisherman, Peter's encounters with Jesus were often based in the sea and in boats. Southwell gets inside this framework of images to demonstrate the disciple's tortured mindset.

Right from the beginning, the lines are stormy. This isn't a tightly enclosed world like "The Burning Babe," but nevertheless metaphors extend and branch throughout. We begin with Peter *becoming* the boat and the tempest. His thoughts are like "torn sails," the wind is his sighs, remorse is his pilot, and the shipwreck is what he deserves. Southwell's trademark alliteration is everywhere, and the iambic pentameter contains imperatives barked to his soul ("Shun," "Stick," "Content thee"). Together, the short words and musical sounds make this a cathartic read. The poem does indeed "give vent"; the noise of the metaphorical storm competes with Peter's cries.

The founder of the Jesuits, St. Ignatius, wrote about the "gift of tears," and this is a theme that Southwell, also a Jesuit, uses throughout the poem. Tears inspired by the Holy Spirit clarify our sight. They allow the faithful to see themselves, including their sins, in relation to God. Peter (here in the poem and no doubt in real life) understands, through grace, the enormity of what he has done. Unsurprisingly, his examination of conscience leads to an outpouring of crying to "wash" and "baptize." This is the road of purification that will lead Peter closer to God. Taken as a whole, the poem is a sometimes exhausting journey that forces us to dwell, with poetic satiation, on the torment of Peter's remorse. Initially there seems to be a shocking finality to his repentance, a terrible self-loathing ("excrement of earth" he calls himself). But this changes, like a wind change at sea, with the final two stanzas. These lines stick to the same rhythm but are quieter in their sounds. The repetition of "Let" has the quality of a trusting lullaby. The conclusion is a much-needed prayer, no less intense in some senses, but filled also with remedy.

Note:

wight: person.

"Saint Peter's Complaint" (Excerpt)

ST. ROBERT SOUTHWELL

Launch forth, my soul, into a main of tears,
Full fraught with grief, the traffic of thy mind;
Torn sails will serve thoughts rent with guilty fears,
Give care the stern, use sighs instead of wind:
Remorse thy pilot, thy misdeed thy card,
Torment thy haven, shipwreck thy best reward.

Shun not the shelf of most deserved shame,
Stick in the sands of agonizing dread;
Content thee to be storms' and billows' game,
Divorced from grace, thy soul to penance wed:
Fly not from foreign ills, fly from the heart,
Worse than the worst of ills is that thou art.

Give vent unto the vapours of thy breast,
That thicken in the brim of cloudy eyes;
Where sin was hatched, let tears now wash the nest,
Where life was lost, recover life with cries;
Thy trespass foul, let not thy fears be few,
Baptize thy spotted soul in weeping dew.

Fly mournful plaints, the echoes of my ruth,
When screeches in my frightened conscience ring,
Sob out my sorrows, fruits of mine untruth,
Report the smart of sin's infernal sting;
Tell hearts that languish in the sorriest plight,
There is on earth a far more sorry wight.

A sorry wight, the object of disgrace.
The monument of fear, the map of shame,
The mirror of mishap, the stain of place,
The scorn of time, the infamy of fame,
An excrement of earth, to heaven hateful,
To man injurious, to God ungrateful.

....

With mildness, Jesu, measure mine offence;
Let true remorse Thy due revenge abate;
Let tears appease when trespass doth increase;
Let pity temper Thy deserved hate;
Let grace forgive, let love forget my fall:
With fear I crave, with hope I humbly call.

Redeem my lapse with ransom of Thy love,
Traverse th'indictment, rigour's doom suspend;
Let frailty favour, sorrows succour move,
Be Thou Thyself, though changeling I offend.
Tender my suit, cleanse this defiled den,
Cancel my debts, sweet Jesu, say Amen!

"The Kissing Sonnet"
from Act 1, Scene 5, of *Romeo and Juliet*

(1591–1596; first performed in 1597)

WILLIAM SHAKESPEARE

In these lines, literature's most famous teenagers are gearing up for their first kiss. And the greatest author in history is sharpening his quill for one of his signature explosions of literary convention.[1]

At the beginning of the play, young Romeo is moon-eyed about a totally different teen: Rosaline. A literary audience of the 1590s might have recognized him as the typical "sonneteer." Sonnets were wildly popular at the time, and many fell into Petrarch's theme of passionately addressing a distant, rather cold love. Romeo is typically hyperbolic about his futile desire. But Shakespeare is never predictable.

When, at his first love-slain meeting with Juliet, Romeo strikes up a sonnet (suggesting, in a roundabout way, that he would like a kiss), Shakespeare's female love-object *pipes up*. As the usually silent counterpart of the sonnet tradition, Juliet steps into the poetry and, taking her cue from Romeo's quatrain, chimes in like a singer in a duet to deliver her own four-liner. She not only flirtatiously picks up his high religious imagery—she obliquely encourages him to go beyond the mere

---

1. A discussion as to why Shakespeare would be included as a Catholic poet, even as critics continue to debate his true identity, is contained in the introduction. This poem and the two that follow demonstrate the Catholic heartbeat that resounds through so much of Shakespeare's work and that has led me to believe, in accordance with many researchers, that the poet kept the Old Faith.

language of seduction and worship and into the physical by sanctioning the touching of hands and likening this innocent contact to a meeting of the lips. By the end of her quatrain, the two are effectively on a roll.

It's not surprising that the fictitious lovers use the language of Catholicism in this love-game: the play is set in Verona. But Shakespeare is demonstrating an acute poetic understanding of both the faith and the Catholic imagination. To begin with, Romeo sets up Juliet as a "holy shrine." English audiences would have been familiar with such places—Walsingham, Canterbury—and seen or heard of their destruction. They would have known that, for pilgrims, such places somehow give access to the inaccessible. For Romeo, it is not enough to touch the "saint" (Juliet); the "pilgrims" are his lips.

Juliet, in turn, is a far cry from the blushing maid or frigid demigoddess. She is the robustly feminine-spiritual woman who shies from neither God nor flesh (very un-Puritan, and very Catholic). Saints, she teases, have hands too, and so do pilgrims, and that's usually how they touch. She plays on the word "palmer" ("holy palmers" were pilgrims to the Holy Land who brought back palm leaves) in consenting to their hands being placed together. Romeo pushes her (don't saints and pilgrims have lips?) and she pushes back (yes, they do—to pray with!). Well, suggests Romeo, let's let our lips do what praying hands do. Juliet's last line here demonstrates the mechanism of intercession. Saints do not move: they are only instruments; through them, prayers are granted. Juliet has placed herself in Romeo's rhetoric by playing at being a passive saint. But it is through her that his prayer takes effect and the kiss happens.

This interlocking dialogue forms one perfect Shakespearean sonnet, beautiful in its symmetry and balance. (Each lover initially has two sentences each. Romeo has two lines more than Juliet overall, but the impression is of equality; they split the final couplet.) The sonnet's sounds increasingly use the lips—"pilgrim," "prayer," "palm," "palmer"—making this all about that much-anticipated conclusion.

As a poem, it is obviously both erotic and spiritual. It uses the language of the sacred to animate human love. (Hadewijch and John of the Cross did the opposite: they unfolded their love for God through images of earthly passion.) The lovers continue in their holy vein further on in the play: at the balcony, Romeo will refer to the emerging Juliet as the sun, and she, in her abundant filling of her role as transcendent love, will answer, "My bounty is as boundless as the sea, / My love as deep. The more I give to thee / The more I have, for both are infinite."[2]

How much the play as a whole is a cautionary tale is highly debatable. Shakespeare was no moral theologian. He was intent on creating a gripping love story and revealing humanity's tragic flaws. But, like any Catholic, he knew that the physical and the spiritual are deeply intertwined. As Benedict XVI wrote, "Eros and agape—ascending love and descending love—can never be completely separated."[3]

---

2. *Romeo and Juliet*, act 2, sc. 2.
3. Benedict XVI, *Deus Caritas Est* 7, encyclical letter, December 25, 2005.

"The Kissing Sonnet"

WILLIAM SHAKESPEARE

ROMEO
If I profane with my unworthiest hand
This holy shrine, the gentle sin is this.
My lips, two blushing pilgrims, ready stand
To smooth that rough touch with a tender kiss.

JULIET
Good pilgrim, you do wrong your hand too much,
Which mannerly devotion shows in this.
For saints have hands that pilgrims' hands do touch,
And palm to palm is holy palmers' kiss.

ROMEO
Have not saints lips, and holy palmers too?

JULIET
Ay, pilgrim, lips that they must use in prayer.

ROMEO
O, then, dear saint, let lips do what hands do!
They pray: grant thou, lest faith turn to despair.

JULIET
Saints do not move, though grant for prayers' sake.

ROMEO
Then move not while my prayer's effect I take.

He kisses her

"Sonnet 116"

(c. 1590)

WILLIAM SHAKESPEARE

Shakespeare's sonnets have always been a source of mystery. To whom was he talking, and what was the nature of their relationship? Are some of the poems coded confessions of a proscribed Catholic faith? Was he involved in a subversive love affair?

The sonnet form usually deals in love. Originating in fourteenth-century Italy, its subject was most often the poet's worshipful love for an unobtainable woman. When the form made it over to England, poets continued with the subject matter—often in long sonnet sequences—but the meter changed to better suit the language, and so did the rhyme scheme.

Unlike the work of other sonneteers, Shakespeare's sonnets do not seem to be a deliberately curated sequence—or at least only in parts. The first 126 appear to speak to a man, and the next twenty-six seem to address a "dark lady." All the sonnets wrestle in some measure with love, but sonnets 1 through 126 have a special preoccupation with time and eternity. Taken alone, sonnet 116 does not seem to be addressed to anyone. It could be argued that, here, Shakespeare's attention is away from his own desires and fixed on heaven.

Shakespearean sonnets are all made up of three four-liners (ABABCDCDEFEF) and a final rhyming couplet to wrap up his "case" (GG). The first quatrain here is a calm petition. The first stressed word, "Let," both implores and insists. Perhaps the speaker is conscious of his own capriciousness, his own passions. Perhaps he is quietly defending what he knows to be pure and unshakeable.

When read aloud, we can hear the compelling alliteration of *m* in the first two lines, and then *l*. The sentences are elegant and parallel in structure; they play with verbs and nouns ("alters"/"alteration," "remover"/"remove") as they insist on the unchanging nature of true love.

The second quatrain refers to an "ever-fixed mark," like an unfaltering star that ships would use for navigation: the star's value might be incomprehensible, but its height (its position for navigation, but also, inescapably, its divinity) is incontrovertible. Readers at that time would have been aware of the Virgin Mary as the metaphorical star by which we navigate storms (and the prohibition in England of thinking of Mary in those terms). But the "ever-fixed mark" of love also has echoes of the indelible nature of a sacrament—in this case, the sacrament of Matrimony. (It is not by chance that the word "marriage" appears in the first line, nor that this is claimed as the most recited poem in modern marriage ceremonies.) Late sixteenth-century and early seventeenth-century readers would have been conscious of the changing nature of worship and the creeping belief among many Protestants that sacraments did not, in and of themselves, bestow grace. The Catholic view, of course, is quite different: a sacrament is powerful. It does not change when it finds a person or situation changed, or "alter when it alteration finds." And neither, says this sonnet, does love. Time itself (appearing as death with his sickle) cannot destroy love, though it may take physical beauty. As St. Paul says, love "endures all things" (1 Cor. 13:7).

"Sonnet 116"

WILLIAM SHAKESPEARE

Let me not to the marriage of true minds
Admit impediments; love is not love
Which alters when it alteration finds,
Or bends with the remover to remove.
O no, it is an ever-fixéd mark
That looks on tempests and is never shaken;
It is the star to every wand'ring bark,
Whose worth's unknown, although his height be taken.
Love's not Time's fool, though rosy lips and cheeks
Within his bending sickle's compass come;
Love alters not with his brief hours and weeks,
But bears it out even to the edge of doom.
   If this be error and upon me proved,
   I never writ, nor no man ever loved.

"I have of late . . ."
from Act 2, Scene 2, of *Hamlet*

(1599–1601; first performed in c. 1602)

WILLIAM SHAKESPEARE

Audiences and critics have argued about this play for centuries.
While T.S. Eliot pronounced it an "artistic failure,"[1] Harold
Bloom described it as a cosmological drama, a "poem unlimited"
that has no parallel in literature.[2]

At first glance, *Hamlet* is simply a revenge tragedy: justice
must be made for the murder of a father and a king. Yet the text
swiftly casts off the cliché of predictability. It is upended by a
devastating psychological and spiritual awareness. Against his
will, Hamlet is entangled in questions of what "is" and "seems"
in discernment of manifestations from beyond the visible
world and how he should react to them. His fate is inextricably
entwined with the question: What is our role in a cast that
includes spirits and angels?

A few years before the writing of this play, Shakespeare lost
his eleven-year-old son Hamnet (*n* and *l* were interchangeable at
that time), probably to the plague. His father had also recently
died. These shocks reverberate through the text. The Ghost
speaks plainly of "fast[ing] in fires" in purgatory and refers
to the quadruple blow of being killed "unhous'led [without
Communion], disappointed [unprepared spiritually], unanel'd

---

1. T.S. Eliot, "Hamlet and his Problems," in *The Sacred Wood: Essays on Poetry and
Criticism* (New York: Alfred A. Knopf, 1921), 90.

2. Harold Bloom, *Hamlet: Poem Unlimited* (New York: Riverhead Books, 2003).

[without extreme unction], / No reckoning made [without confession]."[3] The spirit is expressing the trauma of being violently deprived of religious rites, and this was a deprivation that a proportion of Shakespeare's audience would have been suffering in the real world. (Catholic sacraments were outlawed; the traffic of prayer between the living and the dead was, officially, blocked.) Perhaps no one felt this lack more than the dying—and those who were left behind, feeling that their loved ones were let down at the last.

This is what we witness in *Hamlet*: a grief that is many-barbed. He is embittered by murder with its multiple injustices, paralyzed by prevarication, infused with impotence. This is a grief that demands, "What do I *do* to make amends?" But it is not simply the overwhelming demands of revenge that tax Hamlet. We can see in these lines that, for Hamlet, the place of "noble," "infinite," "admirable" man within the supernatural order has been crippled.

Before this speech from act 2, scene 2, the king and queen have invited Hamlet's friends Rosencrantz and Guildenstern to find out what is behind Hamlet's derangement. In these lines, Hamlet confides to them the darkening of his soul, and simultaneously reveals a luminous understanding of man in Catholic theological terms. The prose structure serves to underline his simple sincerity—the fact he (as well as the iambic pentameter) is undone. But in its conciseness, its figures of speech, and metaphorical structure, this is poetry.

As you read, hear the initial measured tone as Hamlet lays out the anatomy of his mood. The lines then change syntactically as he begins to list the beauties of the earth and sky in gloriously theatrical terms. All of this implies a man once in love with the world and more than able, still,

3. *Hamlet*, act 1, sc. 5.

to apprehend its poetry. Is he playing with his listeners, the craven Rosencrantz and Guildenstern, or is he riffing on his profound disillusionment, rubbing salt into his own wounds by contrasting the innate goodness of creation with his new and lethal cynicism? He ends this poetic waxing with disgust for the world, which then takes us to the center of the speech, its turning point and crux: "What a piece of work is a man."

This expression has passed into modern idiom. "He's a piece of work," we say now, five hundred years on, meaning how corrupt, how low. But here Hamlet is showing us the how of that "work," the divine engineering behind humanity. The lines that follow roll in exclamatory eulogy. He sets out the quintessence of mankind in a religious sense: how on the ladder of being we are elevated, how our "reason" and our "faculties" are far beyond that of animals—we are made in God's image and likeness. On this theme, Shakespeare, through Hamlet's mouth, gives us a Renaissance vision of physical beauty and prowess ("in form and moving"). He goes on to assert the almost angelic capacity of man's actions (and what can this possibly mean aside from his agency in prayer, including, implicitly, the essential action of prayer within the communion of saints, the living and the dead?). He continues by saying that we apprehend almost like gods, intimating *divinization*—that very Catholic awareness of how we are made to receive God into our souls and are destined to be like him (2 Pet. 1:4).

Yet this is now all dust to Hamlet—and, of course, as well as being capable of divinization, man is essentially dust (Gen. 2:7). His father's murder has upended the natural order, and the appearance of his father's ghost from purgatory has disturbed the supernatural status quo. He has broken into the sealed-off world of the living into which Elizabethans had been forced, pronouncing his spiritual debits and making his worldly demands.

Hamlet's concluding "Man delights not me" ends in tetchiness as his two clueless friends smirk at the implication that a *woman's* company would cheer him up. We are left with a sense of the prince being too open to the beauty of creation, yet too bruised by sin, to bear any more chaffing by the idiocy of men.

"I have of late . . ."

WILLIAM SHAKESPEARE

I have of late—but wherefore I know not—lost all my mirth,
forgone all custom of exercises. And indeed it goes so heavily
with my disposition that this goodly frame the earth seems to
me a sterile promontory. This most excellent canopy, the air,
look you, this brave o'erhanging firmament, this majestical roof
fretted with golden fire—why, it appeareth nothing to me but a
foul and pestilent congregation of vapours. What a piece of work
is a man, how noble in reason, how infinite in faculties, in form
and moving how express and admirable, in action how like an
angel, in apprehension how like a god: the beauty of the world,
the paragon of animals! And yet to me what is this quintessence
of dust? Man delights not me—nor woman neither, though by
your smiling you seem to say so.

"The Flaming Heart, Upon the Book and Picture of the Seraphical Saint Teresa" (Excerpt)

(1652)

RICHARD CRASHAW

Richard Crashaw's conversion to the faith was more like a seduction through beauty. Raised as the son of an Anglican cleric with Puritan leanings, Crashaw himself became an Anglican priest—but nursed a devotion to the Blessed Mother and loved censers, crosses, genuflections, and religious paintings. As Puritan sentiment boiled up in England, Crashaw was forced from his homeland and ended up converting to Catholicism in Rome.

His poetry gives us great insight into the nature of his faith. It is baroque in its intricate extravagance and shot through from crown to toe with Catholic theology. He had a profound devotion not only to the Blessed Mother but to saints such as Mary Magdalene and, most particularly, Teresa of Avila. His poetry (which for many years was ignored because of its overtly Catholic flavor) certainly has a tang of the Spanish mystics—and also, more poignantly, of a passionate English mysticism that was being suffocated.

In this piece, Crashaw calls his own heart "hard" and "cold." Reading his work, it seems unlikely that this was true! His experience, recounted here, is of the fiery Teresa of Avila as a channel of illuminated grace. He has read her work; he has meditated on her painting; now, in the poem's title, he

characterizes the Spanish mystic as being like no less than a
seraphim, a six-winged angel of the highest rank. "Seraphic"
means to burn—which makes sense, as seraphim are closest to
God, the source of all light. The historical conflation of Teresa
with a seraph partly arises because of her mystical experience
of being wounded by a spear-wielding angel (see "About Those
Words, 'My Beloved Is Mine'"). But poetically, Crashaw likens
her to an angel of this type because of her own nearness to God.

The first eight lines suggest that Crashaw knew Teresa's
poem about the angel. Just as she was the wounded deer speared
by God, he is a "cold carcass" (suggesting a slaughtered animal)
who will be ravished by the lights contained within her writing.
She will ransack the sin out of him (just as God ransacked
Teresa with his love). Just as Teresa ends up with more when
God takes everything from her, so Crashaw sees Teresa's theft of
his sin (through prayer) as a boon.

"Leave nothing of myself in me," pleads Crashaw to the
mystical saint toward the end. No wonder the Puritans didn't
like him. To anyone who didn't know better, it would seem that
he was idolizing Teresa.

But the poem is simply a prayer for intercession. The
section beginning line-by-line with "By all" is a feast. Crashaw
evidently knew and loved Teresa through her books: he knew
the fierceness of the woman who reformed an order; he knew
her humility; he knew her intellect, love, and desire. "The full
kingdom of that final kiss" reminds us of Bernini's statue of
Teresa about to be speared by that angel, though Crashaw did
not live to see its installation in Rome. The poem's language
is so delicious that it succeeds sublimely as a depiction of
Teresa—"brim-filled bowls of fierce desire"!

Note:

dow'r: dowry.

"The Flaming Heart, Upon the Book and Picture of the Seraphical Saint Teresa" (Excerpt)

RICHARD CRASHAW

O sweet incendiary! show here thy art,
Upon this carcass of a hard cold heart,
Let all thy scattered shafts of light, that play
Among the leaves of thy large books of day,
Combined against this breast, at once break in
And take away from me my self and sin;
This gracious robbery shall thy bounty be,
And my best fortunes such fair spoils of me.
O thou undaunted daughter of desires!
By all thy dow'r of lights and fires,
By all the eagle in thee, all the dove,
By all thy lives and deaths of love,
By thy large draughts of intellectual day,
And by thy thirsts of love more large than they,
By all thy brim-filled bowls of fierce desire,
By thy last morning's draught of liquid fire,
By the full kingdom of that final kiss
That seized thy parting soul and sealed thee his,
By all the heav'ns thou hast in him,
Fair sister of the seraphim!
By all of him we have in thee,
Leave nothing of my self in me:
Let me so read thy life that I
Unto all life of mine may die.

"The Holy Eucharist"

(Seventeenth century)

PEDRO CALDERÓN DE LA BARCA

In seventeenth-century Spain, a soldier and celebrated
playwright was ordained a priest in middle age, and he often
turned the spotlight of his Baroque writing to his faith—in
particular, the Eucharist. This poem is a gem of exegesis and a
hymn to the Church's most beautiful mystery.

Yet the fact of Christ's Flesh and Blood in bread and wine
is not plainly stated within these lines. It is hidden in poetry:
"Godhead here in hiding," as Aquinas would have it via Gerard
Manley Hopkins. Here the truth is not so much taken for
granted as parceled out in strata of biblical reference.

References to the Eucharist are embedded throughout
Scripture, and de la Barca combs through many of them,
beginning with the powerful first line, which recalls Judges
14:8–14, when Samson eats honey from the carcass of a lion
and puts the riddle: "Out of the eater came something to eat"
(Judg. 14:14). As Caesarius of Arles would answer in a sermon,
"Christ is a lion in whose mouth we found the food of honey
after his death."[1]

Honey also comes from a rock in Psalm 81:16, and the image
of a rock is taken up at line four, as we recall Moses knocking for
water for his parched people in Numbers 20. But the Eucharist
is also our storehouse of nourishment, like Joseph's crammed

---

1. Caesarius of Arles, *Sermons* 119.1, in Ancient Christian Commentary on
Scripture, vol. 4, *Joshua, Judges, Ruth, 1-2 Samuel*, ed. John R. Franke (Downers Grove, IL:
InterVarsity, 2005), 147–148.

warehouses of grain in Genesis 41:48 that will feed the populace in times of famine. It is also the dew on Gideon's fleece (Judg. 6:36–40) in that it is a sign of our salvation. And it is a well like the well where Christ promised the Samaritan woman living water and eternal life (John 4:1–42). Furthermore, it is "shew-bread," like the bread of the Old Testament that was kept in the temple as an offering to God (Exod. 25:30).

But, equally, the Eucharist is our daily bread. It is comparable to the manna that rained down on the Israelites during their Exodus, but it is better, as Jesus himself told us (John 6:31–32). It is the wine from the wedding of Cana (John 2:1–12), and it is the bread and wine of "Salem's monarch"—in other words, of the high priest Melchizedek, who gave them to Abram in Genesis 14:18. Finally, it is our medicine, which can restore us physically, mentally, and spiritually.

As Calderón de la Barca demonstrates, the Eucharist, like the Virgin Mary, lends itself to poetry! God has a way of readying us for people and events and helping us to understand them through poetic connections. Throughout Scripture, he prepares our hearts and minds for what he will feed us with at the altar.

"The Holy Eucharist"

Translated from the Spanish by R.C. Trench

PEDRO CALDERÓN DE LA BARCA

Honey in the lion's mouth,
Emblem mystical, divine,
How the sweet and strong combine;
Cloven rock for Israel's drouth;
Treasure-house of golden grain
By our Joseph laid in store,
In his brethren's famine sore
Freely to dispense again;
Dew on Gideon's snowy fleece;
Well, from bitter turned to sweet;
Shew-bread laid in order meet,
Bread whose cost doth ne'er increase,
Though no rain in April fall;
Horeb's manna freely given
Showered in white dew from heaven,
Marvelous, angelical;
Weightiest bunch of Canaan's vine;
Cake to strengthen and sustain
Through long days of desert pain;
Salem's monarch's bread and wine;—
Thou the antidote shall be
Of my sickness and my sin,
Consolation, medicine,
Life and Sacrament to me.

"The Hind and the Panther" (Excerpt)

(1687)

JOHN DRYDEN

Times were fraught in Restoration England, and John Dryden's conversion to Catholicism was more startling and controversial even than most. He had previously worked in the government of the Puritan Oliver Cromwell and written a eulogy for him after his death. Yet when the Catholic King James II ascended the throne, Dryden "poped." Unsurprisingly, this led to accusations of opportunism. But his 2600-line "The Hind and the Panther" that followed was evidence of profound personal and spiritual wrangling.

Dryden's poetry and drama is said to be among the choicest in the English language. He took up Chaucer's heroic couplets and elevated the form to a voice that is stately and authoritative. His lines are assured and unhurried, the rhyming apparently effortless.

We are indebted to him for this poem's initial, indelible image of the Church as a white hind—calling to mind the yearning deer of Psalm 42. The hind is sparkling white and sinless—which then (as now) may have prompted some scoffing. But Dryden is referring to Christ's spotless Church without blemish (Eph. 5:27), not its sinful members. During the Reformation she (the Church) was hunted. But of course, she could not die.

Do pause at the first couplet of the next section and listen to its perfect balance and alliteration ("weight"/"witness";

"private"/"public"). These lines are key to Dryden's epiphany: he realizes the folly of one man's (his own) independent thought overturning centuries of Catholic tradition. He characterizes the Church as a "guide" and "director"—someone essential in our dealings with God, who is hidden in light so bright it blinds like darkness.

The theme of these stanzas is intellectual surrender and acceptance. After all, when faced with the notions of the Trinity, God becoming a baby, and the child growing up to die on a cross, how can the poet quibble about the mysteries of the Church? Dryden casts his pre-conversion life as following false lights, and there is a wonderful image of his pride throwing off "sparkles." It should be noted that, in other ways, in other parts not included here, this poem is quite shocking. Now a convinced Catholic, Dryden doesn't hesitate to pour scorn on other denominations, and he does so by using *animals* to debate the fiercest and most sophisticated theological points. The hind (as we have seen) represents the Catholic Church; a panther represents the Church of England. Various other denominations are present as hare, fox, wolf, boar, etc. Much of these discussions may not be helpful to modern-day apologists!

And in fact, they were not helpful to Dryden. His religious transformation had not easily been swallowed by his peers, poetic or religious. We cannot overestimate the criticism and ridicule that he received for writing and publishing this poem. In places it was insulting. It used talking animals. It was heavily theological. After the deposition of James II, Dryden's faith saw him out of a job and ousted from court.

"The Hind and the Panther" (Excerpt)

JOHN DRYDEN

A Milk-white Hind, immortal and unchanged,
Fed on the lawns, and in the forest ranged;
Without unspotted, innocent within,
She feared no danger, for she knew no sin.
Yet had she oft been chased with horns and hounds,
And Scythian shafts; and many winged wounds
Aimed at her heart; was often forced to fly,
And doomed to death though fated not to die.

....

What weight of ancient witness can prevail,
If private reason hold the public scale?
But, gracious God, how well dost thou provide
For erring judgments an unerring guide!
Thy throne is darkness in th'abyss of light,
A blaze of glory that forbids the sight.
O teach me to believe thee thus concealed,
And search no farther than thyself revealed;
But her alone for my director take,
Whom thou hast promised never to forsake!
My thoughtless youth was winged with vain desires,
My manhood, long misled by wandering fires,
Followed false lights; and, when their glimpse was gone,
My pride struck out new sparkles of her own.
Such was I, such by nature still I am;
Be thine the glory, and be mine the shame.

Good life be now my task: my doubts are done,
What more could fright my faith, than three in one?
Can I believe eternal God could lie
Disguised in mortal mould and infancy?
That the great Maker of the world could die?
And after that trust my imperfect sense,
Which calls in question his omnipotence?
Can I my reason to my faith compel?
And shall my sight, and touch, and taste, rebel?
Superior faculties are set aside;
Shall their subservient organs be my guide?
Then let the moon usurp the rule of day,
And winking tapers show the sun his way;
For what my senses can themselves perceive,
I need no revelation to believe.

"A Virgin Life"

(1688)

JANE BARKER

Virginity, chastity, and faith. By today's secular standards, these aren't words equated with emancipation. On the contrary, to many they have the ring of rigidity and suppression. Yet in this poem, Jane Barker expresses what we might *hope* for from any movement that declares itself "feminist": that women have the right to be on their own terms.

In Barker's time, of course, women's education was limited; ladies rarely worked, they couldn't vote, and they did not inherit. The totter into spinsterhood was consequently considered a tragedy. We might think of our times as far removed from this. Yet even or especially today, virginity, beyond a very young age, has the stigma almost of a chronic illness.

Singleton Jane Barker shook off pity and convention. A Catholic convert, when James II was run out of England by William of Orange, Jane ran with him and a group of Jacobites to France, where she could live her faith and write her poetry and fiction. She returned home some years later and rallied for Catholic resurgence and the canonization of the then-dead James. In other words, she was far from the quiet "Old Maid" her contemporaries would have scorned.

This poem thrashes out how Barker saw her single state. For a start, her virginity is "bestowed," a gift from God, and this poem is a petition to him to save her from what she sees as the subjugation of marital love. The "antiquated name" that all fear is spinsterhood, but she cautions against running into the lion's den of marriage to avoid it. Instead, she redraws the character of virginity (which she now addresses as a person) as a "lovely state" that is "angelical" and "celestial." Virginity empowers her to be "as good a subject as the stoutest man" (meaning robustly moral). She is liberated, in short, to be a good Christian (as St. Paul hinted at in 1 Corinthians 7:8–9). And while many a married woman may have managed, effortlessly, the same, there were (and no doubt are) men and women impeded from this by a suffocating or demanding marriage that they were not called to.

For her jaunty defense of the virginal state, Barker writes in the heroic couplets fashionable at the time, and, in all her sincerity, the voice of a single woman very much her own in God rings out down the centuries.

"A Virgin Life"

JANE BARKER

Since, gracious Heaven, you have bestowed on me
So great a kindness for virginity,
Suffer me not to fall into the power
Of Man's, almost omnipotent amour,
But in this happy state let me remain,
And in chaste verse my chaster thoughts explain,
Fearless of twenty-five and all its rage,
When time and beauty endless wars engage,
And fearless of that antiquated name
Which oft makes happy maid turn hapless dame.
The scorns fixed to that name our sex betray,
And often make us fling our selves away,
As harmless kids which when pursued by men
For safety run into a lion's den.
Ah lovely state! how strange it is to see
What mad conceptions some have made of thee!
As if thy being was all wretchedness,
Or foul deformity in the ugliest dress,
Whereas thy beauty's pure, celestial,
Thy thoughts divine, thy words angelical,
And such ought all thy votaries to be,
Or else they're so but for necessity.
A virgin bears the impress of all good;
Under that name, all virtue's understood.
So equal all, her looks, her mien, her dress,
That nought but modesty seems in excess.

When virgins any treats or visits make,
'Tis not for tattle but for friendship's sake.
The neighboring poor are her adopted heirs,
And less she cares for her own good than theirs,
And by obedience testifies she can
Be as good a subject as the stoutest man.
She to her church such filial duty pays,
That one would think she lived in the pristine days.
Her whole life's business she drives to these ends,
To serve her God, her neighbor and her friends.

"An Essay on Man" (Excerpt)

(1733–1734)

ALEXANDER POPE

In the age of Enlightenment, when our very ways of knowing God were called into question, a Catholic poet published a long poem that sought to advocate for the Creator and the perfection of his design. Another poet, John Milton, had written *Paradise Lost* to "justify the ways of God to men,"[1] but Alexander Pope took this further by aiming to "vindicate the ways of God to man."[2] The French philosopher Voltaire called the result "the most beautiful, the most useful, the most sublime didactic poem ever written in any language."[3]

Pope was a tenacious Catholic. At that time, Catholics were excluded from university, voting, public office, and even, for a period, living in London. The poet was also hobbled by physical disability: he was extremely short, with a hunchback, and critics mocked him for it. His personal struggles make the thrust of his most famous poem even more impressive. He argues for the sheer *rightness* of *all* created things.

Reading "An Essay on Man," with its unsquinting look at the world and what man's place in it should be, we can't help but hear something of the story of Job: "Shall a faultfinder contend with the Almighty?" (Job 40:2). Pope, despite (or perhaps because of) being disabled and marginalized, finds the most glorious

1. *Paradise Lost* 1.26.

2. "An Essay on Man" 1.16.

3. Voltaire, *Lettres Philosophiques*, in *Philosophical Letters* (*Letters Concerning the English Nation*), trans. Ernest Dilworth (Mineola, NY: Dover, 2011), 147.

design in the universe, and he insists that, notwithstanding our knowledge and scientific discovery, our comprehension of creation can only ever be incomplete.

Pope was clear that he had to write his masterpiece in poetry to keep it precise and memorable. His use of heroic couplets has come to define the form as one of authority and didacticism. And, in fact, cascades of lines from this poem have passed into our language and consciousness. His lens is both philosophical and theological: his angels pushing the planets on their course spring from Aristotle; the divine providence that breathes a soul into man is the God of Abraham. The poem sees the world as a "mighty maze but not without a plan."[4]

In our excerpt, which comes at the end of this vast work, Pope confronts us with a view of the universe that is at once telescopic in its sweep of the cosmos and microscopic in its analysis of the "tenth or ten thousandth" piece of the "chain of being."

For Pope, the microscopic elements of the world are crucial: tinkering with the tiniest link in this chain signifies breakage and distortion. The poem's warning is prophetic: meddling in the natural order will unseat the whole, and as a result, those "ruling angels" will be hurled from their posts. And for what? For whom? A "vile worm" such as you. Pope's language is unfashionable these days. His defense is of hierarchy; his challenge is to the hubris of man who thinks he can rule a world he did not create: "What if the foot ordained the dust to tread?"

The fundamental call of this great poem is to "submit." This message might be as indigestible to some today as it was to Adam and Eve. But Pope, with great eloquence, is pleading our unchanging ignorance and asking us not to behave as gods.

4. "An Essay on Man" 1.6.

The final phrase, the famous "Whatever is, is right," both answers and provokes the great discussion of God and suffering in our world.

"An Essay on Man" (Excerpt)

Sections 8–10

ALEXANDER POPE

See, through this air, this ocean, and this earth,
All matter quick, and bursting into birth.
Above, how high, progressive life may go!
Around, how wide! how deep extend below!
Vast chain of Being, which from God began,
Natures ethereal, human, angel, man,
Beast, bird, fish, insect, what no eye can see,
No glass can reach; from Infinite to thee,
From thee to Nothing.—On superior pow'rs
Were we to press, inferior might on ours:
Or in the full creation leave a void,
Where, one step broken, the great scale's destroyed:
From Nature's chain whatever link you strike,
Tenth, or ten thousandth, breaks the chain alike.

And, if each system in gradation roll
Alike essential to th'amazing Whole,
The least confusion but in one, not all
That system only, but the Whole must fall.
Let Earth unbalanced from her orbit fly,
Planets and Suns run lawless through the sky;
Let ruling Angels from their spheres be hurled,
Being on Being wrecked, and world on world;
Heav'n's whole foundations to their centre nod,
And Nature tremble to the throne of God.

All this dread ORDER break—for whom? for thee?
Vile worm!—Oh Madness! Pride! Impiety!

What if the foot ordained the dust to tread,
Or hand, to toil, aspired to be the head?
What if the head, the eye, or ear repined
To serve mere engines to the ruling Mind?
Just as absurd for any part to claim
To be another, in this gen'ral frame:
Just as absurd, to mourn the tasks or pains,
The great directing Mind of all ordains.

All are but parts of one stupendous whole,
Whose body Nature is, and God the soul;
That, changed through all, and yet in all the same,
Great in the earth, as in th'æthereal frame,
Warms in the sun, refreshes in the breeze,
Glows in the stars, and blossoms in the trees,
Lives through all life, extends through all extent,
Spreads undivided, operates unspent,
Breathes in our soul, informs our mortal part,
As full, as perfect, in a hair as heart;
As full, as perfect, in vile Man that mourns,
As the rapt Seraph that adores and burns:
To him no high, no low, no great, no small;
He fills, he bounds, connects, and equals all.

Cease then, nor ORDER Imperfection name:
Our proper bliss depends on what we blame.
Know thy own point: This kind, this due degree
Of blindness, weakness, Heav'n bestows on thee.
Submit.—In this, or any other sphere,
Secure to be as blest as thou canst bear:
Safe in the hand of one disposing Pow'r,
Or in the natal, or the mortal hour.
All Nature is but Art, unknown to thee;
All Chance, Direction, which thou canst not see;
All Discord, Harmony not understood;
All partial Evil, universal Good:
And, spite of Pride, in erring Reason's spite,
One truth is clear, WHATEVER IS, IS RIGHT.

"The Pillar of the Cloud"

(June 16, 1833)

ST. JOHN HENRY NEWMAN

When this poem was written, its author was struggling with
the position of the Anglican Church, of which he was a
determined member at the time, and trapped in a foreign
country. He desperately wanted to go home but couldn't get
there. He had recently seen Rome and felt "there was nothing
[there] of promise to excite or gladden the mind."[1] Falling ill
when he reached Palermo, he could only break down and sob
to his servant that he simply had to get back to England: he
had work to do. At last he was well enough to travel. But the
orange boat on which he found passage was, in turn, blocked
from traveling onward by bad weather. It was in that boat that
he wrote this poem, which would later become set to music as
"Lead, Kindly Light" and be sung by women as they were led to
the Ravensbrück death-camp,[2] by men trapped underground
in one of the worst mining disasters in history[3]—and by many
others, in many other desperate places.

"The Pillar of the Cloud" as a title is very fitting for the
poet's stranded position en route. It refers to the cloud that was
a visible sign of God to the Israelites as they navigated the desert
after the Exodus from Egypt. It speaks of Newman's difficult

1. John Henry Newman, "Home Thoughts Abroad," in *The British Magazine
and Monthly Register of Religious and Ecclesiastical Information, Parochial History and
Documents Respecting the State of the Poor, Progress of Education Etc*, vol. 5 (London:
J. G. & F. Rivington, 1834), 1.

2. Corrie Ten Boom, *The Hiding Place* (London: Hodder & Stoughton, 2004), 178.

3. In 1909 in Durham, England, 168 men lost their lives when a coal mine collapsed.

physical journey but also of his anguished spiritual navigation. More broadly, the poem also points to our radical blindness as human beings: in true crises and despair, we cannot see the future or a way out. The truth of life is that any sight of the future is illusion, and sightless trust in God has to be the more sober reality.

The poem has the flavor of prayer. It is a petition: "Lead!" It has a refrain like the prayers of the Divine Office: "Lead Thou me on!" The lines, which rhyme regularly as ABABCC, are broken in their length by the short, desperate cry of the refrain, which calms in the last stanza to the hopeful "night is gone."

Disillusioned and thwarted, the poet was stumbling with his hand in God's. He had to give up plans and any illusion of control he may have had. He had to shake off his pride. The piece is a living exposition of Jesus' gentle command to not worry about tomorrow (Matt. 6:34).

The final images of night dissolving and the vision of "angel faces" is mysterious. It could be read as recognition that death will bring him into the safest harbor, and he will gain all he has lost. Or "morn" could be a metaphor for the passing of the dark night and the clarity we need to recognize the workings of angels in our lives.

Twelve years after writing the poem, Newman was received into the Catholic Church. He would later become one of England's most celebrated Catholic cardinals and, ultimately, a saint. This work is especially valuable to believers as it is a diary-record of the darkness of one the Church's best and most holy, who is now one of the closest to the Light.

"The Pillar of the Cloud"

ST. JOHN HENRY NEWMAN

Lead, Kindly Light, amid the encircling gloom,
    Lead Thou me on!
The night is dark, and I am far from home—
    Lead Thou me on!
Keep Thou my feet; I do not ask to see
The distant scene,—one step enough for me.

I was not ever thus, nor prayed that Thou
    Shouldst lead me on.
I loved to choose and see my path, but now
    Lead Thou me on!
I loved the garish day, and, spite of fears,
Pride ruled my will: remember not past years.

So long Thy power hath blest me, sure it still
    Will lead me on,
O'er moor and fen, o'er crag and torrent, till
    The night is gone;
And with the morn those angel faces smile
Which I have loved long since, and lost awhile.

"The Dream of Gerontius" (Excerpt)

(1865)

ST. JOHN HENRY NEWMAN

Written quickly, urgently, on scraps of paper, *The Dream* begins "Jesu, Maria—I am near to death / And thou art calling me; I know it now—."

This inspired account of a man's death (Gerontius comes from the Greek meaning "old man") shimmers with authenticity in every line. In elegant blank verse (with some very poignant recourse to rhyme as seen at the end of our excerpt here), Newman dramatizes that deeply Catholic, and highly neglected, of doctrines: purgatory and the necessity of praying for the dead. Yet despite the poem's Catholicity, men and women of other denominations have been struck by its sheer truth and consolation in the face of what we most fear. General Charles George Gordon annotated the poem during the siege of Khartoum, in which he died.

Gerontius is, above all, a gentle poem—which is odd to say in view of its almost painful realism. But the stanzas fill the reader with excitement and hope. There is not a line that appears to have been contrived from human imagination.

The events here are heard not simply through Gerontius' own thoughts but also through the prayers of his priest, family, and friends at his bedside. The poem takes us on and through the no-man's-land between life and death and introduces us to angels, demons, and souls in purgatory on the way. There is no other work in literature, perhaps, that more convincingly records this passage. Unlike the *Divine Comedy*, which is all about painting the unknown and making it knowable, Newman allows for the invisible, the most elusive and barest sensations. He does not (and cannot) lift the veil between this world and the next. But his "hints and guesses," to quote T.S. Eliot, are chillingly close.[1]

In our first excerpt, we are at the point of Gerontius' death. For the first time, the soul speaks apart from the body. The evocation of those moments, as the material world slips away and the prayers of those around Gerontius persist, is utterly convincing. Of note is the deep solitude in which Gerontius finds himself, and also the sense that, at this point, there is "nought else to feed upon" but himself. His existential position is that of being stripped. He is facing the only two things that cannot be avoided: himself and God. At this point he is examining, with unnerving calm, his death-paralysis. His dominion over his own body is gone.

This long narrative poem is, above all, a work of voices, of sounds—of unique sensation. Newman's uncanny guess at how it feels to be conveyed to the afterlife by an angel has a nail-hitting rightness: "Someone has me fast / Within his ample palm; 'tis not a grasp / Such as they use on earth, but all around / Over the surface of my subtle being." With remarkable intuition, Newman has Gerontius' senses mix and overlap in synesthesia: he cannot say if he hears, touches, or tastes music.

In the thrilling section VI, to which we leap ahead, the angel and Gerontius finally come into the "veiled presence" of God. Crucially, the prayers of those on earth can be heard anew. The angel of Gethsemane is reciting a litany of Christ's agony. Like the narrator in "Pearl" as he attempts to cross the stream, Gerontius cannot contain himself: he leaps to the throne of

1. T.S. Eliot, "The Dry Salvages."

the Almighty. But—as Dante would not have been able to without the prayers of the Virgin—Gerontius cannot bear the radiance of the Godhead and lies "scorched, and shrivelled." In his final speech of the section, the soul of Gerontius is singing the song of purgatory, happy in his pain, because he knows this is necessary preparation for heaven and the ultimate, unsurpassable encounter.

Soul of Gerontius

Second and sixth phases

ST. JOHN HENRY NEWMAN

I went to sleep; and now I am refreshed.
A strange refreshment: for I feel in me
An inexpressive lightness, and a sense
Of freedom, as I were at length myself,
And ne'er had been before. How still it is!
I hear no more the busy beat of time,
No, nor my fluttering breath, nor struggling pulse;
Nor does one moment differ from the next.
I had a dream; yes:—someone softly said
"He's gone"; and then a sigh went round the room.
And then I surely heard a priestly voice
Cry "Subvenite"; and they knelt in prayer.
I seem to hear him still; but thin and low,
And fainter and more faint the accents come,
As at an ever-widening interval.
Ah! Whence is this? What is this severance?
This silence pours a solitariness
Into the very essence of my soul;
And the deep rest, so soothing and so sweet,
Hath something too of sternness and of pain,
For it drives back my thoughts upon their spring
By a strange introversion, and perforce
I now begin to feed upon myself,
Because I have nought else to feed upon.

Am I alive or dead? I am not dead,
But in the body still; for I possess
A sort of confidence which clings to me,
That each particular organ holds its place
As heretofore, combining with the rest
Into one symmetry, that wraps me round,
And makes me man; and surely I could move,
Did I but will it, every part of me.
And yet I cannot to my sense bring home,
By very trial, that I have the power
'Tis strange; I cannot stir a hand or foot,
I cannot make my fingers or my lips
By mutual pressure witness each to each,
Nor by the eyelid's instantaneous stroke
Assure myself I have a body still.
Nor do I know my very attitude,
Nor if I stand, or lie, or sit, or kneel.

So much I know, not knowing how I know,
That the vast universe, where I have dwelt,
Is quitting me, or I am quitting it,
Or I or it is rushing on the wings
Of light or lightning on an onward course,
And we e'en now are million miles apart.
Yet . . . is this peremptory severance
Wrought out in lengthening measurements of space,
Which grow and multiply by speed and time?
Or am I traversing infinity
By endless subdivision, hurrying back
From finite towards infinitesimal,
Thus dying out of the expanded world?

Another marvel; someone has me fast
Within his ample palm; 'tis not a grasp
Such as they use on earth, but all around
Over the surface of my subtle being,
As though I were a sphere, and capable
To be accosted thus, a uniform
And gentle pressure tells me I am not
Self-moving, but borne forward on my way.
And hark! I hear a singing; yet in sooth
I cannot of that music rightly say
Whether I hear or touch or taste the tones.
Oh what a heart-subduing melody!

....

ANGEL
Thy judgment now is near, for we are come
Into the veiled presence of our God.

SOUL
I hear the voices that I left on earth.

ANGEL
It is the voice of friends around thy bed,
Who say the "Subvenite" with the priest.
Hither the echoes come; before the Throne
Stands the great Angel of the Agony,
The same who strengthened Him, what time He knelt
Lone in that garden shade, bedewed with blood.
That Angel best can plead with Him for all
Tormented souls, the dying and the dead.

ANGEL OF THE AGONY

Jesu! by that shuddering dread which fell on Thee;

Jesu! by that cold dismay which sickened Thee;

Jesu! by that pang of heart which thrilled in Thee;

Jesu! by that mount of sins which crippled Thee;

Jesu! by that sense of guilt which stifled Thee;

Jesu! by that innocence which girdled Thee;

Jesu! by that sanctity which reigned in Thee;

Jesu! by that Godhead which was one with Thee;

Jesu! spare these souls which are so dear to Thee;

Who in prison, calm and patient, wait for Thee;

Hasten, Lord, their hour, and bid them come to Thee,

To that glorious Home, where they shall ever gaze on Thee.

SOUL

I go before my Judge.

ANGEL

. . . Praise to His Name!

The eager spirit has darted from my hold,

And, with the intemperate energy of love,

Flies to the dear feet of Emmanuel;

But, ere it reach them, the keen sanctity,

Which with its effluence, like a glory, clothes

And circles round the Crucified, has seized,

And scorched, and shrivelled it; and now it lies

Passive and still before the awful Throne.

O happy, suffering soul! for it is safe,

Consumed, yet quickened, by the glance of God.

SOUL

Take me away, and in the lowest deep
     There let me be,
And there in hope the lone night-watches keep,
     Told out for me.
There, motionless and happy in my pain,
     Lone, not forlorn,—
There will I sing my sad perpetual strain,
     Until the morn.
There will I sing, and soothe my stricken breast,
     Which ne'er can cease
To throb, and pine, and languish, till possest
     Of its Sole Peace.
There will I sing my absent Lord and Love:—
     Take me away,
That sooner I may rise, and go above,
     And see Him in the truth of everlasting day.

"The Language of the Church"

(Nineteenth century)

GEORGIANA FULLERTON

To any convert, the notion of the Mass and Divine Office being
continually celebrated and prayed across towns, continents, and
time zones is a particular revelation: it seems like a vast and
endlessly active hive. This poem, written by an English convert,
gives gleefully a sense of that sacred busyness working around
the world, with the coming and going of the day and through
the night.

Admired by Cardinal Newman and highly respected in her
day as a novelist, Georgiana Fullerton helped found Mother
Magdalene Taylor's order of the Poor Servants of the Mother
of God Incarnate, and, following the death of her son, she
became a Franciscan tertiary. In this rolling hymn to the
language of the Church, she praises the ubiquity of key liturgical
phrases in tetrameter (four beats a line) and rhyming couplets.
For newcomers to poetry, or those studying it at school, this
poem is a good one to memorize and recite. The rhymes are
jaunty and the content is quite straightforward. It could also be
a nice introduction for students to some fundamental Catholic
Latin phrases.

Although the language Fullerton is describing throughout
the poem is Latin, the same sense can be applied whether
we are saying "Sanctus," "Saint," "Santo," or "Holy." These
prayers are wheels that carry the Church forward and up. They
disseminate, intercede, supplicate, petition, and evangelize as

long as there are tongues to pray and speak them. Though we may sleep, they do not.

This continual prayer that Fullerton describes helps us to remain aware of the silent response of God and his heavenly host. In Newman's "The Dream of Gerontius," the priest's voice is heard—by Gerontius and the Angel—after Gerontius' death. But, of course, the Angel is also praying, and further on (in our extract) Gerontius discovers that the Angel of the Agony is praying too. The phrases in Fullerton's poem are further witness to one half of a dialogue in which heaven is always participating (and purgatory too, if we refer back to the *Divine Comedy*). Look out also for Gertrud von Le Fort's "The Prayer of the Church," later in these pages. In Catholic poetry, these liturgical prayers are acknowledged as having a transcendent life of their own. And, as Fullerton makes clear in this poem, they seep, like oil, to every corner of the world, through every minute of the day.

"The Language of the Church"

GEORGIANA FULLERTON

Unto all lands thy sound has gone,
With still small voice or clarion tone,
Thou glorious old-Church Latin tongue,
Familiar still the Saints among!
It floats on the chill midnight air,
It ushers in the morn with prayer,
It blends with the soft vesper bell,
And whispers in the convent cell;
Sower of truth's eternal seed,
Tongue of the one unchanging creed
Confessed, where'er the Martyrs bled,
By myriads of the sainted dead;
In every clime beneath the skies
Where Mass is said, where altars rise,
Distant and lone so'er they be:
From pole to pole, from sea to sea,
In high cathedral's sculptured nave,
Or lofty dome, or humble cave,
There does the Church her *Sanctus* sing,
And *Gloria in excelsis* ring;
Throughout the world, in ceaseless round,
The *Credo*'s thrilling accents sound.
Domine non sum dignus leads
The suppliant cry a sinner needs;
And *Ecce agnus Dei* tells
That Christ on earthly altars dwells.

Ora pro nobis swells the prayer
Angels in golden censers bear;
Salve Regina hails the star
By Kings and Prophets seen afar.
Still does the *De Profundis* rise;
The *Stabat Mater* breathes its sighs.
The glad *Te Deum*'s notes upraise
Of joyful hearts th'enraptured praise:
Each solemn rite, each sacred hour,
Still claims thy words of love and power,
Sower of truth's eternal seed,
Tongue of the one unchanging creed!

"As Kingfishers Catch Fire"

(1877)

GERARD MANLEY HOPKINS

Gerard Manley Hopkins crams more poetic acrobatics into one line than most poets do in a sonnet. The busy richness of his verse can seem a little overwhelming—but take heart. Reading Hopkins is like listening to music or looking at art: we have to let its rhythms and colors soak into ourselves. "My verse is less to be read than heard," he wrote to a friend.[1] Do read it aloud. It speaks to the heart; it sings.

The convert Hopkins burnt all of his poems when he joined the Jesuits, fearful that writing would be a distraction from his vocation. His poetic silence lasted seven years and ultimately exploded in the composition of the poems for which he is famous. His poetry is dazzlingly innovative. He ripped up the playbook of writing in regular meter, sentence structure, common vocabulary, and controlled effects. He reshuffled the poetic pack and mega-charged every word. We might even say that Hopkins is the first modern poet of the English language: he threw open linguistic possibility to the poets who came after him. Reading this poem aloud, we first hear a profusion of alliteration and assonance. We should keep in mind that Hopkins uses a kind of synesthesia where senses overlap and swap faculty: the *visual* image of "kingfishers catch fire," for

1. Gerard Manley Hopkins to Robert Bridges, August 21, 1877, in *Gerard Manley Hopkins: Selected Letters*, ed. Catherine Phillips (Oxford: Oxford University Press, 1991), 91.

example, is also onomatopoeic: it *sounds* like the striking of a match.

Listen also to the poet's characteristic "sprung rhythm." Hopkins broke with the predictable regularity of much poetry in the English language (characterized by iambic pentameter). He paid little attention to the number of *un*stressed syllables in a line, concentrating instead on stresses that became, in consequence, bouncy and irregular. Aware of how the reader may be unsure of where to place the stress, Hopkins sometimes accented stressed syllables to ensure that due emphasis was given to them.

As you spring through the text, listen to how the volume of verbs ("catch," "draw," "tumbled," "ring") outweighs the adjectives. His sentences are *active*. Every single word works—in terms of both meaning and sound. And the stresses help hammer images home. Hear how the rhythm makes images sound like what they're describing: the phrase "each hung bell's / Bow swung" swings like a bell itself.

But what on earth is all this about? Well, this is a Petrarchan sonnet, and so a "thesis," or idea, is set up in the first eight lines, and at line nine, this turns (the *volta*, as it is known) to push Hopkins' more precise point and conclusion. Let's unpack it.

All of the things in this poem are actively *doing*, as we have already noted: kingfishers and dragonflies are catching and drawing (like fire); stones are tumbling into a well and ringing; strings (of instruments) are telling; bells are swinging and flinging. Line five is key to these busy descriptions: "Each mortal thing does one thing and the same." Poets know when they are pushing language to its limit, and the most successful will insert pivotal, explanatory lines such as these. Hopkins unites the things described above as doing, in essence, the same thing; that is, they are doing what they were created to do. "Indoors" of line six speaks of the interior working of each thing, which then "deals out" in action. The next lines insist with no less than three verbs—"speaks," "spells," "crying"—exactly this: that everything is called to manifest its own unique essence.

As we leap to the last six lines Hopkins buttonholes us: "I say móre." "The just man," he declares, "justices." A nice new verb! In other words, what we *are*, we *do*. And what we were created to be is Christ. We are made in the image of God. We, in our essence, are called to realize ourselves in the image of our Maker. Christ's verb here is "plays," which evokes both light and music. Christ plays on us and through our features. This is a poem about our profound individuality and vocation, and our even more profound connection to God through how we are made—and what we do.

"As Kingfishers Catch Fire"

GERARD MANLEY HOPKINS

As kingfishers catch fire, dragonflies dráw fláme;
As tumbled over rim in roundy wells
Stones ring; like each tucked string tells, each hung bell's
Bow swung finds tongue to fling out broad its name;
Each mortal thing does one thing and the same:
Deals out that being indoors each one dwells;
Selves—goes itself; *myself* it speaks and spells,
Crying *Whát I do is me: for that I came.*

Í say móre: the just man justices;
Kéeps grace: thát keeps all his goings graces;
Acts in God's eye what in God's eye he is—
Chríst—for Christ plays in ten thousand places,
Lovely in limbs, and lovely in eyes not his
To the Father through the features of men's faces.

"The Windhover"

(1877)

GERARD MANLEY HOPKINS

Just as irregular, densely packed, and beautifully bewildering as "Kingfishers," this is another Petrarchan sonnet by Hopkins. Once again, this is a poem best read aloud, best heard with the heart before the brain. And we should keep its dedication, *To Christ our Lord*, in mind as we journey. The alliteration and poetic working of the language is perhaps even more heightened here, and so are the metaphors, which twist and build like the ascent and descent of the bird it describes.

First, the basics: a windhover is a masterful bird of prey that hovers and rides air currents with great skill. In the first line of the poem, it is described as a "minion" (slave) of morning, and in the second, a "dauphin" (prince). Does this paradoxical embodiment of power and servitude remind us of anyone? The first line also, with deliberate clumsiness, breaks on "king- / dom." (The last word in a line of poetry—here, *king*—is generally very important.) In other words, Hopkins is asking us to see the bird as Christ.

This falcon is "riding" the air as though he were on horseback. "High there, how he rung upon the rein of a wimpling wing"—speak it aloud—rocks us as though we are on the horse too! And he swings us on and into a skating metaphor, as the bird navigates the wind. All of these many active verbs, and no let-up of end-rhyming lines, give muscle and physical prowess to both bird and poem. It is a feathery display. The bird is doing what kingfisher, dragonfly, etc. do in "As Kingfishers Catch Fire"—it is being what it was made to be, with bravura. And Hopkins' heart responds to this; he knows it to be something impressive, something holy in the sense of fulfilling its unique mission.

At line nine, we have the *volta*, the turn of the poem to its conclusion. Hopkins wants this turn in his thoughts to be apparent, and that's why he breaks the stanza—and that's why this whole glorious display now buckles. The bird swoops from its hovering posture and is then more lovely and more dangerous as it completes its mission (seizes its prey). "My chevalier!" (knight) he calls the bird—another word to conjure Christ (who, don't forget, is the person to whom all of this is addressed).

In the penultimate stanza, Hopkins expands this image of the bird brilliantly fulfilling what it was made to do in its final descent. It seems to ignite as it self-actualizes! And, similarly (in the last three lines), the land shines ("sillion" is the furrow in a ploughed field) because of the work, the "shéer plód" of the ploughman. It, too, fulfills its mission. And the dying hearth fire (referred to as "embers" in the penultimate line) also shows us its mission: it breaks open to reveal its still-burning heart. Christ's mission is about his own self-sacrifice, his own destruction, his own *buckling*—and this is the force of his mastery. Christ is the descended windhover. He is the worked, now shining field. He is the hidden but still burning coal that breaks open to reveal "the gold-vermilion"—the spilled blood of the Savior.

And the poem, too, is a worked, beating display just like the things it describes. You'll see at once the repetition of "morning" in the first line, something other poets might have avoided. But Hopkins uses the providential beauty that language throws to him: the repetition provides us with triple alliteration and more stressed assonance ("*morning morn*ing's minion"). Notice also his descriptive compounds: "dapple-dawn-drawn," "bow-bend," "blue-bleak." He milks as much meaning as possible from words through their acoustic relationships. Like the windhover, his visceral, linguistic display invites layers of interpretation.

"The Windhover"

GERARD MANLEY HOPKINS

To Christ our Lord

I caught this morning morning's minion, king-
   dom of daylight's dauphin, dapple-dawn-drawn Falcon,
      in his riding
   Of the rolling level underneath him steady air, and striding
High there, how he rung upon the rein of a wimpling wing
In his ecstacy! then off, off forth on swing,
   As a skate's heel sweeps smooth on a bow-bend: the hurl
      and gliding
   Rebuffed the big wind. My heart in hiding
Stirred for a bird,—the achieve of, the mastery of the thing!

Brute beauty and valour and act, oh, air, pride, plume, here
   Buckle! AND the fire that breaks from thee then, a billion
Times told lovelier, more dangerous, O my chevalier!

No wonder of it: shéer plód makes plough down sillion
Shine, and blue-bleak embers, ah my dear,
Fall, gall themselves, and gash gold-vermillion.

"God's Grandeur"

(1877)

GERARD MANLEY HOPKINS

Hopkins' explosion of masterful sonnets also includes this great paean to nature and, more precisely, God in nature. In Hopkins' poetry there is a profound sensuality connected to the natural world that seems to come directly from the Romantic poet John Keats. But though Hopkins may have grasped this torch of the sensual from Keats' hands, Hopkins runs with it like a man mad for God. Unlike Keats, Hopkins sees the natural world as living evidence of the divine presence. Born into the steamroller progression of the Industrial Revolution, Hopkins is desperate to restore the glorious natural world to Christ.

The images are fecund and ripe; they contain Hopkins' trademark vibrancy in their "sprung rhythm" and alliteration. The images also bear the mark of God's presence—the foil and the compressed oil are both metaphors for how God's greatness shines and is concentrated. But they are also real indicators of the pattern of God through nature. Shining foil is *like* the grandeur of God. But it is also a real sign of the greatness of God written into the world.

What a line break at line three! The "ooze of oil / Crushed." Because of this deliberately awkward break (technically called *enjambment*: one line running into the next with no punctuation or natural pause in the phrase), we are reminded not only of the compression of olives but also of God's power to crush in his wrath. And as the next line goes on, we see man's mindless crushing of the glories of God in his utilitarian attitude to nature.

We can hear the poet's anger in his conglomeration of stressed words: "Why do men then now not reck his rod?" He might be thumping the table. His disgust is amplified in the repetition of "trod" and the rhyming echoes of "seared," "bleared," and "smeared." We have dirtied the world with our mindless work and ignorance of glory. We cannot even feel the earth beneath our bare feet now.

How shocking this would have sounded to Victorian audiences, for whom Christian respectability would have meant wearing a decent pair of shoes at the very least! But this is quintessential Hopkins: the desire the feel the soil between his toes, to feel connected to the earth.

At the shift at line nine, the *volta*, there is a change in tone as he introduces the now-famous phrase "dearest freshness deep down things." This curious mixture of nouns and adjectives places gut feeling—an intuition of the resilience and ever-newness of creation—above genteel grammatical construct. And it heralds Hopkins' final, masterful image of the Holy Ghost as a bird cradling the whole world to its breast and within its wings. Nature, for Hopkins, is indomitable. It does not have the capacity to reject God; it is embraced by its Maker.

"God's Grandeur"

GERARD MANLEY HOPKINS

The world is charged with the grandeur of God.
It will flame out, like shining from shook foil;
It gathers to a greatness, like the ooze of oil
Crushed. Why do men then now not reck his rod?
Generations have trod, have trod, have trod;
And all is seared with trade; bleared, smeared with toil;
And wears man's smudge and shares man's smell: the soil
Is bare now, nor can foot feel, being shod.

And for all this, nature is never spent;
There lives the dearest freshness deep down things;
And though the last lights off the black West went
Oh, morning, at the brown brink eastward, springs—
Because the Holy Ghost over the bent
World broods with warm breast and with ah! bright wings.

"My Own Heart Let Me More Have Pity On"

(1885)

GERARD MANLEY HOPKINS

After the explosion of what came to be called his "bright sonnets" in 1877, Hopkins, still unpublished and unknown as a poet outside his own narrow circle, went to minister as a parish priest in some of the most deprived inner cities. He found the work grueling. We can surmise from his writings that Hopkins was an introvert and frail physically. He was hyper-sensitive. How could anyone doubt this after reading our three previous Hopkins sonnets? They seem written by a man whose mind trembled like antennae at the world's shimmer. Such intuition usually has its downside.

In his final years, Hopkins was sent to Dublin to teach. This move rendered him even more alone: already cut off from his family by a Catholic conversion that had grieved them enormously, he was now in a foreign land. The poems he wrote at this stage are often called "the terrible sonnets." They possibly indicate clinical depression, and certainly alienation. ("To seem the stranger lies my lot," begins another poem.[1])

At first glance, this darkness has a mildly calming effect on Hopkins' language. But at second glance, we quickly rediscover his innovative and inventive ways with words. This poem is also a sonnet. But the stresses are generally more regular than what

---

1. Gerard Manley Hopkins, "To seem the stranger lies my lot," in *As Kingfishers Catch Fire: Selected and Annotated Poems of Gerard Manley Hopkins*, ed. Holly Ordway (Elk Grove Village, IL: Word on Fire Institute, 2023), 35.

we have seen in Hopkins' earlier work. The verbs are fewer and less urgent. The lines speak of an interior state: there are far fewer external objects flying about. Yet this poem is never dull or claustrophobic as less expert poetry about the mind can be.

Hopkins still loves to break a line in strange ways. The first line ends on "let" and the second begins "Me"—a fracture almost any other poet would avoid. The break of line twelve is even stranger: "Smile's" is broken into "smile" and "s." The effect on the reader is discombobulation. But I'm not sure that was Hopkins' aim. Placing "let" and "smile" at the ends of lines give those words great emphasis. And those two words and what they signify are central to the meaning and spirit of this poem.

"Let," the poet says, setting the tone for a piece that is a conversation between one man and himself. His mind torments, his heart suffers. "Let" is a petition to himself to be gentle with himself. The repetition of words in their adjective, noun, or verb forms ("tormented"/"tormenting"; "comfort"/"comfortless") creates the labyrinthine sensation of obsessive thoughts that depression can bring on; it expresses the double bind of situations for which we can see no resolution. There is no comfort in his "comfortless" (again Hopkins eschews grammatical norms), just as there is no day in dark nor thirst in wet.

In the second part of this Petrarchan sonnet, Hopkins continues to give himself a good talking to, referring to himself as "Jackself." "Leave comfort root-room," he is able to say, like a wise and steady confidant to the jaded Jack.

"Smile," the other of those very prominent words, belongs to God. The wise voice in the poem is identifying providence toward the end: "let joy size [increase] / At God knows when to God knows what." And the smile of God is never forced ("not wrung"), but comes to us, says Hopkins, as a slice of sky between mountains. That curious new word "Betweenpie" calls to mind the mountains as pie crusts and sky as the bright filling! But the word is probably a play on "pied" (a term of which Hopkins was fond), conjuring the many-colored mountains and the splash of blue between them.

Even in darkness, Hopkins is open to such great creation—his own, and the Creator's.

"My Own Heart Let Me More Have Pity On"

GERARD MANLEY HOPKINS

My own heart let me more have pity on; let
Me live to my sad self hereafter kind,
Charitable; not live this tormented mind
With this tormented mind tormenting yet.
I cast for comfort I can no more get
By groping round my comfortless, than blind
Eyes in their dark can day or thirst can find
Thirst's all-in-all in all a world of wet.

Soul, self; come, poor Jackself, I do advise
You, jaded, let be; call off thoughts awhile
Elsewhere; leave comfort root-room; let joy size
At God knows when to God knows what; whose smile
's not wrung, see you; unforeseen times rather—as skies
Betweenpie mountains—lights a lovely mile.

"Magna Est Veritas"

(1877)

COVENTRY PATMORE

"Magna Est Veritas" (the truth is mighty) comes from the apocryphal third book of Esdras, and this little ten-line lyric dramatizes the essence of those words. But for the poet Coventry Patmore, truth hid for a while behind an "angel."

Patmore's beloved first wife, Emily, was the inspiration for his long narrative work *The Angel in the House*, a poem that praised what he saw as the high virtue of women in the home. Emily was a Protestant with Puritan tendencies who saw the Catholic Church as a "hideous phantom," according to her husband, and who prophesied before her death, "When I am gone they (the Catholics) will get you!"[1] Coventry had always had Roman leanings, but he found it hard to believe that his wise and virtuous wife could be wrong on such a major issue, so did not convert. However, after Emily's death, he crossed the Tiber to Rome and wrote this poem—a much more to-the-point piece than *The Angel in the House*, and one that is almost reckless in its peace.

Patmore lived for a time in Hastings, England, on the coast. Perhaps it is that stretch of sea that he contemplated and saw as both "purposeless" and "glad." The poet contrives a form (two alternately rhyming quatrains, broken in the middle by a rhyming couplet) and breaks the predictability of line length

---

1. Basil Champneys, *Memoirs and Correspondence of Coventry Patmore*, vol. 2 (London: George Bell & Sons, 1900), 53.

with the briefer "Where twice a day" and "I sit me down." These variations in meter conjure the waves drawing in and out over the sand; the lines come and go, like the sea.

The voice we hear is of a man taking his ease, tired of debate and protestation. Perhaps, like the sea, he is both "purposeless" and "glad." Most importantly, he is realistic about his own self-importance and trusts absolutely that truth will prevail and "the lie shall rot."

This is a complacent poem, in the best sense. The bay, the town, the sea—even Patmore's own self and marital history are dwarfed by Truth. This is complacency as trust.

"Magna Est Veritas"

COVENTRY PATMORE

Here, in this little Bay,
Full of tumultuous life and great repose,
Where, twice a day,
The purposeless, glad ocean comes and goes,
Under high cliffs, and far from the huge town,
I sit me down.
For want of me the world's course will not fail;
When all its work is done, the lie shall rot;
The truth is great, and shall prevail,
When none cares whether it prevail or not.

"The Hound of Heaven"

(1890)

FRANCIS THOMPSON

Reading this famous poem, we may feel that we, too, are
rushing pell-mell through years and streets, being chased by
a "hound" (who is God himself). Although the work is finely
wrought, it seems to ignite from the poet's raw experience. It
has the flavor of being written quickly, of being born, as can
happen with some poems, whole. It is a cry, a paroxysm of panic
and exultation. The reason for its enduring popularity is that its
utter sincerity infects and includes us: it is our story too.

Francis Thompson ended up on the streets of London,
addicted to opium. He had considered becoming a priest, then
studied medicine to please his father, and finally ran away to
pursue poetry. This, his masterpiece, was written when he
was staying with monks at Storrington to recover from his
addiction. It describes how God pursued him down the years—
and how he ran from him, fearing "having Him, I must have
naught beside." It sprints to the beat of Psalm 139: "O LORD, you
have searched me . . ."

The poem should certainly be read aloud, and then read
again, quietly, with pencil in hand to mark out the lines that
speak most forcefully to us. As with any journey, some sights
will strike us more than others. But there are certain road signs
that we can highlight as a guide.

To begin with, let's think about structure: Thompson
begins with traditional iambic pentameter and returns to it

throughout. But it often ruptures, sometimes to three beats a line, sometimes two or one. As well as the varying line lengths, the margins vary wildly. The effect is of a runner who is forced to quicken or slow because of tight corners. Repetition and alliteration accelerate the speed and make this a tongue-twister to say aloud. Thompson is reminiscent of Gerard Manley Hopkins in his linguistic athleticism: "skiey" (of the sky), "plashy" (splashy), "instancy" (insistence, nearness), and "lustihead" (delight, vigor) all have the sound of invented words. They are antique, each uniquely expressive.

The narrative aims for no less than summarizing the world and life itself. We are taken through the "arches of the years"—a wonderful image—as homes, dreams, winds, and savannahs are passed at speed. The discontented speaker urges on time; nature and innocence give him only marginal pause ("Lady-Mother": she is Mother Nature, who cannot, alone, be the answer). We roar on to near destruction of the self, till the narrator stands in dust and smoke. Brokenhearted, he confronts death, who is dressed in "robes purpureal."

But it is the voice of God, at least initially, that holds a sense of menace. We hear him first in line fifteen, and he returns at the end of each section to reiterate in various ways that there is no happiness or security without him: "Naught shelters thee, who wilt not shelter Me." Toward the close, God's voice surrounds the speaker like a "bursting sea." Let's be clear: here we see the Almighty, if not as a brute coercer, certainly as a force from whom there can be no glad escape.

God caught Thompson, just as he catches us if we only give him the tiniest chance (and sometimes it's our exhaustion in our flight that makes this happen). Before we join Thompson on his journey, we need to know that "Fear wist not to evade, as Love wist to pursue" means "Fear knows not how to evade, as Love knows to pursue." And for the last line, which is also in Victorian idiom, we might say, "You pushed love away when you pushed me away."

We should pause here to reflect on how very different this poem is to others of this era. Once again, the sheer passion and unpredictability of this work may put the reader in mind of Gerard Manley Hopkins' sonnets—which would not be published until after Thompson's death. Certainly, as the twentieth century dawned, something new was brewing in the poetic form.

Enjoy the excitement of this newness, as we get set for God's "deliberate speed, majestic instancy."

"The Hound of Heaven"

I fled Him, down the nights and down the days;
    I fled Him, down the arches of the years;
I fled Him, down the labyrinthine ways
    Of my own mind; and in the mist of tears
I hid from Him, and under running laughter.
        Up vistaed hopes, I sped;
        And shot, precipitated,
Adown Titanic glooms of chasmèd fears,
    From those strong Feet that followed, followed after.
        But with unhurrying chase,
        And unperturbèd pace,
    Deliberate speed, majestic instancy,
        They beat—and a Voice beat
    More instant than the Feet—
    "All things betray thee, who betrayest Me."

        I pleaded, outlaw-wise,
By many a hearted casement, curtained red,
    Trellised with intertwining charities;
(For though I knew His love Who followèd,
        Yet was I sore adread
Lest, having Him, I must have naught beside.)
But, if one little casement parted wide,
    The gust of His approach would clash it to
    Fear wist not to evade, as Love wist to pursue.
Across the margent of the world I fled,
    And troubled the gold gateways of the stars,
    Smiting for shelter on their clangèd bars;
        Fretted to dulcet jars

And silvern chatter the pale ports o' the moon.
I said to Dawn: Be sudden—to Eve: Be soon;
    With thy young skiey blossoms heap me over
        From this tremendous Lover—
Float thy vague veil about me, lest He see!
    I tempted all His servitors, but to find
My own betrayal in their constancy,
In faith to Him their fickleness to me,
    Their traitorous trueness, and their loyal deceit.
To all swift things for swiftness did I sue;
    Clung to the whistling mane of every wind.
        But whether they swept, smoothly fleet,
    The long savannahs of the blue;
        Or whether, Thunder-driven,
        They clanged his chariot 'thwart a heaven,
Plashy with flying lightnings round the spurn o' their feet;—
    Fear wist not to evade as Love wist to pursue.
        Still with unhurrying chase,
        And unperturbéd pace,
Deliberate speed, majestic instancy,
        Came on the following Feet,
        And a Voice above their beat—
    "Naught shelters thee, who wilt not shelter Me."

I sought no more that after which I strayed
        In face of man or maid;
    But still within the little children's eyes
        Seems something, something that replies,
They at least are for me, surely for me!
I turned to them very wistfully;
But just as their young eyes grew sudden fair
    With dawning answers there,

Their angel plucked them from me by the hair.
"Come then, ye other children, Nature's—share
With me" (said I) "your delicate fellowship;
    Let me greet you lip to lip,
    Let me twine with you caresses,
        Wantoning
    With our Lady-Mother's vagrant tresses,
        Banqueting
    With her in her wind-walled palace,
    Underneath her azured daïs,
    Quaffing, as your taintless way is,
        From a chalice
Lucent-weeping out of the dayspring."
        So it was done:
I in their delicate fellowship was one—
Drew the bolt of Nature's secrecies.
    I knew all the swift importings
    On the wilful face of skies;
    I knew how the clouds arise
    Spuméd of the wild sea-snortings;
        All that's born or dies
    Rose and drooped with; made them shapers
Of mine own moods, or wailful or divine;
    With them joyed and was bereaven.
    I was heavy with the even,
    When she lit her glimmering tapers
    Round the day's dead sanctities.
    I laughed in the morning's eyes.
I triumphed and I saddened with all weather,
    Heaven and I wept together,
And its sweet tears were salt with mortal mine;
Against the red-throb of its sunset heart

I laid my own to beat,
  And share commingling heat;
But not by that, by that, was eased my human smart.
In vain my tears were wet on Heaven's grey cheek.
For ah! we know not what each other says,
  These things and I; in sound *I* speak—
Their sound is but their stir, they speak by silences.
Nature, poor stepdame, cannot slake my drouth;
  Let her, if she would owe me,
Drop yon blue bosom-veil of sky, and show me
  The breasts o' her tenderness:
Never did any milk of hers once bless
  My thirsting mouth.
  Nigh and nigh draws the chase,
  With unperturbéd pace,
  Deliberate speed majestic instancy;
  And past those noiséd Feet
  A voice comes yet more fleet—
"Lo! naught contents thee, who content'st not Me."

Naked I wait Thy love's uplifted stroke!
My harness piece by piece Thou has hewn from me,
  And smitten me to my knee;
  I am defenceless utterly,
  I slept, methinks, and woke,
And, slowly gazing, find me stripped in sleep.
In the rash lustihead of my young powers,
  I shook the pillaring hours
And pulled my life upon me; grimed with smears,
I stand amid the dust o' the mounded years—
My mangled youth lies dead beneath the heap.
My days have crackled and gone up in smoke,

Have puffed and burst as sun-starts on a stream.
　　　Yea, faileth now even dream
The dreamer, and the lute the lutanist;
Even the linked fantasies, in whose blossomy twist
I swung the earth a trinket at my wrist,
Are yielding; cords of all too weak account
For earth with heavy griefs so overplussed.
　　　Ah! is Thy love indeed
A weed, albeit an amaranthine weed,
Suffering no flowers except its own to mount?
　　　Ah! must—
　　　Designer infinite!—
Ah! must Thou char the wood ere Thou canst limn with it?
My freshness spent its wavering shower i' the dust;
And now my heart is as a broken fount,
Wherein tear-drippings stagnate, spilt down ever
　　　From the dank thoughts that shiver
Upon the sighful branches of my mind.
　　　Such is; what is to be?
The pulp so bitter, how shall taste the rind?
I dimly guess what Time in mists confounds;
Yet ever and anon a trumpet sounds
From the hid battlements of Eternity;
Those shaken mists a space unsettle, then
Round the half-glimpséd turrets slowly wash again.
　　　But not ere him who summoneth
　　　I first have seen, enwound
With glooming robes purpureal, cypress-crowned;
His name I know, and what his trumpet saith.
Whether man's heart or life it be which yields
　　　Thee harvest, must Thy harvest-fields
　　　Be dunged with rotten death?

Now of that long pursuit
Comes on at hand the bruit;
That Voice is round me like a bursting sea:
    "And is thy earth so marred,
    Shattered in shard on shard?
  Lo, all things fly thee, for thou fliest Me!
    "Strange, piteous, futile thing!
Wherefore should any set thee love apart?
Seeing none but I makes much of naught" (He said),
"And human love needs human meriting:
    How hast thou merited—
Of all man's clotted clay the dingiest clot?
    Alack, thou knowest not
How little worthy of any love thou art!
Whom wilt thou find to love ignoble thee,
    Save Me, save only Me?
All which I took from thee I did but take,
    Not for thy harms,
But just that thou might'st seek it in My arms.
    All which thy child's mistake
Fancies as lost, I have stored for thee at home:
    Rise, clasp My hand, and come!"
      Halts by me that footfall:
      Is my gloom, after all,
  Shade of His hand, outstretched caressingly?
    "Ah, fondest, blindest, weakest,
    I am He Whom thou seekest!
Thou dravest love from thee, who dravest Me."

"The Dark Angel"

(1893)

LIONEL JOHNSON

Along with Francis Thompson, Oscar Wilde, and Ernest Dowson, Lionel Johnson was part of the "Tragic Generation," as the poet W.B. Yeats dubbed the group—gifted writers who met as the "Rhymers' Club" in a pub in Fleet Street, London, to talk literature. All were blighted by drink or drugs, decadence or loneliness, and died early deaths. All the men named here, bar Yeats and Thompson (who was a cradle Catholic), converted to the faith.

Johnson struggled with both alcoholism and his sexuality. As the person who introduced Alfred Lord Bosie to his most famous lover, Oscar Wilde, Johnson was repentant and quite viciously condemning: "I hate you with a necessary hate," he wrote in a sonnet thought to be about the Irish playwright.[1]

But "only the lifeless are exempt from the battles of lust," as the monk St. John Cassian said. In this poem, "lust" springs irresistibly to mind. It stands at the end of the first line, alongside the provocative adjective "aching." However, the enjambment (the way that the line runs over to the next) specifies that the dark angel's lust is actually for making humankind unaware of, and unrepentant for, sins of all kinds.

Johnson's language does a thorough and terrifying job of conjuring the passions. The insistent beat, and the extreme yet realistic confession that "no thought, no thing" is untouched by

[1]. The sonnet was Johnson's "The Destroyer of a Soul."

his urges, bounds into imagery of flames and furies. The speaker is a man condemned to have no rest. Every innocent thing is spoiled.

Johnson's Victorian-pastoral attention to natural detail is touching. (As a pastoral poet, he placed himself within the Irish tradition.) But he cannot enjoy nature's peace! The adjectives "beleaguerest, bewilderest" seem to come straight from Thompson's "Hound of Heaven." As readers, we have that same sense of being dragged onward, unable to appreciate the passing view. And, of course, that is what any of the passions—anger, lust, greed, pride, etc.—do to us: they blind us. But unlike "The Hound of Heaven," it is specifically a demon dragging Johnson on and away from the truth of "winter silences" and the "breath of autumn woods," not a misplaced fear of relenting to God.

As all seems lost or poisoned, we are treated to worse: a gothic perspective of tombs and gloom and "haunting laugh." This malevolent presence suggests the devil's role as accuser and father of lies. The speaker's mind is clouded with hopelessness and untruth.

Yet the final vision here is one of hope—of facing down the malicious demon and being united with the divine. The speaker sees that if he wins this battle he will escape from the "second Death." "Yet, what thou dost, is what God saith: / Tempter!" he pronounces, with a feisty echo of Gregory of Nazianzus' confrontation with the devil in his poem "Against the Burden of Sickness." We are reminded that God let Jesus be tempted in the desert, and he permitted Job's dreadful temptations against faith. The dark battle against sin of every kind is ultimately a way of winning sanctity.

"The Dark Angel"

LIONEL JOHNSON

Dark Angel, with thine aching lust
To rid the world of penitence:
Malicious Angel, who still dost
My soul such subtile violence!

Because of thee, no thought, no thing,
Abides for me undesecrate:
Dark Angel, ever on the wing,
Who never reachest me too late!

When music sounds, then changest thou
Its silvery to a sultry fire:
Nor will thine envious heart allow
Delight untortured by desire.

Through thee, the gracious Muses turn,
To Furies, O mine Enemy!
And all the things of beauty burn
With flames of evil ecstasy.

Because of thee, the land of dreams
Becomes a gathering place of fears:
Until tormented slumber seems
One vehemence of useless tears.

When sunlight glows upon the flowers,
Or ripples down the dancing sea:
Thou, with thy troop of passionate powers,
Beleaguerest, bewilderest, me.

Within the breath of autumn woods,
Within the winter silences:
Thy venomous spirit stirs and broods,
O Master of impieties!

The ardour of red flame is thine,
And thine the steely soul of ice:
Thou poisonest the fair design
Of nature, with unfair device.

Apples of ashes, golden bright;
Waters of bitterness, how sweet!
O banquet of a foul delight,
Prepared by thee, dark Paraclete!

Thou art the whisper in the gloom,
The hinting tone, the haunting laugh:
Thou art the adorner of my tomb,
The minstrel of mine epitaph.

I fight thee, in the Holy Name!
Yet, what thou dost, is what God saith:
Tempter! should I escape thy flame,
Thou wilt have helped my soul from Death:

The second Death, that never dies,
That cannot die, when time is dead:
Live Death, wherein the lost soul cries,
Eternally uncomforted.

Dark Angel, with thine aching lust!
Of two defeats, of two despairs:
Less dread, a change to drifting dust,
Than thine eternity of cares.

Do what thou wilt, thou shalt not so,
Dark Angel! triumph over me:
Lonely, unto the Lone I go;
Divine, to the Divinity.

"To Scatter Flowers"

(June 28, 1896)

ST. THÉRÈSE OF LISIEUX

Thérèse of Lisieux has to be one of the most popular saints, if not *the* most popular saint, of modern times. Even Thomas Merton, who admitted to despising the bourgeois world from which she came and the schmaltz that surrounded her cult, came to discover the essential *greatness* of "the Little Flower."

Thwarted in her desire to be a missionary, Thérèse became, in her Carmelite cloister, what we might guess God always wanted her to be: a hothouse flower of sanctity. There is no doubting Thérèse's zeal to travel to faraway lands, but her astonishing work was done in the cloister in prayer—and in her ability to reach millions after her death (even a monk with high literary tastes like Merton).

Thérèse was not, primarily, a poet, though she wrote many poems very much in the style of her time. She is, however, a prime example of someone thriving in the Catholic imagination and contributing to it, as this poem testifies.

The language of flowers dates back to long before Thérèse. The lover in the Song of Solomon is the "rose of Sharon" (Song of Sol. 2:1). Dante in turn used the rose as symbol of heaven. The medieval "There is No Rose of Such Virtue" also has Mary as a rose. And roses, more generally of course, symbolize love in any creed.

Upon her death, Thérèse famously promised that she would let fall "a shower of roses," using the metaphor of rose as prayer or blessing.[1] Catholics everywhere have entered into this poetic exchange, finding roses in odd places and seasons when they pray for her intercession. Catholics naturally use poetic currency: they are good at finding a material thing for the invisible. And that is what this poem is all about.

The flowers in these lines are not simply prayers though. The "plucked petals bright" are also handkerchiefs that dry Christ's tears. They are symbols of the things we "offer up." But beneath the sentimentality and lashings of exclamation points, the young saint was no stranger to pain and darkness. Written in the year before her long and painful death, the sprightly style of this verse belies the suffering Thérèse had recently started to undergo as she went through her own dark night and lost all surety of heaven. Here she lists her "sighs and pains, my heaviest, saddest hours" that become, poetically, the flowers of sacrificial suffering.

But there's more: the flowers are also everything in Thérèse's control. They are her sword (Thérèse was fond of using the analogy of armory and had a special devotion to Joan of Arc); flowers are also her way of saving sinners and disarming the Lord. The petals are her fingers to caress the Holy Face. They are words to pray, her way of speaking about God. They are her language of love.

1. Thérèse of Lisieux, *St. Thérèse of Lisieux: Her Last Conversations*, trans. John Clarke (Washington, DC: ICS, 1977), 62.

"To Scatter Flowers"

Translated from the French by S.L. Emery

ST. THÉRÈSE OF LISIEUX

O Jesu! O my Love! Each eve I come to fling
    Before Thy sacred Cross sweet flowers of all the year.
By these plucked petals bright, my hands how gladly bring,
    I long to dry Thine every tear!

To scatter flowers!—that means each sacrifice,
    My lightest sighs and pains, my heaviest, saddest hours,
My hopes, my joys, my prayers,—I will not count the price.
    Behold my flowers!

With deep, untold delight Thy beauty fills my soul.
    Would I might light this love in hearts of all who live!
For this, my fairest flowers, all things in my control,
    How fondly, gladly I would give!

To scatter flowers!—behold my chosen sword
    For saving sinners' souls and filling heaven's bowers.
The victory is mine: yes, I disarm Thee, Lord,
    With these my flowers!

The petals in their flight caress Thy Holy Face;
 They tell Thee that my heart is Thine, and Thine alone.
Thou knowest what these leaves are saying in my place;
 On me Thou smilest from Thy throne.

To scatter flowers!—that means, to speak of Thee,—
 My only pleasure here, where tears fill all the hours;
But soon, with angel hosts, my spirit shall be free,
 To scatter flowers!

"Nuns of the Perpetual Adoration"

(1896)

ERNEST DOWSON

"They are not long, the days of wine and roses," is one of Ernest Dowson's most famous lines of poetry.[1] Roses also feature in this poem, which is less known, though more sober, more real—and, in some ways, more naïve.

"I cannot imagine the world in which he would have succeeded," said W.B. Yeats of his poet-friend.[2] Dowson was another member of Yeats' Rhymers' Club, another of the Tragic Generation. But this poet's taste for absinthe and the furies it unleashed within him, the company he kept with prostitutes and his broken-hearted love for a teenage girl, his poverty and despair are only worth mentioning as they are the counterpoint to this poem. In some sense, they explain it.

In controlled, unhurried verse, the poet describes and praises the nuns of the Perpetual Adoration at Tyburn, where St. Edmund Campion, St. Henry Walpole, and St. Robert Southwell were martyred. "Calm, sad, secure," he declares in the first line, and those three stressed syllables imbue the line with certainty. Yet the words give us pause. "Calm" the nuns are (or should be): yes. "Secure" seems likely: check. But "sad"?

Does "sad" mean "sober" here? In some ways, the speaker grasps clearly the nature of cloistered life. Time, for these nuns,

---

1. Ernest Dowson, "Vitae Summa Brevis Spem Nos Vetat Incohare Longam."
2. W.B. Yeats, *Memoirs*, ed. Denis Donoghue (London: Macmillan, 1972), 92. For further reading on Ernest Dowson, see Jad Adams, *Madder Music, Stronger Wine: The Life of Ernest Dowson, Poet and Decadent* (London: I.B. Tauris, 2000).

has lapsed into eternity; they are immune to the day ending or beginning in the usual way. Their hours are threaded with Christ's through the Divine Office and Rosary. This is a life untrammeled by binges and hangovers, love-sickness and the wrong kind of poverty. And, in fact, there is nothing sad about this poem—only an almost exhausted peace.

"Outside, the world is wild and passionate," begins stanza four, and the poet sees the nuns rejecting the roses that perfume his other poems. The nuns know how quickly roses fade and put away such things. In "their dream of prayer," they do not, he conjectures, hear the voices of men. It is a naïve line: surely even the most cloistered prayer cannot be divorced from the chaos outside the convent walls. It exists, partly, for that. Again, as with the word "sad," we might guess that this is more about the life of the poet than the nuns. He is looking for escape—from his own madness, the voices in the bars and streets—into a life made simple by God.

At the final stanza, the first line is answered: "Calm and secure," he writes now. Acoustically, this echoes the first line, but through the journey of the poem the sadness has gone. The last line seems to sum up, for this "Tragic Generation," the urge to convert, the peace that they hankered after and ultimately could not reject.

"Nuns of the Perpetual Adoration"

ERNEST DOWSON

Calm, sad, secure; behind high convent walls,
These watch the sacred lamp, these watch and pray:
And it is one with them when evening falls,
And one with them the cold return of day.

These heed not time; their nights and days they make
Into a long returning rosary,
Whereon their lives are threaded for Christ's sake;
Meekness and vigilance and chastity.

A vowed patrol, in silent companies,
Life-long they keep before the living Christ.
In that dim church, their prayers and penances
Are fragrant incense to the Sacrificed.

Outside, the world is wild and passionate;
Man's weary laughter and his sick despair
Entreat at their impenetrable gate;
They heed no voices in their dream of prayer.

They saw the glory of the world displayed;
They saw the bitter of it, and the sweet;
They knew the roses of the world should fade,
And be trod under by the hurrying feet.

Therefore they rather put away desire,
And crossed their hands and came to sanctuary,
And veiled their heads and put on coarse attire;
Because their comeliness was vanity.

And there they rest; they have serene insight
Of the illuminating dawn to be;
Mary's sweet Star dispels for them the night,
The proper darkness of humanity.

Calm and secure; with faces worn and mild;
Surely their choice of vigil is the best?
Yea! for our roses fade, the world is wild;
But there, beside the altar, there, is rest.

"The Ballad of Reading Gaol" (Excerpt)

(1898)

OSCAR WILDE

The downfall of Oscar Wilde stripped him of money, respectability, health, home, family—and more. His stretch in gaol[1] also took away identity and dignified purpose: his "hard labor" consisted in walking a treadmill or untangling tarred ropes until his hands bled. One of the few happy results of his incarceration, though, is this poem. It is, I would argue, a type of living document of Wilde's conversion.

During his sentence of two years for "gross indecency," Wilde wrote that "Christ's place indeed is with the poets."[2] In turn, in this poem, we readers are irresistibly invited to see the face of Christ in the poet Wilde—and his hapless, fellow inmates. What the poem goes on to demonstrate is an elevation of empathy and love-without-judgment that culminates in a crystalline vision of God's mercy.

Published under his prison identification number C.3.3, Wilde's ballad recounts the tale of a new inmate, a trooper of the Royal Horse Guards, who is to be executed for the murder of his wife. As evidenced by the circuitous repetitions and parallelism typical of a ballad, Wilde's observation of the man is compulsive. In mesmerizing rhyming lines of alternately four and three beats, not just Wilde but the whole prison appears rocked by

1. The British English spelling of "jail."
2. Oscar Wilde, "De Profundis." Wilde also writes: "[Christ] realised in the entire sphere of human relations that imaginative sympathy which in the sphere of Art is the sole secret of creation."

anguished identification with the man who will walk by his own coffin to be hanged. Toward the end of the first section, Wilde describes what he himself, as one *not* sentenced to death, will *not* have to go through. But the effect of this thought process works to the contrary: Wilde lives the experience—and so do we through his poem. What results is the most extraordinary account of empathy, that Christian blurring of lines between one man and another—and even between man and his Creator.

Through his empathic gaze, Wilde comes to lament, in his famous refrain: "For each man kills the thing he loves." These words stick in the brain and simultaneously make us ask, "How?" Wilde's knowledge of his own family's pain at his actions must have disclosed to him that killing happens in many different fashions. We are all guilty—including the justice system that deemed itself virtuously Christian and still inflicted torture. In his bleak cell, Wilde must have seen in his mind's eye Christ drawing in sand.

Perhaps he also remembered, "I was . . . in prison and you did not visit me" (Matt. 25:43). Even unconsciously, Wilde imitates Christ's deliberate identification with wrongdoers as he empathizes so vividly with the horse guard.

No doubt he also had Dante's *Purgatorio* and its punishment of the proud on his mind when he wrote of the hefting of rocks. There is no pride nor life left in the beleaguered writer of this poem. His punishments are man-made, graceless, and hopeless.

Thankfully, God's saving mercy rides in at the end as Wilde continues to contrast human justice with divine justice. "Only blood can wipe out blood," says the *Ballad*—meaning not the blood of the horse guard that is shed in retribution but Christ's blood, which cleanses and saves.

On his deathbed, two years after the publication of this deeply Christian poem, Wilde finally succumbed to the "Roman fever" he had suffered throughout his life and was received into the Catholic Church.

"The Ballad of Reading Gaol" (Excerpt)

Sections 1 and 5

OSCAR WILDE

IN MEMORIAM
C.T.W.
Sometime trooper of the Royal Horse Guards,
obit H.M. Prison, Reading, Berkshire
July 7, 1896

He did not wear his scarlet coat,
    For blood and wine are red,
And blood and wine were on his hands
    When they found him with the dead,
The poor dead woman whom he loved,
    And murdered in her bed.

He walked amongst the Trial Men
    In a suit of shabby grey;
A cricket cap was on his head,
    And his step seemed light and gay;
But I never saw a man who looked
    So wistfully at the day.

I never saw a man who looked
    With such a wistful eye
Upon that little tent of blue
    Which prisoners call the sky,
And at every drifting cloud that went
    With sails of silver by.

I walked, with other souls in pain,
    Within another ring,
And was wondering if the man had done
    A great or little thing,
When a voice behind me whispered low,
    "That fellow's got to swing."

Dear Christ! the very prison walls
    Suddenly seemed to reel,
And the sky above my head became
    Like a casque of scorching steel;
And, though I was a soul in pain,
    My pain I could not feel.

I only knew what hunted thought
    Quickened his step, and why
He looked upon the garish day
    With such a wistful eye;
The man had killed the thing he loved
    And so he had to die.

*

Yet each man kills the thing he loves,
    By each let this be heard,
Some do it with a bitter look,
    Some with a flattering word.
The coward does it with a kiss,
    The brave man with a sword!

Some kill their love when they are young,
　　And some when they are old;
Some strangle with the hands of Lust,
　　Some with the hands of Gold:
The kindest use a knife, because
　　The dead so soon grow cold.

Some love too little, some too long,
　　Some sell, and others buy;
Some do the deed with many tears,
　　And some without a sigh:
For each man kills the thing he loves,
　　Yet each man does not die.

He does not die a death of shame
　　On a day of dark disgrace,
Nor have a noose about his neck,
　　Nor a cloth upon his face,
Nor drop feet foremost through the floor
　　Into an empty space.

He does not sit with silent men
　　Who watch him night and day;
Who watch him when he tries to weep,
　　And when he tries to pray;
Who watch him lest himself should rob
　　The prison of its prey.

He does not wake at dawn to see
    Dread figures throng his room,
The shivering Chaplain robed in white,
    The Sheriff stern with gloom,
And the Governor all in shiny black,
    With the yellow face of Doom.

He does not rise in piteous haste
    To put on convict-clothes,
While some coarse-mouthed Doctor gloats, and notes
    Each new and nerve-twitched pose,
Fingering a watch whose little ticks
    Are like horrible hammer-blows.

He does not feel that sickening thirst
    That sands one's throat, before
The hangman with his gardener's gloves
    Comes through the padded door,
And binds one with three leathern thongs,
    That the throat may thirst no more.

He does not bend his head to hear
    The Burial Office read,
Nor, while the anguish of his soul
    Tells him he is not dead,
Cross his own coffin, as he moves
    Into the hideous shed.

He does not stare upon the air
   Through a little roof of glass:
He does not pray with lips of clay
   For his agony to pass;
Nor feel upon his shuddering cheek
   The kiss of Caiaphas.

     . . . .

*

But though lean Hunger and green Thirst
   Like asp with adder fight,
We have little care of prison fare,
   For what chills and kills outright
Is that every stone one lifts by day
   Becomes one's heart by night.

With midnight always in one's heart,
   And twilight in one's cell,
We turn the crank, or tear the rope,
   Each in his separate Hell,
And the silence is more awful far
   Than the sound of a brazen bell.

And never a human voice comes near
   To speak a gentle word:
And the eye that watches through the door
   Is pitiless and hard:
And by all forgot, we rot and rot,
   With soul and body marred.

And thus we rust Life's iron chain
   Degraded and alone:
And some men curse, and some men weep,
   And some men make no moan:
But God's eternal Laws are kind
   And break the heart of stone.

And every human heart that breaks,
   In prison-cell or yard,
Is as that broken box that gave
   Its treasure to the Lord,
And filled the unclean leper's house
   With the scent of costliest nard.

Ah! happy they whose hearts can break
   And peace of pardon win!
How else may man make straight his plan
   And cleanse his soul from Sin?
How else but through a broken heart
   May Lord Christ enter in?

*

And he of the swollen purple throat,
   And the stark and staring eyes,
Waits for the holy hands that took
   The Thief to Paradise;
And a broken and a contrite heart
   The Lord will not despise.

The man in red who reads the Law
   Gave him three weeks of life,
Three little weeks in which to heal
   His soul of his soul's strife,
And cleanse from every blot of blood
   The hand that held the knife.

And with tears of blood he cleansed the hand,
   The hand that held the steel:
For only blood can wipe out blood,
   And only tears can heal:
And the crimson stain that was of Cain
   Became Christ's snow-white seal.

"The Donkey"

(1900)

G.K. CHESTERTON

G.K. Chesterton was not, primarily, a poet. This essayist, journalist, novelist, and apologist wrote a startling amount of everything, which we might expect of a man of such astonishing physical and intellectual proportions. Like any true journalist, his writing, in most forms, was about a message that needed to be communicated. As a Christian, then Catholic convert, his evangelical message was so poetic that poetry seems to have been an obvious genre for him to use.

On one level, this little poem in the voice of the Easter donkey is the stuff of children's anthologies—and younger readers certainly love it. But there is poetic bite and true hope here, which anyone can appreciate. Written in rhyming quatrains, with alternating stresses of four and three per line, and peppered with alliteration, this is a dark but touching piece that manages to say so much about Christianity.

At the start, Chesterton conjures a moment in which something seems to have gone awry with nature. There is an element of dark superstition in the moon turning to blood and trees walking when this creature is born. It seems akin to Shakespeare's *Macbeth*, when the witches prophesy that Great Birnam wood will uproot and march. It smacks of the sky darkening at Christ's final breath. Nature itself winces at the ugly affront of this beast being born into the world.

Historically, through many cultures, the deformed or different have been shut away or even killed. Humanity ogled and mocked "the Elephant Man" and many like him. This donkey is an embodiment of any variation in nature. His ears are alarming and unfathomably big. There is no music in his voice.

Chesterton was known as the "Prince of Paradox," though the name might apply more aptly to Jesus Christ himself. With Christ's coming, weakness and difference were turned upside down: the ugly became beautiful, the weak became strong, the last will be first. We are used to imagining Jesus as conventionally lovely in face and form. But Isaiah prophesied he would be "as one from whom others hide their faces" (Isa. 53:3).

The parallel between the donkey of this poem and Jesus is made plain in the third stanza: he invites the world to "starve, scourge, deride" him—the last two words being an integral part of Christ's Passion.

For the donkey, like Christ, will have his day. He will come to be himself in God and do what he was brought into being to do: carry God into Jerusalem, from where he will be carried out into the world. To this day, of course, donkeys are born with a dark cross on their back.

And yet the donkey keeps his silence. Today, this notion of keeping quiet about our religious experience is alien to many of us. Early Christians often had to keep quiet about their religion, and many still do in different parts of the world. But the donkey's silence is chosen. In the parameters of the poem's logic, where a donkey is writing poetry, his muteness is a rational choice. He is following in the footsteps of the person closest to God, Mary, who pondered such things in her heart (Luke 2:19). He does not transform into the conventionally beautiful. He does not stand on his two back legs and speak. This is not a fairytale; no true conversion is. For the donkey, the fact of God's nearness is enough to sustain him through the rest of his days.

"The Donkey"

G.K. CHESTERTON

When fishes flew and forests walked
   And figs grew upon thorn,
Some moment when the moon was blood
   Then surely I was born.

With monstrous head and sickening cry
   And ears like errant wings,
The devil's walking parody
   On all four-footed things.

The tattered outlaw of the earth,
   Of ancient crooked will;
Starve, scourge, deride me: I am dumb,
   I keep my secret still.

Fools! For I also had my hour;
   One far fierce hour and sweet:
There was a shout about my ears,
   And palms before my feet.

"The Unknown God"

(1901)

ALICE MEYNELL

In this lucid lyric, the poet describes the experience of the
Holy Mass from an extraordinary point of view. Perhaps we
are used to contemplating the closeness of Christ during
Communion. As we kneel, it may seem that each person in
the church is a closed vessel concentrated entirely on what is
happening within themselves.

Yet, as Alice Meynell intuits, Christ is not only in our hearts.
He is in the heart of the man or woman next to us, and the
teenager behind us, and the first communicant out front, and
the returning churchgoer who prays in a back pew. He abides in
them too. They are also his temple. How well Meynell describes
this other person—not only the physicality of their breaths
and heartbeat but the "stronghold" of their will and their
impenetrable mystery. We can almost see Christ in this dark,
hidden place: he is working in them.

Scripture, too, asks us to see Christ in every man, especially
the least (Matt. 25:40). But Meynell pushes this idea further: she
writes of the man praying by her side as a place she can confess
God—as though he were a church that she can, spiritually, enter.
Her prayer is not exactly for herself and not exactly for him.
Rather, it is an engagement with the narrator's positioning of
herself within the Body of Christ. It also illuminates something
of what happens when we pray for other people. God is within

our neighbor. If we reach out to him, if we pray for him, if he prays for us, we encounter, in a mysterious way, the Creator.

The litany of the final stanza, "Christ in his numbered breath," recalls St. Patrick's "The Deer's Cry": "Christ in the heart of every man who thinks of me . . ." In other words, we should pray as much for Christ to be alive in others as we pray for him to be alive in us.

It was Alice Meynell and her husband, Wilfrid, who first published the poetry of Francis Thompson. They not only brought Thompson's poetry to light; they took him off the streets and into their home and helped him into recovery for his addiction.

Meynell's deeply spiritual poem is imbued with this same capacity for empathy. It brings to mind the famous quote attributed to St. John Chrysostom: "If you can't find Christ in the beggar at the door, you won't find him in the chalice."[1] But Meynell is asking us to venture into a place even more of us ignore: the small temple of a fellow congregant's soul.

1. See John Chrysostom, *Homilies on Matthew* 50.4.

"The Unknown God"

ALICE MEYNELL

One of the crowd went up,
And knelt before the Paten and the Cup,
Received the Lord, returned in peace, and prayed
Close to my side. Then in my heart I said:

"O Christ, in this man's life!—
This stranger who is Thine—in all his strife,
All his felicity, his good and ill,
In the assaulted stronghold of his will,

"I do confess Thee here,
Alive within this life; I know Thee near
Within this lonely conscience, closed away
Within this brother's solitary day.

"Christ in his unknown heart,
His intellect unknown—this love, this art,
This battle and this peace, this destiny
That I shall never know, look upon me!

"Christ in his numbered breath,
Christ in his beating heart and in his death,
Christ in his mystery! From that secret place
And from that separate dwelling, give me grace!"

"The Closed House"
of *Five Great Odes* (Excerpt)

(1907–1908)

PAUL CLAUDEL

The *Five Great Odes* of Paul Claudel are vast meditations on
passion, poetry, and faith. Actually, "meditation" is too calm
a word for writing that is all at once anguished, penitent,
rhapsodic, and consoling. A glance at Claudel's life reveals much
of what sets the poetry ablaze.

As a young man, Claudel had a conversion experience in the
cathedral of Notre Dame: something in the singing of Vespers
brought the eternity of God to him in the moment of a song. He
wondered about becoming a monk but ended up as a diplomat.
He embarked on a "conflagration"[1] of a love affair with a
married woman but finished as a family man "growing fat."[2] He
ached for God and Wisdom but was ransacked by sin. ("Who can
contain the human flame?" he writes earlier in the *Odes*.[3]) We
take our excerpt from the fifth ode, "The Closed House," where
the portly diplomat is squaring up to eternity from what he has
come to see as the cloister of his marriage.

Written in the long lines of "versets" (that have come to
be called *le verset claudélien*, after their creator, and that were
inspired by the Vulgate translation of the Psalms), this poetry
is far different from some of the tight poetic forms we have

1. Paul Claudel, *Five Great Odes*, trans. Jonathan Geltner (Brooklyn, NY:
Angelico, 2020), 35.
2. Claudel, 92.
3. Claudel, 35.

previously seen. Claudel's focus is on image and natural rhythm.
The shortening and lengthening of the lines is driven purely
by emotion and content rather than any outwardly imposed
structure. The poet calls this particular poem a "song," and he
consecrates it to the new century. But what is also startling
about this religious ode, aside from its form, is its emphasis on
the *finite* (hence, "The Closed Room"), not the *infinite*. "We have
found / your Creation is finite," Claudel asserts partway through
this passage, addressing God. What can he mean?

Well, what Claudel calls "finite" we might think of as
"formed" or "made." He is writing against the formlessness
of the void that we read of at the beginning of Genesis. He is
recognizing the common purpose of poet and God: to create
something that shores up the overwhelming nature of the
infinite. He is observing God's consecrating presence in all
things (particularly the Church, which this passage eulogizes)
and how this makes the cosmos knowable—especially for a poet
who is given to finding connections between disparate things,
whether they be larvae, stars, or brothers and sisters in Christ.
The "measure" of God, Claudel says, is "nowhere absent." In
other words, through the structures, rituals, and edifices of the
Church and the communion of saints, nothing is lost to chaos.

Claudel's vision of the Church is cosmic, its members
multitudinous. His references to stars (think of God's promises
to Abraham in Genesis 26:4 that his descendants will be as
numerous as the stars in the sky), fish (think of Christ's promise
to Peter and Andrew that they will be fishers of men), and the
long territories of the "old maps" paint a picture of the Church
as a vast seething organism stretching to the ends of time and
space. Everything is connected; everything is linked. The use of
the small "c" in "catholic" is intentional here: it is all-inclusive,
all-embracing. These lines might be seen as a response to

our speech from Shakespeare's *Hamlet*, which also saw the
glorious structures and connections of creation and man's place
within them—but with far less hope. These lines, in contrast
to Hamlet's, resound with gratitude for the indestructible
brotherhood of catholic men and women.

"The Closed House" of *Five Great Odes*
(Excerpt)

Translated from the French by Jonathan Geltner

PAUL CLAUDEL

I see before me the Catholic Church,
   which is the whole universe.
Oh, prize and miraculous catch! Oh, million stars
   caught in the mesh of our net,
like a great booty of fish, dangling fresh over the sea,
   scales flashing lively light under the ship's torches.
We have conquered the world and we have found
   your Creation is finite,
and that the imperfect has no place among your finite works,
   that our imagination cannot add
a single figure to this Number, which is
   ecstatic before your unity.
As once, when Columbus and Magellan had rejoined
   the two halves of the earth
and all the monsters of the old maps vanished,
   so heaven no longer holds terror for us, knowing
however far world might extend
   your measure is nowhere absent. Your goodness is not absent.
And we look with peace at your stars in the sky,
   as at fattened sheep and grazing flocks,
as numerous as the seed of Abraham.

As you can see little spiders or larvae
like precious stones hidden in a satin purse,
   so I have seen a whole brood of stars still folded
in the cold curtains of the nebula,
   and so I see you, all my brothers, in the muck and mire
and as disguised as those suffering stars.
   All is mine, for I am catholic, not one of you,
my beloved brothers, is reft from me.

"The Portal of the Mystery of Hope"
(Excerpt)

(1910)

CHARLES PÉGUY

In the last part of the nineteenth century, Nietzsche took the pulse of God and pronounced him dead. From the ashes of hope, nihilism rose like black smoke across the new age. But in the midst of this bleak creep, humanity received a gift: a poetic treatise on the theological virtue of hope.

Its author, Charles Péguy, lived a short life, obsessed with the quest for truth. Initially abandoning his faith in favor of socialism, he returned to the Catholicism of his birth—but his atheist wife, with whom he had a civil marriage, would not follow him, nor would she let their children be baptized. In his remaining years, Péguy found himself living in that restless hinterland where exclusion and grace collide.

This extract, from the second part of a trilogy, characterizes faith as a loyal wife, charity as a mother, and both of them as *unsurprising* to God. After all, Péguy says earlier in the voice of the Creator, who wouldn't be faithful, looking on all of creation, and who wouldn't be charitable, seeing suffering all around them? But "what surprises me, says God, is hope. / And I can't get over it. / This little girl hope who seems like nothing at all."

The way in which Péguy gives voice to God is cheeky, but somehow never grating. We are let into the mind of God (a literary device and not divine dictation, as the poet would have been well aware) as he ruminates on the shocking fact that mankind (mostly) manages to get out of bed every morning with renewed hope for the day ahead. "I'm surprised by it myself," says God. This epic hope begins in the fount of blood from Christ's pierced side, and it transforms into mankind's fragile hope, which Péguy characterizes as the tiny fragile flame at the tabernacle.

But it is the personification of hope as a little girl that slays us. His image of her playing with her snowman and her Christmas manger scene brings to mind the heartbreaking vulnerability of any small child—their weakness and their uncanny resilience. The snowman, of course, will melt; the baby Jesus will grow up to be crucified. How can we bear it? But somehow this little girl endures "the weight of worlds." Somehow, she is the lynchpin of all the virtues. Without this little girl, we would not have the strength to love and to be faithful.

This is oral poetry. It is casual and chatty, and forms part of a multi-volumed verse drama. The versets are irregular and powered by the deepening of Péguy's thought. The punctuation is idiosyncratic and jerky; it suggests a difficult, emotional contemplation. But the lines are enchanting. They use repetition and extensive metaphor to draw us into a drama that includes God, hope, and us.

At the age of forty-one, Charles Péguy was killed in battle at the start of the First World War. He fought because he believed it would be the war to end all wars. He gives us what can be the only response to his own tragedy: "One flame will pierce the eternal shadows."

His wife and most of their family, who he had entrusted to the Blessed Virgin, would later be baptized.

"The Portal of the Mystery of Hope" (Excerpt)

Translated from the French by David Louis Schindler, Jr.

CHARLES PÉGUY

But hope, says God, that is something that surprises me.
Even me.
That is surprising.

That these poor children see how things are going and believe
     that tomorrow things will go better.
That they see how things are going today and believe that they
     will go better tomorrow morning.
That is surprising and it's by far the greatest marvel of our
     grace.
And I'm surprised by it myself.
And my grace must indeed be an incredible force.
And must flow freely and like an inexhaustible river.
Since the first time it flowed and since it has forever been
     flowing.
In my natural and supernatural creation.
In my spiritual and carnal and yet spiritual creation.
In my eternal and temporal and yet eternal creation.
Mortal and immortal.
And that time, oh that time, since that time that it flowed like
     a river of blood, from the pierced side of my son.
What must my grace, and the strength of my grace, be so that
     this little hope, vacillating at the breath of sin, trembling
     with every wind, anxious at the slightest breath,

be as constant, remain as faithful, as righteous, as pure; and
    invincible, and immortal, and impossible to extinguish;
    as that little flame in the sanctuary.
That burns eternally in the faithful lamp.
One trembling flame has endured the weight of worlds.
One vacillating flame has endured the weight of time.
One anxious flame has endured the weight of nights.
Since the first time my grace flowed for the creation of the
    world.
Since my grace has been flowing forever for the preservation of
    the world.
Since the time that the blood of my son flowed for the salvation
    of the world.

A flame impossible to reach, impossible to extinguish with the
    breath of death.

What surprises me, says God, is hope.
And I can't get over it.
This little girl hope who seems like nothing at all.
This little girl hope.
Immortal.

Because my three virtues, says God.
The three virtues, my creatures.
My daughters, my children.
Are themselves like my other creatures.
Of the race of men.
Faith is a loyal Wife.
Charity is a Mother.
An ardent mother, noble-hearted.
Or an older sister who is like a mother.

Hope is a little girl, nothing at all.
Who came into the world on Christmas day just this past year.
Who is still playing with her snowman.
With her German fir trees painted with frost.
And with her ox and her ass made of German wood. Painted.
And with her manger stuffed with straw that the animals
    don't eat.
Because they're made of wood.
And yet it's this little girl who will endure worlds.
This little girl, nothing at all.
She, alone, carrying the others, who will cross worlds past.

As the star guided the three kings from the deepest Orient.
Toward the cradle of my son.
Like a trembling flame.
She alone will guide Virtues and Worlds.

One flame will pierce the eternal shadows.

"The House of Christmas"

(1912)

G.K. CHESTERTON

It is fair to say that G.K. Chesterton had no truck with literary Modernism. He used structure, as the old balladeers used to, to tell stories and to entertain. In poetry and literature generally, he was not interested in opacity or complication. His poetic style made for memorable, popular pieces that appeal to poetry skeptics as much as poetry lovers.

Christmas was a subject that Chesterton wrote much about. A childless man, he was apparently a favorite uncle with children, which shouldn't surprise us given his vivid stories, his rhymes, and also his joy. There is no moping in his poetry (another thing that sets him apart from many poets).

This Christmas poem *must* be read aloud, preferably after dinner by the fire on Christmas Eve. His rollicking rhythm goes fast and urgent. He does this by using four and three stresses per line alternately (typical of the ballad form) until the all-rhyming lines five, six, and seven, which all have four stresses—thus upping the emotional and rhetorical ante. Each stanza sticks to plain, square rhymes, and this gives the glad certainty of a nursery rhyme.

The deliberately repetitive vocabulary (Rome, home, homeless) is meant to hammer home his premise: that our only home is with Christ, in the barn where he was homeless. (And even the Church of Rome is built on this precarious homelessness.)

No one can fashion lines like Chesterton for sheer memorability: "This world is wild as an old wives' tale" will never be forgotten once read. "Our rest is as far as the fire-drake swings / And our peace is put in impossible things" is worthy of a meditation in itself. In his own inimitable style, Chesterton is exploring themes of the spiritual life seen from the beginning of Christian writing, in texts such as St. Augustine's *Confessions*: "I have burned for Thy peace."[1] In his alliterative conjuring of man's homesickness (we are "strangers under the sun"), we hear something of Dowson's longing for a godly place in "Nuns of the Perpetual Adoration." Chesterton's rhythm takes us on quickly, but as well as reading this aloud, it is worthwhile pausing quietly with a pencil and going through the jewels to be found here in every line.

1. Augustine, *Confessions* 10.27.

"The House of Christmas"

G.K. CHESTERTON

There fared a mother driven forth
Out of an inn to roam;
In the place where she was homeless
All men are at home.
The crazy stable close at hand,
With shaking timber and shifting sand,
Grew a stronger thing to abide and stand
Than the square stones of Rome.

For men are homesick in their homes,
And strangers under the sun,
And they lay their heads in a foreign land
Whenever the day is done.
Here we have battle and blazing eyes,
And chance and honor and high surprise,
But our homes are under miraculous skies
Where the yule tale was begun.

A Child in a foul stable,
Where the beasts feed and foam;
Only where He was homeless
Are you and I at home;
We have hands that fashion and heads that know,
But our hearts we lost—how long ago!
In a place no chart nor ship can show
Under the sky's dome.

This world is wild as an old wives' tale,
And strange the plain things are,
The earth is enough and the air is enough
For our wonder and our war;
But our rest is as far as the fire-drake swings
And our peace is put in impossible things
Where clashed and thundered unthinkable wings
Round an incredible star.

To an open house in the evening
Home shall men come,
To an older place than Eden
And a taller town than Rome.
To the end of the way of the wandering star,
To the things that cannot be and that are,
To the place where God was homeless
And all men are at home.

"Trees"

(1913)

JOYCE KILMER

Joyce Kilmer is best remembered as being the author of this simple and famous poem. The clear vision of "Trees"—its memorable rhyming couplets, its storybook personifications of nature, its wry self-deprecation—have made this piece a favorite with readers and anthologists.

Published the same year that Kilmer and his wife, Aline Murray, were received into the Church, "Trees" also garnered its share of scorn from the literati of the time. (See Ogden Nash's parody about billboards.[1]) Its couplets were too cute, its sentiments too sugary, to appeal to the Modernists or any serious students of poetry. So why include it here? Well, the roots of "Trees" go deep, so to speak.

The poem has its foundations in a mystical sensibility that runs through the entire Catholic canon. I don't want to make any great claim as to the sophistication of the text. It is, in many ways, a poem for children. But children, as we all know, sniff out the phony very quickly. Like the elements in Columcille (the "heaving waves . . . When they chant music to their Father") and the book of Daniel ("Let the earth bless the Lord" [Dan. 3:74]), Kilmer's trees praise God. They are personified as worshiping beings who know fellowship with birds and rain. We hear echoes of this spiritual kinship with nature down the poetic ages—in Manchán, St. Francis, and Gerard Manley Hopkins.

1. Ogden Nash, "Song of the Open Road."

In its final witty lines, Kilmer knows his poem's place as "God's grandchild," to quote Dante. Both Kilmer and Dante knew that nature is the prime creation: God's child. Poems are only crafted by men in imitation of God: "Your art strives to follow, as it may / Nature—you are the pupil, she the teacher. / So we might say that human industry / Is the grandchild of God."[2] In other words, as Kilmer says, the tree is the greater poem.

This little poem works because of the sound truths underpinning it, its utter rhyming simplicity, and also the lightness that belies the poet's suffering. (At the time of its writing, Kilmer's daughter was suffering from poliomyelitis, an experience that helped him to conversion.) The lines speak of his joyous faith.

2. Dante Alighieri, *Inferno*, trans. Anthony Esolen (New York: Modern Library, 2003), canto 11, line 106.

"Trees"

JOYCE KILMER

I think that I shall never see
A poem lovely as a tree.

A tree whose hungry mouth is prest
Against the earth's sweet flowing breast;

A tree that looks at God all day,
And lifts her leafy arms to pray;

A tree that may in Summer wear
A nest of robins in her hair;

Upon whose bosom snow has lain;
Who intimately lives with rain.

Poems are made by fools like me,
But only God can make a tree.

"I See His Blood upon the Rose"

(1916)

JOSEPH MARY PLUNKETT

This poet, Joseph Mary Plunkett, is also known for his part in the Irish Easter uprising of 1916. The British executed him at the age of twenty-eight, seven hours after his marriage to Grace Gifford. After his death, his sister published his controlled and often passionate poems.

Centuries before this lyric was written, Irish poets with whom we have already visited—St. Columba, Manchán, the anonymous author of "The Crucifixion"—were waxing about the presence of the divine in the natural world. St. Francis also recognized God in nature in a way that was fresh and yet as ancient as Scripture. For the Psalms themselves have the elements praising God (Ps. 148) and talk of his footsteps on the sea (Ps. 77:19).

But, for Plunkett, the Incarnation of Christ makes God present in particular ways. The very flesh of Jesus and his Passion are written in the bloody color of flowers, in the skies, and among the snows, where his body "gleams." For Plunkett, Christ does not just walk through the sea; he stirs it with his heartbeat. The poet gives careful expression to the Creator in all things. Every flower, each bird's song, each rock is written or carved by him. This is the poet as God's explainer, his watcher and praiser.

The vision of the poem is mystical; it sees God everywhere. It has the mind and heart of ceaseless prayer, in which all things

point to the divine. Yet there is a simplicity and an artlessness
about the piece, despite its immeasurable vision. Its rhyme
scheme gives the air of a song. Though the two middle lines
of each stanza have the traditional five stresses a line, the first
and last lines are shorter and lend a memorable awkwardness.
It seems as if they declare bald and poignant facts: "His cross is
every tree."

This is an intimate confession of God in flesh and in nature.

"I See His Blood upon the Rose"

JOSEPH MARY PLUNKETT

I see his blood upon the rose
And in the stars the glory of his eyes,
His body gleams amid eternal snows,
His tears fall from the skies.

I see his face in every flower;
The thunder and the singing of the birds
Are but his voice—and carven by his power
Rocks are his written words.

All pathways by his feet are worn,
His strong heart stirs the ever-beating sea,
His crown of thorns is twined with every thorn,
His cross is every tree.

"The Prayer of the Church" (Excerpt)

(1922–1924)

GERTRUD VON LE FORT

Baroness Gertrud von Le Fort was at a point of personal and political crisis. The First World War had ended, and the seeds of the Second World War were germinating. Her mother had died, and her brother was caught up in a right-wing rebellion. Though Protestant, Le Fort took to attending a Benedictine liturgy near her home in Munich.[1] This encounter with Catholicism inspired her to write a cycle of poems about the Church. In them, the Church is personified as a glorious woman. The images Le Fort uses are undoubtedly familiar. As you begin to read, the poem will seem much like a psalm spoken to God. But keep in mind that this is a poem spoken specifically to the Church. And watch how she rises before us in these lines like a queen.

As we know, the Church is already referred to as the Body of Christ, his Bride; she is our Mother, and she is Mary. Using the long lines of the Psalms (versets) and their parallelism (a succession of phrases that are repetitive in terms of structure or content), Le Fort works the Psalmist's charm of turning abstractions (like prayer, thought, doubt, and hope) into solid landscape. The Church's prayers are "bolder than all the mountains of thought." But they are also "bridges" and "ships" sent out into "wilderness." The Church seems almost like a military general—or a god itself. In Le Fort's hands, the sheer strength of the Church's prayer is revealed as sublime, and "the

---

1. Helena Tomko, "The Golden-Hearted Imagination of Gertrud von Le Fort," *Logos: A Journal of Catholic Thought and Culture* 23, no. 2, (Spring 2020): 129–144.

world shudders" in fear. Toward the end of the first stanza, Le Fort, who had just lived through a world war, writes of the Church as someone returning from "the desert," "the abyss," a scene of "destruction." It is not hard to imagine the young woman, faced with so much existential anxiety, coming to recognize the Benedictine altar as the place on which the world and its worries could be safely placed.

The second stanza speaks of the loneliness of the world and the loneliness of God, and the Church rising from the shadows to unite them both. The gift Le Fort gives us here is seeing the Body of the Church in supernatural terms. After all, the Church is, in some ways, only people. In reality, men and women are staggering out of bed with indigestion or mental lists clouding their brains as they pick up their breviaries and shuffle into chapel. But the Church, Le Fort is saying, is more: "You wash the face of the earth with your songs, you bathe it in your prayer till it is clean." Again, Le Fort uses very familiar scriptural and liturgical terms (the dawn, the dew) to convey this sense of the Church blessing, daily, a world very much in need of blessing.

We end on what seems to be Le Fort's decisive moment of conversion: at the beginning of stanza three, she acknowledges that the Catholic Church speaks for God. And in doing so, it expresses God's *silence*. Prayers, the Church knows, are only "heralds" of what cannot be said. The Church knows that there is something beyond all of the words, songs, and buildings in which she seems to consist—something that cannot be quantified nor even described. The Church can only point the way. Everything falls down in the face of God's silence: the Church falls down before God. But on our altars, he lays himself down for us.

Two years after completion of this long cycle, Le Fort was herself received into the Church.

"The Prayer of the Church"
from *Hymns to the Church* (Excerpt)

Translated from the German by Margaret Chanler
Stanzas 1–3

GERTRUD VON LE FORT

Your prayers are bolder than all the mountains of thought.
You build them like bridges over shoreless waters, you fly them
    like eagles to measureless heights.
You send them out as ships into unknown seas, like great
    frigates into a wilderness of fog.
The world shudders at your folded hands and trembles at the
    ardour of your kneeling.
From sheer terror its lips utter mockery, and it bolts itself up in
    the chambers of doubt.
For you consign it to eternity as a living body, its years to
    corruption before they have run their course.
Behold, the ways that issue from your mouth are ways into
    another life and where your soul reaches all creatures
    have an end.
But you return from the desert adorned as a bride, bathed in
    brightness from the wings of the night.
You come from the abyss as one living, from the eternal solitude
    as one whose prayers have been answered.
You return from destruction as one who has found strength,
    out of the invisible you return with form and stature.

While cities are still sunk in their feverish sleep and dank
    hamlets seem lost in earthy mists from the fields,
When neither bird nor beast has yet stirred and the loneliness
    of the Lord is encamped over the world,
Then you raise your voice in the shadows, as spirit rises out of
    blind matter.
You shuffle sleep from your limbs and wrestle in darkness with
    the shudder of dawn.
For the sins of the night are like poisonous vapours, and sleep
    lies on creatures with the heaviness of death.
No man knows if there will be another day.
But you kindle your soul that she may run before the morning
    like a ray of hope.
Before the dew falls you fall on your knees to the Lord.
You lift up your heart rejoicing before the lark rises, your joy
    drives away all fear with the praise of your Maker,
You wash the face of the earth with your songs, you bathe it in
    your prayer till it is clean.
You turn to the Lord as a new face.
Then the Lord breaks from His solitude and receives you with
    arms of light—and the whole world awakens in His grace.

Now I know that the Lord speaks from you, because you have
    mastered His silence.

You have learned it like a mighty speech, your words are only
    its heralds.

When it begins, the clamor of your cathedrals is hushed, your
    mighty organs hold their breath.

Your psalms fall down before it and your choirs cease their song.

It is as though the waves of the sea were bending low, as though
    great storms folded their wings.

The Great Unrest of men dies like a child.

It passes away with incense and lighted tapers. The end is fair,
    it is blest.

The death-note is a song of praise.

You lay it on your last prayers before the Lord comes; they are
    snow-white as though your voice dazzled:

No man can hear them.

For now His light is upon you for whom you became darkness;
    behold, He before whom you humbled yourself has
    humbled Himself to you.

"Mass at Dawn"

(1930)

ROY CAMPBELL

Catholics are often characterized as "rule-followers." South African Roy Campbell, who converted to the faith at the age of thirty-four, bucked this trend—and every other of his time. Anti-apartheid decades before it was socially acceptable in his native country, anti-bohemian when he tangled with London's "Bloomsbury Set," Franco supporter in the Spanish Civil War: right or wrong, Campbell was a man who practically invited cancellation—and, in fact, his work has been somewhat overlooked.

His poetry is as riotous as his life. Though it rhymes and sticks to regular meter, there is nothing predictable about his colors or images. Though he uses tropes that, as we shall see, are profoundly familiar to Catholics, in his hands they have the air of being newly washed and rearranged.

Part of the charm of this poem is that we cannot know how much of it is literal and how much is metaphor. Campbell was a sailor (as well as a soldier), and the piece zings with the flavor of a real experience—a boatman drifting to harbor after a night's fishing.

But the poet lifts the event out of the ordinary by comparing his boat to a bride and by the radiant description of his catch. Any poet of faith that uses sea and fish imagery knows that they are evoking Gospel stories. Any poem that signals religion in its title and then speaks of a boat coming in will suggest the fishermen-disciples on the morning that they spotted Christ on the shore, where he cooked them breakfast (John 21). The beauty of this poem lies in the fact that this allusion is worn lightly; it is an echo we can almost hear.

At the same time we see, in plain terms, sunlight and shade. We know the real tiredness of the sailor and the mechanics of the sail. The final image of being met at the quayside sounds very much like a happening in the poet's real life: breakfast after a long night fishing, children waiting for him with bread and wine. But children are never just children in poetry, and bread and wine in Catholic poetry are never just bread and wine. What the speaker is arriving at is innocence, home, the stuff of nourishment, and, potentially, Christ's Flesh and Blood.

But read the poem again. What if this is not a personal poem? What if it is Christ himself in the boat? The boat becomes the same boat in which he slept; the fish are fish he caught with his disciples; the children are ourselves, waiting. I do not claim that this was the poet's intention or that it's the "right" interpretation. But this is a poem of mystery. It lends itself to different views. It is a poem of arrival and greeting and feeding. As such, it is not about one man's story, but about our fundamental experience of God healing our weariness and becoming our food, our home.

"Mass at Dawn"

ROY CAMPBELL

I dropped my sail and dried my dripping seines
Where the white quay is chequered by cool planes
In whose great branches, always out of sight,
The nightingales are singing day and night.
Though all was grey beneath the moon's grey beam,
My boat in her new paint shone like a bride,
And silver in my baskets shone the bream:
My arms were tired and I was heavy-eyed,
But when with food and drink, at morning-light,
The children met me at the water-side,
Never was wine so red or bread so white.

"To God the Father"

(1939)

ST. TERESA BENEDICTA OF THE CROSS
(EDITH STEIN)

This poem is undoubtedly a prayer, written by someone who was not interested in impressing the reader with poetic display. At the same time, it is undoubtedly a poem: it is articulated in careful and penetrating images that are not necessarily meant for God's ears alone but for the needy ears of many.

Many is a word that leaps to mind when reading the text. Given what was to follow during the years of the war, and the writer's own death in Auschwitz, the poem reads not simply as a cry from the writer's own heart and life but as a lamentation for multitudes. It is impossible to disentangle historical context and biography from this piece.

Edith Stein was born into a devout Jewish family, and her conversion to the Catholic faith as a young woman and philosopher was painful, and no doubt puzzling, to her mother. (Her father had died.) Through Stein's writings, there resonates a deep consciousness of others. As a cloistered nun, she knew that she was privileged in having time for contemplation, and she would always pray for those who were praying outside in the workaday world. As a Catholic nun rounded up by the Nazis because of her Jewish blood, she knew that she was shouldering the cross, an agony that so *many* had to go through, and she suffered it in solidarity with them—and with Christ. She was calm and resigned, her fellow prisoners in the deathcamp said, and deeply occupied with caring for those around her.

There is something prophetic in this poem. At the time of its writing, Stein did not know what her end would be, but reading these lines, we might feel that she did. Certainly, persecution of the Jews was well underway in Germany, and the war was beginning. In the first stanza here, Stein acknowledges the isolation we feel in misery.

As she writes of "the passage of moths at night," it seems, given what we now know, impossible not to think of the crowds of suffering people transported on trains during the war. We are not like those moths, she is saying. We fear the darkness and the unknown. Her words invoke also the dark path of John Henry Newman in his "Pillar of the Cloud": like Newman, Stein knew that, in suffering, we cannot see the next step. Nonetheless, she seems to presage her own end and, of course, the end of so many others, as she asks God to "bless the distress of men." "My mourning clothes," she says, "You never yet removed." The Jewish people traditionally tear their clothes after a bereavement to physically show the tears in their hearts. The words seem to be a profound acknowledgment of Stein's identity as a Jewish woman contemplating the pain of so many, and her own, which she pledges to bear "in penitence." The taking of the name "Benedicta of the Cross" already demonstrates that Stein knew her life was intimately bound up in sacrifice. A sole woman, Edith Stein was very conscious of her sisterhood with all other women in their feminine vocation, of her extended Jewish family, and of her new calling as a Carmelite nun to take all of these identities and offer them up with and for so many innocents. This is a poem of great resignation and peace, and, due to the events in which its author would find herself, can be read as one of the great supplications from the horrors of the twentieth century.

"To God the Father"

Translated by Susanne M. Batzdorff

ST. TERESA BENEDICTA OF THE CROSS
(EDITH STEIN)

Bless the mind deeply troubled
Of the sufferers,
The heavy loneliness of profound souls
The restlessness of human beings,
The sorrow which no soul ever confides
To a sister soul.

And bless the passage of moths at night,
Who do not shun specters on paths unknown.
Bless the distress of men
Who die within the hour,
Grant them, loving God, a peaceful, blessed end.

Bless all the hearts, the clouded ones,
Lord, above all,
Bring healing to the sick.
To those in torture, peace.
Teach those who had to carry their beloved to the grave,
    to forget.
Leave none in agony of guilt on all the earth.

Bless the joyous ones, O Lord, and keep them under your wing.
My mourning clothes You never yet removed.
At times my tired shoulders bear a heavy burden.
But give me strength, and I'll bear it
In penitence to the grave.

Then bless my sleep, the sleep of all the dead.
Remember what Your son suffered for me in agony of death.
Your great mercy for all human needs
Gives rest to all the dead in Your eternal peace.

"Still Falls the Rain"

(1940)

EDITH SITWELL

In the Blitz of 1940, poet Edith Sitwell compared the bombs that were raining down around her to the inexhaustible London rain. In those months, the deaths seemed endless, the ugliness unnavigable, as streets were obliterated and families cowered (or sang) in shelters through the night. The words of Sitwell, an aristocrat and fan of that great formal poet Alexander Pope, reflect this sense of brokenness; they honor it. For Sitwell, a Modernist, none of the traditional, formal poetics could adequately convey what she was witnessing. Mechanical warfare meant previously unsurpassed destruction was being visited on ordinary streets and in family homes. Sitwell's nose was up against the taped windowpane, and her disjointed, unsettling poetic form reflects it.

Think of the six times repeated "Still falls the Rain" as joists: this phrase unites Sitwell's ever-deepening images. The rhymes among the irregular lengths of lines ("loss"/"Cross," "beat"/"feet") are like still-standing walls in a falling building, among falling rain. This rain is likened to the "nineteen hundred and forty nails / Upon the Cross" (1940—the year of the poem). In other words, Christ is suffering with the people of this city.

The image of rain morphs through the piece: it becomes nails, a heartbeat, hammer-beats, impious feet—until we see it, near the end, as a gushing fount of mercy from Christ's side.

In this multiplicity of metaphor, Sitwell is a daughter of the medieval mystic Julian of Norwich, who wrote that Christ's drops of blood looked like rainwater falling from eaves; that they were so plentiful, they looked like herring scales on his forehead.[1] Sitwell's rain covers "the Potter's Field," which the high priests bought as a place to bury foreigners when Judas returned his thirty pieces of silver (Matt. 27:7); it covers the tomb, Cain's worm (which never dies [Mark 9:48]), Dives, and Lazarus. The rain is as inclusive as God's mercy. (Lazarus' sores and Dives' gold are "as one.")

All of the world's wounds, even those of a "baited bear," are contained in Christ's heart. And Sitwell is unflinching in her belief that this blood-as-rain, this redemptive suffering, will save us. The lines "O Ile leape up to my God: who pulles me doune— / See, see where Christ's blood streames in the firmament" are from a speech by Christopher Marlowe's Doctor Faustus as he is dragged into hell. The doctor, who sold his soul to the devil, needs only one drop of Christ's blood for his salvation—but he has given himself over to evil; it is too late.

We, on the other hand, Sitwell insists, are being bathed in Christ's blood, if we would only choose to stretch out our hands to this rain (his blood, our suffering) and accept it.

Christ's voice in the last line once again seems to speak of Julian, that other English literary woman from so many centuries before, who recorded Christ's willingness to suffer more for her, for all of us. He is still shedding his blood for us.

Still falls the rain, hammers the poem—the evil continues. But, says the poem in equal measure, so still falls his saving blood.

1. Julian of Norwich, *Revelations of Divine Love*, chap. 7.

"Still Falls the Rain"

EDITH SITWELL

(The Raids, 1940, Night and Dawn)

Still falls the Rain—
Dark as the world of man, black as our loss—
Blind as the nineteen hundred and forty nails
Upon the Cross.

Still falls the Rain
With a sound like the pulse of the heart that is changed to the
    hammer-beat
In the Potter's Field, and the sound of the impious feet

On the Tomb:
       Still falls the Rain
In the Field of Blood where the small hopes breed and the
    human brain
Nurtures its greed, that worm with the brow of Cain.

Still falls the Rain
At the feet of the Starved Man hung upon the Cross.
Christ that each day, each night, nails there, have mercy on us—
On Dives and on Lazarus:
Under the Rain the sore and the gold are as one.

Still falls the Rain—
Still falls the Blood from the Starved Man's wounded Side:
He bears in His Heart all wounds,—those of the light that died,
The last faint spark
In the self-murdered heart, the wounds of the sad
    uncomprehending dark,
The wounds of the baited bear,—
The blind and weeping bear whom the keepers beat
On his helpless flesh . . . the tears of the hunted hare.

Still falls the Rain—
Then—O Ile leape up to my God: who pulles me doune—
See, see where Christ's blood streames in the firmament:
It flows from the Brow we nailed upon the tree
Deep to the dying, to the thirsting heart
That holds the fires of the world,—dark-smirched with pain
As Caesar's laurel crown.

Then sounds the voice of One who like the heart of man
Was once a child who among beasts has lain—
"Still do I love, still shed my innocent light, my Blood, for thee."

"Soldiers Bathing"

(1942)

F.T. PRINCE

During the Second World War, a band of soldiers strip off and wash in the sea. Poet and convert F.T. Prince paints the scene (he was actually working at Bletchley Park at the time), and in doing so, confronts us with issues of the flesh and our Catholic attitudes toward it.

Prince's measured and masterful couplets are calm in the naked detail. The soldiers' bodies have been "gross" and "bestial"—but only because of what they have been doing (killing) and where they have been (the battlefield). The sea, like an absolution, makes their nudity "fragile and luminous."

There are, of course, several views of nudity in the Catholic imagination: the blessed state of innocence in which Adam and Eve wandered through the garden; our glorious physicality through identification with God-made-man; and the ashamed covering-up that tells us we are no longer innocent. This latter is highlighted in the quote from *King Lear* at line eleven: "Poor bare forked animal." In our fallen state, we are only pitiable beasts with our breeches off, Shakespeare's king is saying. But Prince does not really seem to think so. In fact, he is almost romantic about the soldiers' innocent and sensual delight in their flesh. They seem to regain their childhood playing in the waves—almost as though they were in another world, away from the corruption of war.

349

Prince then brings in two drawings, one by Michelangelo and one by Pollaiuolo, of similar scenes. Michelangelo's uncompleted sketch shows the surprised buttocks and limbs of soldiers taken unawares by an enemy attack. Pollaiuolo's is, in a sense, even more shocking: the warriors are naked as they slaughter.

But there is another type of nudity that is at the heart of this poem: Christ's nakedness on the cross. It is interesting to consider that Christ's uncovered flesh may be harder for us to deal with as a culture than his injuries. Churches frequently house graphic statues of the flagellated Jesus, but artists almost never fail to cover his genitals. And yet Christ's nudity was central to his Passion. Like Lear (yet so unlike Lear), he is a king stripped of everything and thoroughly humiliated. But Christ's nudity also points to his role as the New Adam. In his body, there is no shame.

Prince is bafflingly specific about the importance of the Crucifixion in this poetic mix of war and flesh. He plays with the reader. Saying that the cross is the "obverse" of the scene of war (fairly easy to comprehend), he goes on to claim that the cross "is the explanation" of the rage of battle. And later he maintains that God's "great love" has driven man to such violence. What on earth can he mean?

The answer lies in the extraordinary power of the crucified Christ, who does not fight back. His vulnerability is total and *naked* like the soldiers'—and yet they would, if caught like Michelangelo's men, seize their bayonets and kill like Pollaiuolo's men.

The fact that Christ died so devastatingly for us, accepting his nakedness and *not* fighting back, should shake us to our core: it *asks* of us. And so, as Prince concludes, "we prefer / The freedom of our crimes."

Yet what "strange delight," what "strange gratitude" the speaker feels at the scene, "as if evil itself were beautiful." Fundamentally, this nuanced poem is about the relationship between innocence and corruption—which, for Catholics, holds the endless possibility of transformation and redemption.

"Soldiers Bathing"

F.T. PRINCE

The sea at evening moves across the sand.
Under a reddening sky I watch the freedom of a band
Of soldiers who belong to me. Stripped bare
For bathing in the sea, they shout and run in the warm air;
Their flesh worn by the trade of war, revives
And my mind towards the meaning of it strives.
All's pathos now. The body that was gross,
Rank, ravenous, disgusting in the act or in repose,
All fever, filth and sweat, its bestial strength
And bestial decay, by pain and labour grows at length
Fragile and luminous. "Poor bare forked animal,"
Conscious of his desires and needs and flesh that rise and fall,
Stands in the soft air, tasting after toil
The sweetness of his nakedness: letting the sea-waves coil
Their frothy tongues about his feet, forgets
His hatred of the war, its terrible pressure that begets
A machinery of death and slavery,
Each being a slave and making slaves of others: finds that he
Remembers his old freedom in a game
Mocking himself, and comically mimics fear and shame.
He plays with death and animality;
And reading in the shadows of his pallid flesh, I see
The idea of Michelangelo's cartoon
Of soldiers bathing, breaking off before they were half done
At some sortie of the enemy, an episode
Of the Pisan wars with Florence. I remember how he showed
Their muscular limbs that clamber from the water,

And heads that turn across the shoulder, eager for the slaughter,
Forgetful of their bodies that are bare,
And hot to buckle on and use the weapons lying there.
And I think too of the theme another found
When, shadowing men's bodies on a sinister red ground
Another Florentine, Pollaiuolo,
Painted a naked battle: warriors, straddled, hacked the foe,
Dug their bare toes into the ground and slew
The brother-naked man who lay between their feet and drew
His lips back from his teeth in a grimace.
They were Italians who knew war's sorrow and disgrace
And showed the thing suspended, stripped: a theme
Born out of the experience of war's horrible extreme
Beneath a sky where even the air flows
With *lacrimae Christi.* For that rage, that bitterness, those blows,
That hatred of the slain what could they be
But indirectly or directly a commentary
On the Crucifixion? And the picture burns
With indignation and pity and despair by turns,
Because it is the obverse of the scene
Where Christ hangs murdered, stripped, upon the Cross.
     I mean,
That is the explanation of its rage.
And we too have our bitterness and pity that engage
Blood, spirit, in this war. But night begins,
Night of the mind: who nowadays is conscious of our sins?
Though every human deed concerns our blood,
And even we must know, what nobody has understood,
That some great love is over all we do,
And that is what has driven us to this fury, for so few
Can suffer all the terror of that love:
The terror of that love has set us spinning in this groove

Greased with our blood.
                    These dry themselves and dress,
Combing their hair, forget the fear and shame of nakedness,
Because to love is frightening we prefer
The freedom of our crimes. Yet, as I drink the dusky air,
I feel a strange delight that fills me full
Strange gratitude, as if evil itself were beautiful,
And kiss the wound in thought, while in the west
I watch a streak of red that might have issued from Christ's
     breast.

"A Poor Christian Looks at the Ghetto"

(1943)

CZESŁAW MIŁOSZ

To write poetry after Auschwitz is barbaric, said the German philosopher Theodor Adorno.[1] The superlative human cruelty of the twentieth century seemed beyond the redemptive capacity of art, or even, for some, beyond the redemptive power of God himself. The perspective of poetry had no place, some felt, in what the Jewish people had faced. This poem, by a poet who was in Warsaw at the time of the ghetto, with its deportations to the death camps and its final, hideous destruction, implicitly takes on what poetry can say in the face of such evil. It also confronts what religion can say—or, more precisely, how those who profess to be Christian can face God.

Gone are the sweeping poetic proclamations of centuries past, seen in the likes of Alexander Pope's poetry. The scale of mass destruction sometimes has an inverse effect on the poetic eye: it asks for the small, singular image. Perhaps we cannot comprehend stories of mass suffering; perhaps we were never meant to. We are given instead, through poetry—and God—the threads, the individual stories and people with which to understand.

The first two lines here are brutally specific and yet full of beauty. Nature's relentless creativity continues, even as humanity tries to unpick it. The litany of civilization being

1. Theodor Adorno, "Cultural Criticism and Society," 1949.

355

torn apart in lines three and four is beautiful; it is meant to be. The repetition in the first two lines and then the second two, the color, the detail, and even the shocking yellow flare of destruction at line six—all this shows us the inescapability of love and beauty, and how it is only our perversion of this matter and essence that hurts us.

Tens of thousands were murdered in the final destruction of the ghetto. But the poet does not show us directly the bodies in the streets. A lesser poet would do so. The television news would do this—albeit with faces of the dead obscured for decency's sake. Again Miłosz descends to the level of insects, their miniscule beauty and instinctive capacity for creation. All else is razed to "one leafless tree." This is humankind's dread skill. But life begins again with building.

Who is the mole of the penultimate stanza of whom the poet is so much afraid? Miłosz leaves behind his forensic eye at this point and shows us his spiritual preoccupations as he describes the vapors of the dead and their different hues. Something is giving off from them—not simply rot, but something ethereal that is unique to each.

The speaker reveals himself now as a body who was present at the scene. And the mole, it seems, is some kind of angel, sorting wheat from chaff: a spiritual triage; a prophet, swollen with wisdom. The speaker is "A Jew of the New Testament," someone awaiting the Second Coming—in other words, a Christian as well as a Jew. Destroyed, he will be handed to Jesus, and he fears his own innate, inescapable guilt. The poem is saying: Do we not all participate in the evil around us, in millions of small ways? *"Through my fault, through my fault, through my most grievous fault . . ."*

"A Poor Christian Looks at the Ghetto"

Translated from the Polish by the poet

CZESŁAW MIŁOSZ

Bees build around red liver,
Ants build around black bone.
It has begun: the tearing, the trampling on silks,
It has begun: the breaking of glass, wood, copper, nickel,
   silver, foam
Of gypsum, iron sheets, violin strings, trumpets, leaves,
   balls, crystals.
Poof! Phosphorescent fire from yellow walls
Engulfs animal and human hair.

Bees build around the honeycomb of lungs,
Ants build around white bone.
Torn is paper, rubber, linen, leather, flax,
Fiber, fabrics, cellulose, snakeskin, wire.
The roof and the wall collapse in flame and heat seizes the
   foundations.
Now there is only the earth, sandy, trodden down,
With one leafless tree.

Slowly, boring a tunnel, a guardian mole makes his way,
With a small red lamp fastened to his forehead.
He touches buried bodies, counts them, pushes on,
He distinguishes human ashes by their luminous vapor,
The ashes of each man by a different part of the spectrum.
Bees build around a red trace.
Ants build around the place left by my body.

I am afraid, so afraid of the guardian mole.
He has swollen eyelids, like a Patriarch
Who has sat much in the light of candles
Reading the great book of the species.

What will I tell him, I, a Jew of the New Testament,
Waiting two thousand years for the second coming of Jesus?
My broken body will deliver me to his sight
And he will count me among the helpers of death:
The uncircumcised.

"The Reed"

(1945)

CARYLL HOUSELANDER

This tall, slender poem stands on the page in the shape of the reed it describes. Houselander wrote much about this image: the Virgin Mary as a hollow reed, ready for the breath of God to make music in her.[1] This poem has that same Marian sense of space and silence. The structure of the poem asks us to go slowly and to let each word resound.

It isn't only God who makes the reed of the poem vibrate. The lines also echo the reality of the war in which they were written. Houselander was a sensitive and permeable person. Filled by the suffering and noise she saw around her in bombed-out London, she was engaged with finding a way to pray without ceasing. "We are really part, as it were, of a vast rhythm," she wrote to a friend.[2] Drawn to the Jesus Prayer, which consists in repeating "Lord Jesus Christ, Son of God, have mercy on me a sinner" over and over again, she wanted to write repetitive lines and memorable images that would beat through her whatever she was doing, despite a lack of solitude and silence. Her poetry was intended to weave with the city's rhythm: she knew she couldn't block out what was around her, and so she used it as part of the rhythmic prayer-poetry she was writing. She wanted her words to "rock" people, just as Mary does in this poem, into

1. See Caryll Houselander, *The Reed of God* (Notre Dame, IN: Christian Classics, 2020).

2. Caryll Houselander, "From a Letter to Maisie Ward," in *The Flowering Tree* (New York: Sheed & Ward, 1945), vi.

prayer and contemplation in the midst of traffic, bombs, trains, and chatter. We can hear her intense meditative silence as we read these limpid images of Mary absorbing God. Certain parts, like the crystallized image of Mary as a reed resounding to God's music in stanza four, can remain imprinted in our hearts.

There is an inevitable darkness to this wartime poem. Twice the poet says that the world is "round and sorrowful." But Mary's arms are a circle that transforms this bleak shape into a cradle for God himself. Mary is presented as the great protagonist of our reality, the great agent of change: she is "answering for the whole world" when she says "Be it done to me"; she lays her child "in every cot."

Houselander then presents a list of images of the hope that is engendered, beginning with "the Child in the wooden bed, / the light in the dark house." It is lines like these, a kind of litany, that the poet hoped would be taken by ordinary people out into the world, or into their fearful mouths, as bombs fell.

Most of all the poem is a petition to Mary that she will make us as soft and receptive and fertile as she: "be the thaw that melts." Be, we ask of her, the arms that rock the whole world.

Houselander had a charism of care as well as poetry, and during the war she counseled the traumatized. A crucial aspect of her mysticism was being vitally alive to Christ in every person and situation. She was hyper-attuned to others' suffering and vulnerable herself. Though single and childless, poems such as these were her lullabies to us, her prayers.

"The Reed"

CARYLL HOUSELANDER

She is a reed,
straight and simple,
growing by a lake
in Nazareth:

a reed that is empty,
until the breath of God
fills it with infinite music:

and the breath of the Spirit of Love
utters the Word of God
through an empty reed.

The Word of God
is infinite music
in a little reed:

it is the sound of a Virgin's heart
beating in the solitude of adoration;
it is a girl's voice
speaking to an angel,
answering for the whole world;

it is the sound of the heart of Christ,
beating within the Virgin's heart;
it is the pulse of God,
timed by the breath of a Child.

The circle of a girl's arms
has changed the world—
the round and sorrowful world—
to a cradle for God.

She has laid love in His cradle:
in every cot
Mary has laid her Child.

In each
comes Christ;
in each Christ comes
to birth;
comes Christ from the Mother's breast,
as the bird from the sun
returning—
returning again to the tree he knows,
and the nest,
to last year's rifled nest.

Into our hands
Mary has given her Child:
heir to the world's tears,
heir to the world's toil,
heir to the world's scars,
heir to the chill dawn
over the ruin of wars.

She has laid Love in His cradle,
answering, for us all,
"Be it done unto me":

The Child in the wooden bed,
the light in the dark house,
the life in the failing soul,
the Host in the priest's hands,
the seed in the hard earth,
the man who is child again,
quiet in the burial bands,
waiting his birth.

Mary, Mother of God,
we are the poor soil
and the dry dust;
we are hard with a cold frost.

Be warmth to the world;
be the thaw,
warm on the cold frost;
be the thaw that melts,
that the tender shoot of Christ,
piercing the hard heart,
flower to a spring in us.

Be hands that are rocking the world
to a kind rhythm of love;
that the incoherence of war
and the chaos of our unrest
be soothed to a lullaby;
and the round and sorrowful world,
in your hands,
the cradle of God.

"Maidens Like White Lilies"

(1945)

TAKASHI NAGAI

"I want to tell you something," Doctor Takashi Nagai wrote
in a letter. "A lot of Junshin girls were killed by the A-bomb.
They devoted their lives to Mary, singing hymns beautifully.
This spring, I had a monument built and I want a ceremony to
console their souls. I wrote a poem . . ."[1]

Doctor Nagai was a convert to the Catholic faith. On August
9, 1945, he was working in Nagasaki's radiology department
when the second atomic bomb was dropped. With devastating
injuries and sickness, he devoted the rest of his life tending to
those afflicted by the unprecedented destruction. His wife was
killed. Her rosary beads, melted in the blast, are preserved in a
museum dedicated to her husband's work and prayer for peace.

The "Junshin girls" referred to in the lines above were
students at the Junshin Catholic University in Nagasaki, which
was catastrophically impacted that August day.

The question of suffering, of how to respond to suffering—
or, more urgently, of how to bear suffering—burns through the
words of Nagai. Poetry and music are instruments, however
seemingly small, to begin the contemplation of trauma. They
are a natural overflowing of prayer.

"Holocaust is a ceremony in the Old Testament," the
doctor wrote. "Pure lambs were burnt at an altar and they were

---

1. Letter from Dr. Takashi Nagai to Fumio Kino, in *A Resurrection* (Nagasaki:
Junshin Catholic University, 2018), p. 2, https://www.n-junshin.ac.jp/univ/mt_profile
/a_resurrection.pdf.

offered to God as a sacrifice." Nagai wrote that he saw the slain students as lambs: "I was deeply impressed by the purity of the girls who were killed."[2] In his poem the girls become white lilies, symbols of purity; Mary's flowers.

The classical Japanese poetic forms, *waka*, are short. They use crisp, crystallized images, often of nature, to evoke emotion or a scene. Nagai's lines conform to this brevity, but his images are Catholic: the flames, the lilies, and the song symbolize sacrifice, purity, and praise.

This poem is testimony to the raw need for poetry and to how, in the millions of pieces resulting from such destruction, man will, somehow, begin to create again. Even something so small resounds more than a thousand words, and its lightness reaches to heaven.

2. Letter from Dr. Takashi Nagai, in *A Resurrection*, https://www.n-junshin.ac.jp /univ/mt_profile /a_resurrection.pdf.

"Maidens Like White Lilies"

Translated from the Japanese by Paul Glynn

TAKASHI NAGAI

Maidens like white lilies
Consumed in the burning flames
As a whole burnt sacrifice
And they were singing.

"Advent"

(1947)

PATRICK KAVANAGH

Patrick Kavanagh, one of Ireland's most beloved poets, was acutely realistic in his portrayal of the bleakness of life in rural Ireland. But he could never leave behind the almost mystical nostalgia with which he viewed the rural world of his childhood. He not only eulogized that world; he hankered after seeing with a child's eyes again. In this Advent poem, this childlike way of seeing is wholly associated with the ability to know God.

At the beginning, two lovers are in a darkened room eating black bread and drinking sugarless tea. It is Advent, a time for fasting and drawing in as they await the light of the world. The narrator of the poem is identified as a son of Adam—he and his lover have not only "tasted" but "tested" too much (the similarity in the sound of those verbs says a lot). He knows that for "wonder" to return, expanses of light and sensation must be shut out. Only this way can the fouled-up knowledge they have acquired be returned to "Doom."

This is fundamentally a poem about wonder, that "newness" Kavanagh had as a child—and lost. In our next poem, "A Childhood Christmas," the poet will show us fully this enchanted vision—of a hill, for example, where the three wise kings (which were really bushes) seemed to walk. But in this pre-Christmas poem, the hill is only seen in its bleak reality as a "black slanting Ulster hill." And the old man (perhaps it is he who in the next poem speaks of the melodeon's eloquence) is only "an old fool." By fasting and darkness, the narrator seeks to restore the "spirit-shocking / Wonder," the "prophetic astonishment" of the child we will meet in the next poem.

"Advent" is all about the ability to be surprised, to *see* when we have grown blind with seeing. In its final gallop of longing for the coming of Christmas, there are no stanza breaks: Kavanagh wraps up the next two blocks of seven lines into one, and his end-rhymes, which were plentiful, come even thicker and faster, falling over each other ("searching," "burning," "churning," "lurching"). Once Christmas has come, newness will be restored, he imagines: they will no longer have to try and make the tired old phrases sound novel. There will be no more sterile searching for material pleasure, no more dry knowledge and lusting after reason and money. It is openness and docile acceptance of mystery that the narrator hungers for: "the why of heart-breaking strangeness in dreeping hedges" (that vivid adjective conjuring greenery lowering under the weight of leaves and wetness).

What will come will come as an image, as a Word— something to be apprehended in new ways. This is, finally, a poem that sings with hope. It is about the return and the rediscovery of God, who comes in ways we cannot arrange but is best prepared for in darkness, silence, and seeing the ordinary with the startled eyes of a child.

"Advent"

PATRICK KAVANAGH

We have tested and tasted too much, lover –
Through a chink too wide there comes in no wonder.
But here in the Advent-darkened room
Where the dry black bread and the sugarless tea
Of penance will charm back the luxury
Of a child's soul, we'll return to Doom
The knowledge we stole but could not use.

And the newness that was in every stale thing
When we looked at it as children: the spirit-shocking
Wonder in a black slanting Ulster hill
Or the prophetic astonishment in the tedious talking
Of an old fool will awake for us and bring
You and me to the yard gate to watch the whins
And the bog-holes, cart-tracks, old stables where Time begins.

O after Christmas we'll have no need to go searching
For the difference that sets an old phrase burning –
We'll hear it in the whispered argument of a churning
Or in the streets where the village boys are lurching.
And we'll hear it among decent men too
Who barrow dung in gardens under trees,
Wherever life pours ordinary plenty.
Won't we be rich, my love and I, and please
God we shall not ask for reason's payment,
The why of heart-breaking strangeness in dreeping hedges
Nor analyse God's breath in common statement.
We have thrown into the dust-bin the clay-minted wages
Of pleasure, knowledge and the conscious hour –
And Christ comes with a January flower.

"A Christmas Childhood"

(1947)

PATRICK KAVANAGH

After the longing of Kavanagh's "Advent," here we meet the child who knew wonder. Kavanagh vividly recreates Christmas through the eyes and ears of his childhood—a viewpoint that animates and enchants. This is a portrait of lost innocence from deep in the Irish countryside. It was written far from home in terms of miles and years, and he is weakening to the painful beauty of nostalgia and taking us with him.

The poet begins, and then is railroaded before the first section is done, in thinking of how he exiled himself from this Eden of his early years. But he returns to the small observed details of his old world that expand beyond measure and flood us with his memory.

So much of this poem is sounds, and those sounds are transformed by perception. The child puts his ear to the paling post and hears music. He hears music also from his mother milking the cow. (We can almost hear the milk squirting into the tin pail, the clanking of the bucket on the stone flags). And sights are no less transfigured: the child sees heaven in a chink of light and three whin bushes become the three wise men. It is the poet's job to transfigure, to see with the freshness of the child's eye, and when poet's and child's eye coincide, we are doubly illuminated. The Irish way of saying comes in, too, as a passing old man comments: "Can't he make it talk—the melodion." The expressiveness of the instrument speaks, then, to us too.

Memory is made up of sounds and sights we think we never noticed and never would have imagined that we would remember. They become the fabric of childhood when (at least in those days) so much was observed and listened to—in the dead time before church, or waiting for tea, when parents were busy with chores and play had, momentarily, run dry. No detail is lacking: the crunch of ice, the light of the lamp like the Bethlehem star, the narrator tightening his coat in preparation for Mass.

The rhymes are natural, and the music is accentuated in assonance—in "Lennons and Callans" and "strange thing had happened"; in "Cassiopeia" and "Cassidy's."

At the end, rhyme works to crystallize the final image. His prayer is unspoken; perhaps it will be as unthinking as a child's participation in the Mass. But it is there, as unarguable and concrete as his mother's milking or his father's playing: no less than a white rose pinned to the blouse of Our Lady. Something so real, like this poem to us, that he can practically see, touch, and smell it.

"A Christmas Childhood"

PATRICK KAVANAGH

I

One side of the potato-pits was white with frost—
How wonderful that was, how wonderful!
And when we put our ears to the paling-post
The music that came out was magical.

The light between the ricks of hay and straw
Was a hole in Heaven's gable. An apple tree
With its December-glinting fruit we saw—
O you, Eve, were the world that tempted me

To eat the knowledge that grew in clay
And death the germ within it! Now and then
I can remember something of the gay
Garden that was childhood's. Again

The tracks of cattle to a drinking-place,
A green stone lying sideways in a ditch,
Or any common sight, the transfigured face
Of a beauty that the world did not touch.

II

My father played the melodion
Outside at our gate;
There were stars in the morning east
And they danced to his music.

Across the wild bogs his melodion called
To Lennons and Callans.
As I pulled on my trousers in a hurry
I knew some strange thing had happened.

Outside in the cow-house my mother
Made the music of milking;
The light of her stable-lamp was a star
And the frost of Bethlehem made it twinkle.

A water-hen screeched in the bog,
Mass-going feet
Crunched the wafer-ice on the pot-holes,
Somebody wistfully twisted the bellows wheel.

My child poet picked out the letters
On the grey stone,
In silver the wonder of a Christmas townland,
The winking glitter of a frosty dawn.

Cassiopeia was over
Cassidy's hanging hill,
I looked and three whin bushes rode across
The horizon—the Three Wise Kings.

An old man passing said:
"Can't he make it talk—
The melodion." I hid in the doorway
And tightened the belt of my box-pleated coat.

I nicked six nicks on the door-post
With my penknife's big blade—
There was a little one for cutting tobacco.
And I was six Christmases of age.

My father played the melodion,
My mother milked the cows,
And I had a prayer like a white rose pinned
On the Virgin Mary's blouse.

"Saint Isaac's Church, Petrograd"

(1925; revised in 1947)

CLAUDE MCKAY

In 1922, the celebrated African American poet Claude McKay visited communist Russia and gave a speech at the Communist International conference. He was inspired by the country's proletarian revolution. He saw communism as a way of fighting *all* injustice, including the blight of racism. During his trip, the young man stopped in a cathedral, as travelers do, and was—to put it plainly—bowled over. He went home and wrote a poem about his experience, but he apparently flipped his feeling of being overwhelmed into a critique of man's domination and corrupting wealth.[1] Only later, when McKay became disillusioned with communist ideology and turned to Catholicism as the locus of truth, did he rewrite the poem. It was published in Dorothy Day's *Catholic Worker* paper in 1947.

There is a double grace in this poem. As a raging light of the Harlem Renaissance, there is no doubt that McKay's finest work was produced in his youth. It sprang from his restless search for spiritual truth, from his furious desire for justice, from his indignation at the cruel treatment of African Americans that he witnessed. He did continue writing poetry after his conversion, but something—perhaps the stroke he suffered, or the calming effect of the peace he received at last—took the wind out of his

---

1. Nick Ripatrazone, "Poet Claude McKay's Catholic conversion," Angelus News, July 20, 2018, https://angelusnews.com/arts-culture/poet-claude-mckays-catholic -conversion/.

final verse. We are left with a sense that his best work is not Catholic, and his Catholic work is not his best.

However, because this poem was written in the heyday of his communist rage, then rewritten after his conversion, we have both: the Truth grasped, and the restless spirit that sought it out still in pulsing evidence. His language is truly alive. Written formally, in his hands the regimens of a rhyme scheme shimmer in ways rarely seen.

The lyricism here is intense and captivating; the assonance of "bow down" and its seven-time repetition evokes that instinctive physical obeisance that we feel before the presence of God. For a man so seduced by the power of comradeship in political terms, he now sees that the hegemony of our relationship with God is right and good—and entirely personal. He bows. He is, now, "humble and alone"; divorced, for this intimate encounter, from the masses.

The first eight lines of the sonnet alternate between what is created art and what cannot be seen ("holy silences" / "marble man"; "angel host" / "jeweled glory"). The architecture seems to penetrate him even physically—lifting him and taking his breath.

In the last six lines, we see acknowledgement of man's talent in the creation of all of this. But this culminates in the final two lines, in which he recognizes that art is the glorious meeting point between the human and the divine.

"Saint Isaac's Church, Petrograd"

CLAUDE MCKAY

Bow down my soul in worship very low
And in the holy silences be lost.
Bow down before the marble man of woe,
Bow down before the singing angel host.
What jeweled glory fills my spirit's eye!
What golden grandeur moves the depths of me!
The soaring arches lift me up on high
Taking my breath with their rare symmetry.

Bow down my soul and let the wondrous light
Of beauty bathe thee from her lofty throne
Bow down before the wonder of man's might.
Bow down in worship, humble and alone;
Bow lowly down before the sacred sight
Of man's divinity alive in stone.

"To the Immaculate Virgin, on a Winter Night"

(1949)

THOMAS MERTON

When Thomas Merton became a Trappist monk, he wondered, like his great forerunner Gerard Manley Hopkins, if writing poetry would harm his vocation. Thank God he was encouraged to write by his superior and came to know that the work of every Christian artist is "restoring all things in Christ."[1]

In the 1940s, Merton wrote this piece, presumably on or around the eighth of December. Addressed to Our Lady, it laments not simply war but the fact that mankind does not know *how* to pray for peace. "To some men," Merton wrote, "peace merely means the liberty to exploit other people without fear of retaliation or interference." He concludes, "If you love peace, then hate injustice, hate tyranny, hate greed—but hate these things *in yourself*, not in another."[2] This is the nub of the remarkable poem that we have here.

Merton writes in free verse, and he is a master of the form (for free verse can be anything but formless). His line and stanza lengths are predicated entirely on sense, music, and impact: so "The last train cries out" is left alone on a line to heighten its desolation. The rightness of the language lies in assonance ("blood"/"come" and "drops"/"cross" in the first stanza). And

---

1. Thomas Merton, *Echoing Silence: Thomas Merton on the Vocation of Writing*, ed. Robert Inchausti (Boston: New Seeds Books, 2007), 45.
2. Thomas Merton, *New Seeds of Contemplation* (New York: New Directions, 2007), 122.

stresses and alliteration emphasize the weight of what it is he is condemning: "In a day of *blood* and many *beatings*."

Listen to the way he achieves quietness, darkness, and devastation. The utter stillness of the first stanza is conveyed through the progress of night falling, the "bleeding" of the sunset, and the stars appearing. It is through these almost imperceptible movements that we know both the Virgin's and the poet's motionlessness.

"Where in the world has any voice," says the beginning of the second stanza, suggesting helplessness or lack of protest. But this is swiftly explicated by the enjambment (continuation to the next line with no punctuation): "Prayed to you, Lady . . ." The problem, the poet is saying, is that we are not even really praying; we do not even really understand what it is that we want.

The blood, the beatings, are far off. We are talking about the actions of "governments" and "soldiers" that perhaps the poet is only reading about or seeing on the news. But still they affect the things of this night: the "birds are dead," "the fields are mute," "trees make gallows." Once again, we see the pathetic fallacy of our defective relationship with God. Even nature cries out—or is stunned to silence. "Where will Christ be killed again?" the poet asks—meaning, perhaps, that every victim of war is Christ himself.

In the last devastating stanza, poet and world conflate and merge in empathy: the night "has got us by the heart." He is walking to the Virgin "on water"—evoking the ice and snow of the poem but also the miracles of her Son. And the very last line tells us everything about the problem of man and war.

"To the Immaculate Virgin, on a Winter Night"

THOMAS MERTON

Lady, the night is falling and the dark
Steals all the blood from the scarred west.
The stars come out and freeze my heart
With drops of untouchable music, frail as ice
And bitter as the new year's cross.

Where in the world has any voice
Prayed to you, Lady, for the peace that's in your power?
In a day of blood and many beatings
I see the governments rise up, behind the steel horizon,
And take their weapons and begin to kill.

Where in the world has any city trusted you?
Out where the soldiers camp the guns begin to thump
And another winter time comes down
To seal our years in ice.
The last train cries out
And runs in terror from this farmer's valley
Where all the little birds are dead.

The roads are white, the fields are mute
There are no voices in the wood
And trees make gallows up against the sharp-eyed stars.
Oh where will Christ be killed again
In the land of these dead men?

Lady, the night has got us by the heart
And the whole world is tumbling down.
Words turn to ice in my dry throat
Praying for a land without prayer,

Walking to you on water all winter
In a year that wants more war.

"The Assumption—An Answer"

(1950)

ALFRED NOYES

Writing in formal quatrains, the convert Alfred Noyes delivers
a beautiful poetic defense of the dogma of the Virgin Mary's
Assumption into heaven. Noyes was a convert, and we might
imagine him making these arguments to curious friends and
fellow writers over dinner. This is honed and expert apologia
in verse.

What is initially so surprising about the poem is that a
man could be so sensitive to the Virgin Mary's experience of
pregnancy. The image of the Christ child's "small soft feet" in
utero gets inside the mother's mind and womb and creates a
picture of the unsurpassable intimacy between her and
her child.

These days, science tells us that a baby will leave a small
scattering of his cells in the mother's body that will remain
there for many years. In stanza two, Noyes describes something
strikingly similar in Mary's case: Christ continues to live in
her in a particular way precisely because of his initial, physical
presence. She is mixed with him. It is a kind of exchange, he
will go on to say: Christ came to earth through Mary, and so
of course, Mary, whose "life-blood once had throbbed in Him,"
is assumed to heaven through Christ. They are inextricable.
Of course, we, too, are party to this divine entanglement. In
the penultimate stanza, Noyes evokes the Eucharist, a physical
reminder that Christ is still here in Flesh (ready to be consumed

by our flesh), thanks to Mary, who prays with us still. The logic of Catholicism is plain—and it is physical.

These ideas, and others throughout the poem, are structured around a series of rhetorical questions beginning "Think you . . . ?" What Noyes is asking the reader each time is, given the facts—the existence of heaven shown in Murillo's painting, God's sharing of lifeblood with this woman—how can the Assumption *not* be true?

A final point to look out for in this deft piece of apologetics: notice the way the third line runs into the fourth (enjambment). Noyes is telling us, after imagining Christ's tiny feet within Mary, that he is "her own." But this thought is broken by the unpunctuated swing into the fourth line and the ominous yet marvelous "Once." For Jesus belongs, of course, to everyone.

And yet, as the rest of the poem insists, to no one like his mother.

"The Assumption—An Answer"

ALFRED NOYES

Before earth saw Him she had felt and known
   The small soft feet that thrust like buds in Spring.
The body of Our Lord was all her own
   Once. From the Cross her arms received her King.

Think you that she, who bore Him on her breast,
   Had not the Word still living in her heart?
Or that, because once voice had called her blest
   Her inmost soul had lost the better part?

Henceforth all generations . . . Ah, but that
   You think was but an ancient song she knew!
Millions this night will sing Magnificat,
   And bring at least one strange prediction true.

Think you His Heaven, that deep transcendent state,
   Floats like Murillo's picture in the air?
Or that her life, so heavenly consecrate,
   Had no essential habitation there?

Think you he looked upon her dying face,
   And throned above His burning seraphim,
Felt no especial tenderness or grace
   For her whose life-blood once had throbbed in Him?

Proof of his filial love, His body on earth
    Still lives and breathes, and tells us, night and day,
That earth and Heaven were mingled in His birth
    Through her, who kneels beside us when we pray.

Kneels to the Word made flesh; her living faith
    Kneels to incarnate Love, "not lent but given,"
Assumed to her on earth, and after death
    Assuming her to His own Heart in Heaven.

"Embraced by New Time"

(1950)

KAROL WOJTYŁA (POPE ST. JOHN PAUL II)

Karol Wojtyła was an actor, dramatist, and poet before he was a priest, and he continued writing after his ordination. There are not many who would call Wojtyła a great poet. But he is one of our finest examples of the contemplative mind moved to such sensitivity that it overflows into brilliance of expression—not necessarily in the usual forms that a more conventional poet might use, but in a fearless exploration of little chartered territory: man's relationship with God through prayer. Yet, despite his engagement with abstractions, the work of the man who would become a saint is very human.

Given his theatrical leanings, it is unsurprising that Wojtyła often wrote dramatic monologues. And yet they are not "theatrical" in the showy sense; they are all about the interior state. Reading them, reading this poem, is like stepping into someone else's mind, someone else's experience of God. His empathy shimmers. Wojtyła was particularly attuned to the experience of the Virgin Mary, her femininity, her love and calling, and her motherhood.

At the first line of this poem, we step into the first person of Mary like a warm bath, and it tells us much: she is *seen*. This is the key to her existence, that locked gaze between herself and God. "I told no one the expression of your eyes," she says, and we are brought into the unique and private experience of a woman who saw and sees God in a way that no one else ever will. Once you have read the poem, go back and read this first stanza again. Meditate on it. It will tell you so much about Mary's relationship with God. It is also deliberately ambiguous: Is the narrator talking of her motherly relationship with the Christ child, or is this the intangible encounter with the Father? These possibilities rightly shift and merge.

God's gaze is also a stillness, one that she lifts herself toward. Here we are up against the abstract: How does a person lift themselves to a stillness? Yet the line is vivid, especially when we learn that one day this acceptance of stillness will allow her to absorb the divine so deeply that she will be like "water vanishing / into a dry riverbed" (though, as the poet adds, her body remains at death; she is assumed into heaven). This is the "new time" to which the title refers, this new existence when Mary's life will no longer be "weighed deep in . . . blood."

The poem ends on song. Again, we are recalled to Mary's "Magnificat." Her life, her meaning, and her vocation were expressed in that song that births in every man and woman an encounter with Christ. This is the "Event" she speaks of: the meeting with God, which, through her, gave God to everyone.

The lines are prayer spilled into poetry. It is as if Wojtyła (as far as this is possible) steps into Mary's ontological existence of closeness to God and her seamless passage to the afterlife. Inescapably, the poem also speaks of prayer more generally. The author plainly knew something of that gaze of God of which he writes. He knew of that stillness and that song. He knew how all would be "full at the last."

"Embraced by New Time"

Translated from the Polish by Jerzy Peterkiewicz

KAROL WOJTYŁA (POPE ST. JOHN PAUL II)

My depths are seen into, I am seen through and through.
Open to sight I rise, in that vision gently submerge.
For a long time nobody knew of this;
I told no one the expression of your eyes.

How attentive your stillness: it will always be part of me.
I lift myself toward it, will one day grow so used to it
that I will stand still, transparent as water vanishing
into a dry riverbed—though my body will remain.
Your disciples will come, and hear that my heart beat has
    stopped.

My life will no longer be weighed deep in my blood,
the road will no longer slip away from my weary feet.
New time now shines in my fading eyes:
it will consume me, and dwell with my heart.
And all shall be full at the last, and left for thought's delight.

I will open out my song and I know its smallest sound,
I will open out my song intent on the whole of your life,
my song possessed by the Event so simple and clear,
which begins in every man, visibly there, yet secret.

In me it was made flesh, was revealed in song with grace,
and came to many, and in them found its own space.

"The Prophet Lost in the Hills of Evening"

(1951)

HILAIRE BELLOC

Many readers will know Belloc's poetry without knowing that they know it. They will know Matilda, who told such dreadful lies, and Rebecca who slammed doors, "a trick that everyone abhors." Belloc, a great friend of Chesterton and the other half of the monster "Chesterbelloc," was also an essayist, historian, travel writer, politician, and apologist. But as a poet, he will surely be remembered for his incomparable use of comic rhyme.

Yet he turned his versifying to other remarkable ends. This poem has the ring of a final confession. For a man who was very sure in his defense of the faith, this is a poem that has the faltering tone necessary when speaking of a relatable encounter with God. The very term "lost prophet" means someone gifted with crystal-clear religious sight who has, for now, mislaid his bearings. Even the most forthright apologists, the seemingly doubt-free, sometimes find themselves in "hills," with their dips and shadows as well as their heights. They come to their own "evening": the fearful sense that life is drawing to a close.

The surety of Belloc's quatrains does nothing to ease a true sense of humility. Like Dante at a similar point of age-related reckoning, the poet is metaphorically lost in a landscape of segregated parts—the frozen summits and the "haunted waters" are intimations of hell itself. The voice here is pleading to God as he realizes that he is at the mercy of "sense and dreadful fate."

He is indeed in a state of spiritual crisis: the very presence of Christ under the appearance of bread and wine is unavailable.

Belloc's first two stanzas are smooth, however dismal in tone. (He achieves this smoothness by making each one a complete sentence.) The shortening sentences toward the middle of the poem then convey jagged unease. At the truncated "I hunger and I have no bread," we feel his fear. The lines become choppier until his more fluid penultimate stanza, which returns to being one sentence.

The burden of the narrator's plea lengthens this to five lines. It is a hopeful and heartfelt reminder to the Almighty that he sang God's praises always and "kept the Faith."

As a poem, this has its obvious antecedents in the spiritual life—not only Dante's *Commedia* but also John Henry Newman's "The Pillar of the Cloud." Belloc's poetic touch is smooth, but his themes are no less weighty and disturbing. And coming from a man who radiated certainty in other genres, the piece should reassure us that doubt is as natural to us as our innate ability to know God.

"The Prophet Lost in the Hills of Evening"

HILAIRE BELLOC

Strong God which made the topmost stars
   To circulate and keep their course,
Remember me; whom all the bars
   Of sense and dreadful fate enforce.

Above me in your heights and tall,
   Impassable the summits freeze,
Below the haunted waters call
   Impassable beyond the trees.

I hunger and I have no bread.
   My gourd is empty of the wine.
Surely the footsteps of the dead
   Are shuffling softly close to mine!

It darkens. I have lost the ford.
   There is a change on all things made.
The rocks have evil faces, Lord,
   And I am awfully afraid.

Remember me: the Voids of Hell
   Expand enormous all around.
Strong friend of souls, Emmanuel,
   Redeem me from accursed ground.

The long descent of wasted days,
   To these at last have led me down;
Remember that I filled with praise
The meaningless and doubtful ways
   That lead to an eternal town.

I challenged and I kept the Faith,
   The bleeding path alone I trod;
It darkens. Stand about my wraith,
   And harbour me—almighty God.

"To an Old Philosopher in Rome"

(1952)

WALLACE STEVENS

Wallace Stevens was a poet whose body of work wrestled with what is real and what is imagined. Famously, he described thirteen ways to see a blackbird: his multiplicity of perspectives was sharp and implicitly destabilizing. As a student at Harvard, Stevens came across the atheist philosopher George Santayana. The men had in common a preoccupation with ways of seeing and imagination. What Santayana did concede, although he never wavered from his atheism, was the poetry of the Catholic faith; in fact, he called himself an "aesthetic Catholic." Perhaps, then, it is not surprising that he chose to spend his last years being looked after by nuns in Rome. To read this poem (especially in the context of its inclusion in this book), it is helpful to know that, unlike Santayana, Stevens converted to the faith in his final weeks.[1]

The poem presents the atheist philosopher Santayana on a threshold: between life and death, between the earthly and heavenly Eternal Cities. And in doing so, it engages with the issue of shifting perception. But the poem's material setting (the domes, the bells, the candles, the nuns of Rome) is far from a neutral backdrop. By entering into the discussion of what *is* and *seems* (as Hamlet might say), Stevens is playing the Roman Church at its own game—and seems to want to lose.

---

1. See Paul Mariani, *The Whole Harmonium: The Life of Wallace Stevens* (New York: Simon & Schuster, 2016).

To begin with, there is the ordinary sense of people becoming small from the perspective of one high hospice bed. How, in the confusion of terminal illness, "banners" may seem to be angels' wings in a patient's mind. But this shifting is heightened by the nature of the city itself and what it represents on earth. Anyone who has been to Rome (Stevens had not) will recognize the almost surreal dislocation of perception that it produces: everything from the light to the dwarfing statues gives new dimension. Everything points *up*. "The extreme of the known in the presence of the extreme / Of the unknown"—this poem names a bleeding between this world and the next, which might be located in the febrile instability of illness or in the simple reality of what is taking place between man and God.

For Rome is not only holder of the greatest symbols of *forever*. It is the place where *is* and *seems* are thrown into more flux than any other mortal place: where the *seems* of bread becomes the *is* of Flesh. The city, says Stevens, is "a shape within the ancient circles of shapes, / And these beneath the shadow of a shape"—which calls to mind Joseph Ratzinger's positioning of the Church as something between "shadow and reality."[2]

Stevens' poetry is full of symbols. But a candleflame and what it represents here can finally, in *this* city, become "the celestial possible." Now, Santayana can escape from the factual fire of that candle flame and become part of what it symbolizes: the Spirit of God.

From stanza seven, we enter with the poet into the philosopher's existential dilemma between wakefulness and sleep, life and death, belief and unbelief, as, in his misery, he is "impatient for the grandeur" that he needs "in so much misery."

2. See Joseph Ratzinger, *The Spirit of the Liturgy*, trans. John Saward (San Francisco: Ignatius, 2000), 43, 60, 138.

But that grandeur is inextricable from poverty and misery. By default, Stevens is entering the Christian narrative.

The poem is not prescriptive. Necessarily, we are left to wonder in which of these "two worlds" Santayana might be "penitent" and "impenitent." Stevens is careful to wrap his mentor's death in a spun cloak of beauty, privacy, and mystery. There is no simple telling; this is all beautiful guessing.

"To an Old Philosopher in Rome"

WALLACE STEVENS

On the threshold of heaven, the figures in the street
Become the figures of heaven, the majestic movement
Of men growing small in the distances of space,
Singing, with smaller and still smaller sound,
Unintelligible absolution and an end—

The threshold, Rome, and that more merciful Rome
Beyond, the two alike in the make of the mind.
It is as if in a human dignity
Two parallels become one, a perspective, of which
Men are part both in the inch and in the mile.

How easily the blown banners change to wings . . .
Things dark on the horizons of perception
Become accompaniments of fortune, but
Of the fortune of the spirit, beyond the eye,
Not of its sphere, and yet not far beyond,

The human end in the spirit's greatest reach,
The extreme of the known in the presence of the extreme
Of the unknown. The newsboys' muttering
Becomes another murmuring; the smell
Of medicine, a fragrantness not to be spoiled . . .

The bed, the books, the chair, the moving nuns,
The candle as it evades the sight, these are
The sources of happiness in the shape of Rome,
A shape within the ancient circles of shapes,
And these beneath the shadow of a shape

In a confusion on bed and books, a portent
On the chair, a moving transparence on the nuns,
A light on the candle tearing against the wick
To join a hovering excellence, to escape
From fire and be part only of that which

Fire is the symbol: the celestial possible.
Speak to your pillow as if it was yourself.
Be orator but with an accurate tongue
And without eloquence, O, half-asleep,
Of the pity that is the memorial of this room,

So that we feel, in this illumined large,
The veritable small, so that each of us
Beholds himself in you, and hears his voice
In yours, master and commiserable man,
Intent on your particles of nether-do,

Your dozing in the depths of wakefulness,
In the warmth of your bed, at the edge of your chair, alive
Yet living in two worlds, impenitent
As to one, and, as to one, most penitent,
Impatient for the grandeur that you need

In so much misery; and yet finding it
Only in misery, the afflatus of ruin,
Profound poetry of the poor and of the dead,
As in the last drop of the deepest blood,
As it falls from the heart and lies there to be seen,

Even as the blood of an empire, it might be,
For a citizen of heaven though still of Rome.
It is poverty's speech that seeks us out the most.
It is older than the oldest speech of Rome.
This is the tragic accent of the scene.

And you—it is you that speak it, without speech,
The loftiest syllable among loftiest things,
The one invulnerable man among
Crude captains, the naked majesty, if you like,
Of bird-nest arches and of rain-stained-vaults.

The sounds drift in. The buildings are remembered.
The life of the city never lets go, nor do you
Ever want it to. It is part of the life in your room.
Its domes are the architecture of your bed.
The bells keep on repeating solemn names

In choruses and choirs of choruses,
Unwilling that mercy should be a mystery
Of silence, that any solitude of sense
Should give you more than their peculiar chords
And reverberations clinging to whisper still.

It is a kind of total grandeur at the end,
With every visible thing enlarged and yet
No more than a bed, a chair and moving nuns,
The immensest theatre, the pillared porch,
The book and candle in your ambered room,

Total grandeur of a total edifice,
Chosen by an inquisitor of structures
For himself. He stops upon this threshold,
As if the design of all his words takes form
And frame from thinking and is realized.

"Mosaic: St Praxed's"

(1954)

R A I S S A   M A R I T A I N

When Rome is hot, churches give an abundance of shade. On entering, their darkness hits the eye; the silence is only broken by the whispers of tourists blowing through. Sometimes it is hard to see paintings or statues: heads block the way, lit phones are waved high. But in a side chapel in one of the city's oldest churches, Saint Praxed's near Saint Mary Major, is a mosaic of the Blessed Virgin that glows steadily in this darkness. Often, it, too, is surrounded by a crush of people. But she abides. The overwhelming impression is of finding someone tucked safe in a rock, someone who silently shines.

Raissa Maritain stumbled on this mosaic during her stay in Rome. She had left Russia for France to escape anti-Semitism and to study. For her, studying was more than a matter of garnering qualifications; it was a search for truth. She soon met a fellow searcher, the philosopher Jacques Maritain, and they were married. The pair—atheist Jewish and agnostic—were so jaded by the pointless materialism of the world that they seriously considered suicide. Before it came to that, and after prayers to the Blessed Virgin when Raissa was ill, they converted to the Catholic faith.

This small but luminous poem, translated by Thomas Merton, is a stunning description of the mosaic that Raissa saw. The initial image, Mary as a bird in a hollowed rock, makes the Virgin seem vulnerable but at the same time sheltered—and bestowing shelter. The "stone needled tapestry" is the mosaic itself. And Maritain speaks of Mary as being made not of stones but of love, art, and poetry. We see the logic of this in the fact the she is the mother of the Word and Love itself.

Despite or because of the chapel's darkness, the mosaic is radiant, and the colors are jewels "flaming," as Maritain has it. The "conch" she writes of is Mary herself. She is a "refuge" to the poet, like the refuge and rock of the Psalms, which is also called to mind by the rock of the first line.

The last three lines speak of evil, and though we can't know which evil Maritain had on her mind, we know that, as a Jew, she lived through two World Wars. In the final analysis, though, Mary hauls her up to joy by her own shining joy.

The poem has no punctuation, and the effect of this is a leveling of the lines and a foregrounding of every single word. There are no "dead" words here, no explaining or rhetorical flourishes, no semicolons to trip on. The impression is that the images, the ideas, are too simple, too luminous, to be pinned down or divided up by grammar. The poet asks us to consider each word on its own terms. Childlike and calm, the poem overflows with love.

"Mosaic: St Praxed's"

Translated from the French by Thomas Merton

RAÏSSA MARITAIN

So like a quiet pigeon in a hollowed rock
You stand there in the wall's curve
Made of stone needled tapestry
In this dim sheltered paradise
Mary made of love art and poetry

In the obscure and flaming chapel
Where gold and ruby hold the azure
Conch of sweetly burning peace
You welcome me refuge pure
To see you O soul's delight

Deeply forgetful of the evil by our side
We sail above our strange agony
Chained utterly Mary to your joy

"On Approaching Forty"

(1957)

MARIO LUZI

Nel mezzo del cammin di nostra vita: halfway through the journey
of our life. These words begin Dante's *Divine Comedy*, and they
resound through this poem by Italian poet Mario Luzi. The
title tells us clearly where we are: that moment in life where
time telescopes, life rushes, and we evaluate the point—or
pointlessness—of it all.

Luzi is described as a "hermetic" poet (his work isn't
always easy to figure out) who believed that the mysteries of life
could best be explored in the mysterious language of poetry.
A favorite of Pope John Paul II and a man whose work is steeped
in Catholicity, Luzi argued that only poetry can save us: "The
word is everything: it is the Word. It is the primary sense of the
divine in us."[1]

This is a limpid and moving poem, permeated by the
consciousness of not just this life but eternity. In many ways,
the premise itself is simple enough: a middle-aged man drives
through a "dreary town" and is assailed by the fleetingness of
his life. The images are suggestive, not prescriptive: the black
fleck of a chimney swift is thrown into disproportionate relief
by the distant mountains. It would be reductive to say that the
bird represents the man's life and the mountains eternity, and

---

1. Mario Luzi, *Frammenti di Novecento: conversando con il poeta protagonista e
testimone di un secolo*, ed. Renzo Cassigoli, *Le Lettere* (January 2000): 60; quoted in
Luciano Zapella, "La parola è tutto: Mario Luzi e la Bibbia," in *Il mondo della Bibbia* 113
(June–August 2012): 49–51; editor's translation.

the poet doesn't ask us to draw those simple conclusions. It is enough that we drive with him and feel those distances.

For the external world is soon inextricable with the poet's psyche. Life is one "gust" of March wind. But there are "delays" in the form of loves, which he characterizes as "straining hands," "haunts," and "customs." It is these things, these attachments, which give form to life, he seems to be saying; they slow it down, locate it in a moment when the world seems to stop turning. But this crisis—the "thought" that he refers to in the first line, this Dantean reflection—has "crushed" his calm.

In stanza three, the poet reveals to us the meaning of existence in all of this flux. He takes the real road and uses it for the familiar trope of life's too quickly passing journey. What saves him is a sense that love and attachment, and how we dance with passing time, is all part of life's "work." The eternal intersects with the open road to present him with a place where the living and the dead are comrades, where every love and loss make the world clearer. Nothing is for nothing; all is restored with a faith (which the poet certainly possessed) that tells us we are one Body, that we have immortal souls, and that navigating all of this is work that makes the "impenetrable world" become clearer. Luzi's vision, far from being impenetrable, is penetrating. He sees the invisible in the same way he sees a bird. This, we might say, is his "fire."

The poem is poignantly comforting rather than depressing, though the final, mysterious image raises questions. What is the fire to which he refers, and what is the flame? Having sunk into a beautiful acceptance of the afterlife, Luzi is—like Dante, Newman, Claudel, Belloc, Stevens, and so many others—contemplating that grand threshold. What must be purged when we make that step? And what will remain?

"On Approaching Forty"

Translated from the Italian by Dana Gioia

MARIO LUZI

The thought pursues me through this dreary town
where the wind sweeps down from the high plateau
and where a diving chimney swift can cut
the slender thread of mountains far away.

So soon come forty years of restlessness,
of tedium, of unexpected joy,
quick as a gust of wind in March is quick
to scatter light and rain. Soon come delays,
snatched from the straining hands of those I love,
torn from my haunts, the customs of my years
suddenly crushed to make me understand.
The tree of sorrow shakes its branches . . .

The years rise like a swarm around my shoulders.
Nothing has been in vain. This is the work
which all complete together and alone,
the living and the dead, to penetrate
the impenetrable world, down open roads,
down mineshafts of discovery and loss,
and learned from many loves or only one,
from father down to son—till all is clear.

And having said this, I can start out now,
easy in the eternal company
of all things living, of all things dead,
to disappear in either dust or fire
if any fire endures beyond its flame.

"The Annunciation"

(1957)

THOMAS MERTON

Many poems have been written about the Annunciation, that
encounter between a young girl and an angel that changed
God's relationship with mankind forever. The scene has also
been painted thousands of times. In these paintings, Mary is
often decked out in clothes particular to the native country of
the artist and also their period of history. Mary can be simply
dressed or clothed in regal gowns. She may sit with cherubim or
peacocks or near medieval Italian towns. But every poet has to
make his subject new. For a convert like Thomas Merton, this
meant digging to the spiritual truth of the scene, acknowledging
what might have been the reality of that scene, and giving a nod
to all of those old representations. What he achieves is a layered
encapsulation of Mary's role in the salvation of the world.

To begin with, Merton embraces the abstract. His view of
the world is post-apocalyptic. We see nothing but ashes and
fire. Then the Incarnate Lord walks in (stanza two) and "puts
our substance on." Here we are seeing the entry of the physical
Christ into the world in a new way. We don't see Mary (yet). We
don't see the angel. We witness the Spirit making the flesh of
God in the world and the "sparks" that this sends out. This is a
kind of supernatural sowing.

Mary enters in stanza three, and Merton is keen to show
her as she was (as far as possible) in her surroundings. The room
is very simple. Here Merton nods to those many Renaissance

paintings of the Virgin in far more luxurious and complex surroundings—but he effectively dismisses them as inaccurate. Instead, he looks to the many references to Mary in the Old Testament (as Wisdom, as the Ark of the Covenant, and as the Tower of David). The manna is here, in her womb. Through this stanza, and the whole poem, we are witnessing the many strata of the Virgin in our consciousness and in theology. She is a mere girl, and yet she is much more. She was born in the New Testament, and yet she inhabits the Old.

Merton pushes on with Mary's presence, signifying something more than the life of one mortal woman. She cuddles the whole world. (Abishag was a girl who chastely kept King David warm in 1 Kings 1:1–4; Mary does the same to us, Merton is saying.) She is the New Eve who is instrumental in saving us exiles from the Garden of Eden. She is the one who brings us into Christ's mysteries. As Marian devotees know, she is the one who gives us to Christ. Merton's heart as a smiling flower in the hand of Mary stands in riveting poetic contrast to the nihilism described in stanza one. Through the Annunciation, the time of blooming has begun.

"The Annunciation"

THOMAS MERTON

Ashes of paper, ashes of a world
Wandering, when fire is done:
We argue with the drops of rain!

Until One comes Who walks unseen
Even in elements we have destroyed.
Deeper than any nerve
He enters flesh and bone.
Planting His truth, He puts our substance on.
Air, earth and rain
Rework the frame that fire has ruined.
What was dead is waiting for His Flame.
Sparks of His Spirit spend their seeds, and hide
To grow like irises, born before summertime.
These blue things bud in Israel.

The girl prays by the bare wall
Between the lamp and the chair.
(Framed with an angel in our galleries
She has a richer painted room, sometimes a crown.
Yet seven pillars of obscurity
Build her to Wisdom's house, and Ark, and Tower.
She is the Secret of another Testament
She owns their manna in her jar.)

Fifteen years old—
The flowers printed on her dress
Cease moving in the middle of her prayer
When God, Who sends the messenger,
Meets His messenger in her Heart.
Her answer, between breath and breath,
Wrings from her innocence our Sacrament!
In her white body God becomes our Bread.

It is her tenderness
Heats the dead world like David on his bed.
Times that were too soon criminal
And never wanted to be normal
Evade the beast that has pursued
You, me and Adam out of Eden's wood.
Suddenly we find ourselves assembled
Cured and recollected under several green trees.

Her prudence wrestled with the Dove
To hide us in His cloud of steel and silver:
These are the mysteries of her Son.
And here my heart, a purchased outlaw,
Prays in her possession
Until her Jesus makes my heart
Smile like a flower in her blameless hand.

"One Flesh"

(1966)

ELIZABETH JENNINGS

Elizabeth Jennings bucked the trend of many twentieth-century women poets who often wrote in inventive free verse. Jennings' forms and images are quieter. She was also a quietly fervent Catholic. Eccentric and vulnerable, Jennings ended as a drifter who looked more like a bag lady than a celebrated poet, spending her days in a coffee shop next to a coach station in Oxford. But despite her vulnerability and struggles with mental health, Jennings' work is an embodiment of control, the gentle charming of the uncontrollable, and the naming of the unnamable. Her disheveled dress and personal disconnection belied the sane order of her art.

The title of this poem is taken from Christ's description of marriage in Matthew 19, and it is a poignant meditation on an older couple who are now sleeping in separate beds. The measured pace and rhyme both rein in and accentuate the feeling of the first two stanzas. These are two people occupying not just separate beds but separate worlds in their thoughts.

The acoustic similarity of "flotsam" and "passion" in the first line of the second stanza throw us into the newly-old territory of what their physical relationship once was. The next line is then broken in two (a caesura), like the couple themselves. Jennings dwells delicately and incisively on this chaste relationship—what touch means in this context. Though it may be seen as sad that this pair are now more like brother and sister, Jennings is steering us to see that this is simply a new season for them, and one that required preparation like any other.

In the last stanza, the form changes to alternate rhymes that are more noticeable to the reader. This has the effect of binding the poem's subjects (the two people) together and injecting more blood and pace into the verse. It is here that Jennings brings us to the nub of this otherwise inexplicable situation: the weft of the sacrament that the Church sees as indissoluble. The distance between the couple is, paradoxically, also a closeness. Their silence is something that unites them; it is a thread the particular tension of which is not to be messed with. ("What are you thinking? What are you doing?" a less experienced spouse might pipe up in this situation.) The image of time as a feather is mysterious and subtle: it is too light to weigh but too tangible to ignore.

The final presentation of the couple as the poet's parents is like a punchline. And she, by virtue of a now-dead fire, is like a phoenix rising from its ashes. But while generations of British schoolchildren have studied this as a set text and may have found it dispiriting, Jennings has focused the reader's mind early on with her choice of title. The interlocking rhymes and images of the pair are inextricable. What binds them is invisible. But though they have now "grown cold," they represent something larger than themselves. They are a part of nature's cycle of fusion, birth, and a gentle letting go, which—by the virtue of grace—does not let them fall apart. Her service through her words is to give flesh to what Catholics know as reality through the sacrament of Matrimony.

"One Flesh"

ELIZABETH JENNINGS

Lying apart now, each in a separate bed,
He with a book, keeping the light on late,
She like a girl dreaming of childhood,
All men elsewhere—it is as if they wait
Some new event: the book he holds unread,
Her eyes fixed on the shadows overhead.

Tossed up like flotsam from a former passion,
How cool they lie. They hardly ever touch,
Or if they do it is like a confession
Of having little feeling—or too much.
Chastity faces them, a destination
For which their whole lives were a preparation.

Strangely apart, yet strangely close together,
Silence between them like a thread to hold
And not wind in. And time itself's a feather
Touching them gently. Do they know they're old,
These two who are my father and my mother
Whose fire from which I came, has now grown cold?

"A, a, a, Domine Deus"

(1974)

DAVID JONES

A a a Domine Deus ecce nescio loqui quia puer ego sum. These
words from Jeremiah 1:6 ("Ah, Lord GOD! Truly I do not know
how to speak, for I am only a boy") are the reference for the
anguished cry that is the title of this poem. The initial question
of the piece—"Ah! what shall I write?"—echoes Jeremiah's
complaint. God puts words into Jeremiah's mouth. But the poet
here seems to have to gather, frantically, his own.

Painter and poet David Jones was in many senses a broken
man. He served extensively on the front lines during the
First World War and suffered afterward from post-traumatic
stress disorder. After the war, Jones converted to Catholicism,
remarking in a letter that "the Mass makes sense of *everything.*"[1]

But, as a poet, Jones was destined, or condemned, to
make his own particular sense of life's horrors through his
writing. In this jagged poem, he is searching for God in a newly
technological society—a place of pillars and pylons, colors and
lights. He cannot find him.

Poets like Gerard Manley Hopkins seemed to find God's
presence with great ease (though Hopkins, too, knew mental
darkness). But Hopkins was living at a time of uncluttered
skies, not among the "automatic devices" and "inane patterns"
that Jones writes of here. Jones, like so many Catholic poets,

---

1. David Jones, "Two Letters to Saunders Lewis," *Agenda* vol. 11, no. 4/vol. 12, no. 1
(David Jones, Special Issue, 1973/1974).

is searching for the physical Christ in his immediate world. Plunkett saw him in a rose. Sitwell saw him in a bomb-pelted city. Jones is looking for "Wounds" and "the Living God" in machines and tin—and his failure to find the divine is bleakly horrific. Nonetheless, with the urgency of the lover in the Song of Solomon, he tries in so many ways—by running his hand, by wondering, by watching—to find his God.

You will notice that the poem looks, quite literally, broken on the page, and intentionally so. We talk of lines of poetry "running," but the litany of Jones' search for God ("I looked," "I have looked," "I have run") runs then stumbles into indented lines. This irregular, fractured style only changes at the potentially terrifying conclusion in prose-poetry, as the poet declares that, for all his looking, he has found only "stage-paste." The effect of these last, longer lines seems to be an acceleration of the speaker's mania. The ending (at first glance) is not happy.

Modernist poetry is sometimes seen as a symptom of a loss of faith in religion, in structure and hierarchy. While it is true that artists and writers are called to make form from chaos, God (and therefore beauty) is also in the destroyed and the disrupted; he is everywhere. He is, as Jones surely knew, there on the battlefields, in the reeking trenches, in death and terror. He is here in Jones' fractured lines that seem like the fault lines and crevices of despair.

But the poem ends on a cry to God, just as it began. Despite everything, Jones keeps on crying out precisely because he knows that God is there. The real question of the poem might be: How do we cope in a world of machines in which it is often so difficult to find him?

"A, a, a, Domine Deus"

DAVID JONES

I said, Ah! what shall I write?
I enquired up and down.
                (He's tricked me before
with his manifold lurking-places.)
I looked for His symbol at the door.
I have looked for a long while
                at the textures and contours.
I have run a hand over the trivial intersections.
I have journeyed among the dead forms
causation projects from pillar to pylon.
I have tired the eyes of the mind
                regarding the colours and lights.
I have felt for His Wounds
                in nozzles and containers.
I have wondered for the automatic devices.
I have tested the inane patterns
                without prejudice.
I have been on my guard
                not to condemn the unfamiliar.
For it is easy to miss Him
                at the turn of a civilisation.
    I have watched the wheels go round in case I might see the
living creatures like the appearance of lamps, in case I might see
the Living God projected from the Machine. I have said to the
perfected steel, be my sister and for the glassy towers I thought I
felt some beginnings of His creature, but *A, a, a, Domine Deus*,
my hands found the glazed work unrefined and the terrible
crystal a stage-paste . . . *Eia, Domine Deus.*

"Total Virgin"

(1976)

JESSICA POWERS

The Virgin Mary is the most painted woman in history. Whether she is lithe and sensual, as Caravaggio would have her, or limpid and silent, like Lippi's Madonna, a wealth of gazes has influenced the way we see the most *unimaginable* woman in history. For any other woman, these gazes, these representations, might be destabilizing. Of course, Mary's outlandish fame began after her time on earth, but one can't help wondering how her Son's notoriety, how people's longing for him, impacted on her. How did she see herself? Above all, how did she cope with the way that God saw her—as someone fit to be the mother of his Son?

These ways of being seen might be the "house of mirrors" that cloistered nun and poet Jessica Powers is speaking of in the first line of this poem. It is the mission of the text to capture the essence of Mary, which is "Virgin."

"She never sat down with her own innocence," Powers writes, in an incisive portrait of Mary's unselfconsciousness. Of all generations, maybe we will understand the sense of this the most. In the twenty-first century, it seems that we sit down with ourselves fairly regularly to evaluate our characters, accomplishments, and place in the narrative of history. Mary did not sit down with her own innocence because she was sitting down with God and had all the definition she needed from him. She was, as the epigraph to this poem says so well, Virgin "even of herself"—that is, she was not self-regarding.

In a mysterious sense, journeys are the theme of the second stanza. Mary was not static. She was living in the moving, tumultuous world. At the same time, what pushed her on was with her: "he hid in her heartbeat" and "behind her breath." Mary carried all "without touching or tasting." I don't think we are supposed to take, from that curious phrase, that Mary had a puritanical reserve regarding things of the physical world. Rather, she did not lose herself in external trappings. She traveled onward. The direction was to God.

This poem is a complex Marian meditation. It investigates her exceptional ability to be in the world but not of it, and how to search for God while knowing he is in us. Powers uses free verse to expertly parse out the complexity of her contemplative conclusions. Each line contains enough of a thought to hit the reader's mind and allow them to reflect before journeying on. Her poetic skill lies in allowing each line to breathe and shine with its own meaning. For example, "whom she was always seeking" in the second stanza, would, in prose, be drained by the clause before it. In poetry, it has the space to ring out. In the dynamics of Powers' free verse, not one strand of meaning is suffocated.

The poem's last three lines are masterful. Life is "a virgin to us all," she says: it comes into our hands untainted and new, bursting with hope. Only Mary, as Immaculate Conception, was able to preserve this virginity. Time, in relation to her, was "inviolate": she belonged to eternity; her days were written in the eternal consciousness of mankind. She cannot know decay. In the deepest spiritual sense, the poem seems to say, Mary was unbruised by the world. And in turn, like time, we can certainly know that the world was unbruised by her.

"Total Virgin"

JESSICA POWERS

"She was virgin even of herself"—Père Francois O.C.D.

In a house of mirrors that coveted her image
she never walked
with her own beauty
nor made a feast of her goodness,
inviting friends from the far and wide.
She never sat down with her own innocence
to dialogue together,
nor called a stranger in
to sit at her hearth and be glorified.

She was a maiden promised to one lover
whom she was always seeking.
Though he hid in her heartbeat and settled himself
behind her breath,
he was distance, too. Journeys dwindled to places
beside her own, and miles melted beneath
her steps of wanting. She could by-pass all
meadows that trap us with their poisonous flowers
and their solicitous pools
and winding lanes that skirt the only death.

She was out on a road alone, hastening onward,
gathering all as a gift, the small and great
fragments of mystery and reality.
Everything was for Him, even her own being.
Since love marks neither measurement or weight
she carried all, without touching or tasting.

Life which comes as a virgin to us all,
most safely came to her.
Time, when she passed, remained inviolate.

"A Confession"

(1985)

CZESŁAW MIŁOSZ

The first "sin" that this poetic confession refers to is strawberry jam—which is as innocent as a First Communion confession. Seemingly, it is no sin at all. Yet the jam segues into the parallel "dark sweetness of a woman's body," and the image of the jar melts in our mind into the shape and color of a female form. The poem is mischievous and honest, and it becomes a mouth-watering menu when the poet catalogues smells and tastes. Where is the sin?

The clincher of this piece—the locus of its vulnerability—is Miłosz's question to God: "What kind of prophet am I?" The Romans called poets *vates*, which meant "prophets," and this conflation of the two roles has persisted through history. Our earliest poets in this anthology had a prophetic role. The Fathers of the Church used poetry as a way to reveal truth and to understand the relationship between past, present, and future. All of the mystics in this book turned, on a shining pinhead of prophecy, to poetry. For prophecy is only seeing very clearly, and that is exactly what poets are called to do. Poets not only see; they *understand*—not always and not everything but in flashes. Or as Pope St. John Paul II wrote, they are granted "spark[s] of his own surpassing wisdom."[1] These sparks will come to any real poet at least once in his or her lifetime.

1. John Paul II, "Letter to Artists" 1, April 4, 1999.

Miłosz was a great poet, as he probably knew. And yet, as the strawberry jam image shows, he was also just a man. And the jam is the least of it, as he continues, playfully. The speaker's sins are human, harmless many might say, and funny. And who would think to expect monastic purity from a writer? This, really, is the downfall of the poet, any real poet. They are gifted with a kind of clairvoyance, but it is spasmodic and incomplete. They know, perhaps more than others, what *else* there is in and beyond the world, but their feet are still made of clay. They are left with what can only be classed as second best in the realm of God and truth: literature.

We last spent time with Miłosz in his 1943 poem "A Poor Christian Looks at the Ghetto." By the time of the writing of this poem, he was in exile in the United States. But his self-excoriation persists, though here it is more of an amiable self-deprecation. "No Catholic thinks he is a good Catholic; or he would by that thought become a bad Catholic," wrote G.K. Chesterton.[2] In Miłosz's knowledge of good and bad within himself and the world, and his masterful use of image, he gives us a wry yet penetrating analysis of both the poet's calling and his downfall.

2. G.K. Chesterton, "The Don and the Cavalier," in *The Well and the Shallows* (San Francisco: Ignatius, 2006), 119.

"A Confession"

Translated from the Polish by the poet and Robert Hass

CZESŁAW MIŁOSZ

My Lord, I loved strawberry jam
And the dark sweetness of a woman's body.
Also well-chilled vodka, herring in olive oil,
Scents, of cinnamon, of cloves.
So what kind of prophet am I? Why should the spirit
Have visited such a man? Many others
Were justly called, and trustworthy.
Who would have trusted me? For they saw
How I empty glasses, throw myself on food,
And glance greedily at the waitress's neck.
Flawed and aware of it. Desiring greatness,
Able to recognize greatness wherever it is,
And yet not quite, only in part, clairvoyant,
I knew what was left for smaller men like me:
A feast of brief hopes, a rally of the proud,
A tournament of hunchbacks, literature.

"Ikon: The Harrowing of Hell"

(1989)

DENISE LEVERTOV

Perhaps you have seen Byzantine icons of Christ hauling the
tremulous dead out of their tombs. These icons are "written,"
their makers say: the act of creating an icon is seen as prayer,
something divinely guided. Convert Denise Levertov calls this
poem an "ikon" in that same vein: she is "painting" (I would
guess prayerfully) a place she has not seen. Like a painted
icon, this poem journeys beyond the observable and into the
experience of Christ himself.

Having moved to America from England at a young age,
Levertov was on her own journey, both of poetry and truth.
Her verse became bolder, even as she moved from a vague
spirituality and humanism to the decisive creed of Catholicism.
This poem is almost a living painting of the continuation of that
movement. It begins with familiar images of the harrowing of
hell and ends by penetrating the mind of Christ—showing us
how he might *feel*—with the freshest of perception.

The progression of the poem comes with no helpful stanza
breaks, almost as though what Levertov is exploring is too
riveting for interruption or formal constriction. It is as though
she were taking us with her down to this strange netherworld
of which Scripture speaks and about which we pray on Holy
Saturday. Whether she had a particular icon in mind when she
wrote this or it was her own invention, we do not know. But
in her vision, Christ goes through an arch within the tomb to

access what she calls "limbo." (Sheol was, of course, simply a darkness to which all the dead were sent before the coming of Christ. Levertov may be evoking the secular sense of limbo as a place of waiting.) The image of Christ then "gathering" the dead and pulling them from their tombs sounds like many a Byzantine icon. Some are "almost unwilling"—a nod to how complacent and lazy we can become in our darkness and despair. The good thief is described as still "streaked" in dust: Christ is making good his promise to him.

But it is in the last twenty lines that Levertov hones in on Christ's experience in ways that are most illuminating and unusual. There is a gear change away from what we see in painted icons to "that struggle / no human presumes to picture." *This* is the essence of poetry: how it can burrow so very deeply into truth. Here Levertov is investigating an aspect of Christ's experience that we may never have contemplated.

His life, his death, and this descent are of a different nature to what he must achieve now—a kind of painful birth that he must go through to gain access back to the tomb, out into the world, and into the structure of "days and weeks." She describes his glorified body as being "lit from within." (And here we have the nub of why Mary Magdalene will not recognize him at dawn. We cannot know what a glorified body will look like.) Christ is full, now, of an ache we cannot imagine; it is an unnatural wrench to leave "*them*" (the dead) and give in again to human hunger. As God, he must again surrender to that most merciful and yet, in pre-Christian ways, ungodly act of accepting help and food from men. He must become vulnerable. He must choose, again, to be fed by us—just as we choose to be fed by him.

"Ikon: The Harrowing of Hell"

DENISE LEVERTOV

Down through the tomb's inward arch
He has shouldered out into Limbo
to gather them, dazed, from dreamless slumber:
the merciful dead, the prophets,
the innocents just His own age and those
unnumbered others waiting here
unaware, in an endless void He is ending
now, stooping to tug at their hands,
to pull them from their sarcophagi,
dazzled, almost unwilling. Didmas,
neighbor in death, Golgotha dust
still streaked on the dried sweat of his body
no one had washed and anointed, is here,
for sequence is not known in Limbo;
the promise, given from cross to cross
at noon, arches beyond sunset and dawn.
All these He will swiftly lead
to the Paradise road: they are safe.
That done, there must take place that struggle
no human presumes to picture:
living, dying, descending to rescue the just
from shadow, were lesser travails
than this: to break
through earth and stone of the faithless world
hack to the cold sepulchre, tearstained
stifling shroud; to break from *them*
back into breath and heartbeat, and walk

the world again, closed into days and weeks again,
wounds of His anguish open, and Spirit
streaming through every cell of flesh
so that if mortal sight could bear
to perceive it, it would be seen
His mortal flesh was lit from within, now,
and aching for home. He must return,
first, in Divine patience, and know
hunger again, and give
to humble friends the joy
of giving Him food—fish and a honeycomb.

"The Animals"

(1995)

JOSEPHINE JACOBSEN

"Poetry is like walking along a little, tiny, narrow ridge up on a precipice. You never know the next step, whether there's going to be a plunge. I think poetry is dangerous. There's nothing mild and predictable about poetry."[1] So said poet Josephine Jacobsen to a journalist. The poem we have here pulses with this poet's utmost respect for language—and the surprising danger of language of which she was talking. Through this poem, we do not know where she is leading us. And it is highly probable that when Jacobsen wrote it, she did not know entirely where she was going either. But, as a Catholic, Jacobsen was alert to mystery and symbol. She was mistress of repetition and musical inevitability that somehow still manages to haunt and surprise us.

The world that Jacobsen describes here is mystical and nocturnal. She takes the reader to a place beyond the veil of consciousness where man is no longer writing the story or calling the shots. She is taking us deep into the unconscious mind of humanity, where God's symbols work tirelessly, even or especially as we sleep. She takes us into the quasi-dreamscape of Scripture, to pluck out animals that carry (like Chesterton's donkey) a burden of symbol.

Animals have always had a poetic meaning in the embroidered tapestry by which man understands the universe.

1. Interview, *The Baltimore Sun*, 1990.

From earliest times, man has used animals as symbols for the mythical and mystical. Owls were seen as messengers between the living and the dead. Cats were holy, according to the ancient Egyptians. Cows are still revered by Hindus. So it is unsurprising that God's poetry would use these symbols to help us understand epic and otherwise ineffable truths.

Of course, the poem feels unpeopled. The one specified man present is a part of the quartet who is described in the book of Revelation as having six wings and many eyes, the creatures who surround the throne of God singing "Holy, holy, holy" (Rev. 4:6–9). The other people, mentioned in line 5, are faceless and silent.

In her dream, Jacobsen takes us to a desperate and arid landscape where we meet the scapegoat, which the priests of the Old Testament would cast out into the wilderness with mankind's sins heaped upon it (Lev. 16:21). We meet the cock that crowed three times when Peter denied Christ. We meet the sparrow (whose demise the Creator knows and cares about; see Matt. 10:29), and its fall—at three o'clock, the time of day when its Creator died—is quietly epic. There is the serpent writing its strange music of evil (Gen. 3:1). And finally there is the dove, as messenger of hope (Gen. 8:11). This silent carnival of praise, sacrifice, betrayal, death, evil, and redemption spins through our silences and otherworldly edifices of night, as the prayers of Georgiana Fullerton's "Language of the Church" spin across time zones and territories.

And the parade of animals is lent depth and ominous atmosphere through Jacobsen's use of language. The half-rhymes at the first and last line of each stanza create a sense of things being right, and yet not quite right. The repetition ("animals came and shone / . . . but silent shone the animals") and the abundance of alliteration (see stanza two: "watched," "waterless wilderness"; "granite," "goat"; "people," "praying"; "sin," "sunken") serve to make this seem a deliberately thought-out scene—albeit one that we cannot always understand. The language gives the poem the weird rightness of a dream.

Jacobsen was right: there is nothing mild and predictable about this poem. It engages with the fabric of mystery.

"The Animals"

JOSEPHINE JACOBSEN

At night, alone, the animals came and shone.
The darkness whirled but silent shone the animals:
The lion the man the calf the eagle saying
Sanctus which was and is and is to come.

The sleeper watched the people at the waterless
    wilderness' edge;
The wilderness was made of granite, of thorn, of death,
It was the goat which lightened the people praying.
The goat went out with sin on its sunken head.

On the sleeper's midnight and the smaller after hours
From above below elsewhere there shone the animals
Through the circular dark; the cock appeared in light
Crying three times, for tears for tears for tears.

High in the frozen tree the sparrow sat. At three o'clock
The luminous thunder of its fall fractured the earth.
The somber serpent looped its coils to write
In scales the slow snake-music of the red ripe globe.

To the sleeper, alone, the animals came and shone,
The darkness whirled but silent shone the animals.
Just before dawn the dove flew out of the dark
Flying with green in her beak; the dove also had come.

"The Shortest Days"

(1998)

ANNE PORTER

Anne Porter's long life was, in many ways, hidden. Or at least her poetry was hidden. Mother of a large family and wife of the artist Fairfield Porter, it was not until she was in her late seventies that her poems began to be published. It is fitting, then, that we include a poem of hers about old age. This elderly lady was a convert and a third order Franciscan who took the social teachings of the Church to heart and shared St. Francis' joy in nature.

Porter's writing is natural in every sense. Not only does she write exquisitely of leaves and light; she is a great observer of people. Her eye for detail is acute. We can see people bent over their kettle, exactly as she sees them, and hear the whispering of her prayer on the bus. She scoops up the marginalized and places them center-page. She understands the heartbreak of an eighty-year-old in a hospital bed and carries this sorrow with her, alongside the mother's natural vicarious joy and suffering for her children.

This naturalness, this humanity, breathes through her poetic diction. Her lines find their own endings, often with the rhythm of natural conversation. Even the rhythms of her petition ("Hold out your hands") and her litanies ("Through . . . Through . . . Through . . ." in the penultimate stanza) sound like someone talking to herself or confiding to a friend over a cup of tea.

But Porter's writing is not simply of the natural order. In Porter's work, God's immanence is vivid. She has the eye of Hopkins for his sublime light, and the determination of Dorothy Day (to whom she wrote when she was contemplating conversion[1]) to abide in that light and let it sweep her closer to the brokenhearted.

Like the sacrifice of thanksgiving in Psalm 50, the poem exalts the Lord in its recognition of his presence. It reflects the world back to its Maker; it shows God how the poet has seen and understood what she has been given, and it shows others where he is in his everyday creation.

The poem is also evidence of "a broken spirit" (Ps. 51:17)—the old lady's in the hospital bed, the poet's in her confession of her fears. She knows that we break in his hands. Most of all, the poet is acknowledging her end: her own inevitable "unknown death" and the deaths of those she loves. But she hands all of this over. Fundamentally, from the very first line, this poem is a "promissory note" for God. The piece is her version, on one particular day, in one particular poem, of Ignatius' "Suscipe": "Take, Lord, and receive all my liberty, my memory, my understanding, and my entire will, all that I have and possess. Thou hast given all to me. To Thee, O Lord, I return it. All is Thine, dispose of it wholly according to Thy will. Give me Thy love and Thy grace, for this is sufficient for me."[2]

1. Dana Greene, "To Praise and Live as 'Love's Apprentice': The Poetry of Anne Porter," *Renascence* 66, no. 4 (Fall 2014): 273–282, https://doi.org/10.5840/renascence201466420.

2. Ignatius, *Spiritual Exercises*, in *Ignatian Collection*, ed. Holly Ordway and Daniel Seseske (Park Ridge, IL: Word on Fire Classics, 2020), 80.

"The Shortest Days"

ANNE PORTER

Hold out your hands, God my Father,
Because I want to give you my old age,
Or at least, try to give you my old age

Beginning with the dusk of this morning in Advent.
In the small frame houses round the station
Honey-colored light fills up the kitchens
Where old handymen and widows, pensioners and spinsters
Are boiling water for the day's first coffee or tea
While the tiny maple-leaves are curling like birds' feet round
    the frost,
Through all the whispering to you in buses
As I ride to see grandchildren
Or to greet the eighty-year-old heart breaking in a hospital bed,
The hands that served you strapped to the rails of the bed,
(And may that heart be broken into your hands.)

Through all your lights, sparkling glowing
glittering flashing blazing,
And truth, your terrible light,
Through fears for my old husband and grown children,
    and joys when they have joy,
Through "clouds, calms, and all weathers,"
Through all the unknown history
    through the unknown sicknesses through the unknown
      death.

God my Father, hold out your hands
So I may place in them this promissory note, this title-deed,
This poem, here on this page.

"Lux Perpetua"

(1996)

GEORGE MACKAY BROWN

The convert George Mackay Brown once wrote, "That such an institution as the Church of Rome—with all its human faults—had lasted for nearly two thousand years, while parties and factions and kingdoms had had their day and withered, seemed to me to be utterly wonderful. Some mysterious power seemed to be preserving it against the assaults and erosions of time."[1]

Time is what this last poem is about—not the historical time of wars, borders, and technological advances, but time as lived by every man, with its inevitable quietness and flickers of God.

This poem has as much time, space, and silence as the cold island of Orkney on which it was written. Mackay Brown's is a style that teaches us the power of few words and little explanation. He allows his visual images to tell their own tales, to create their own associations in our minds. This poem begins as a list of light, written out in pictures. Each element speaks a book. Each conjures a whole story, whether it is the birth of Christ, a farmer's or fisherman's workday, a cozy evening, or a prayer for the dead. Each is thrown sparely onto the mind of the reader, where it blooms.

Mackay Brown foregoes punctuation here. The silence at the end of a line is sacrosanct; the writer expects the reader to

---

1. Maggie Fergusson, *George Mackay Brown: The Life* (London: John Murray, 2006), 39.

know and respect it. Adjectives are very few. Fittingly, a star breaks the two stanzas.

The conclusion of the final two lines is profound. It tells us that these "glimmers" are lamps, lights along the road until we reach God. They are intimations of that immense Lux Perpetua, or perpetual light, that Dante was confronted with during his last moments in paradise. They are like everyday flecks of that "mysterious power" about which Mackay wrote above.

Again, we have the poetic currency of light and dark, God breaking through and into our existence. Yet this poem does not speak of ecstasy or great mystical union, but rather of work and ordinary scenes.

It is in these fragments that we know the Creator, the lines say: in the silence and clarity of the everyday; in poetry.

"Lux Perpetua"

GEORGE MACKAY BROWN

A star for a cradle
Sun for plough and net
A fire for old stories
A candle for the dead

*

Lux perpetua
By such glimmers we seek you.

A Glossary of Relevant Poetic Terms

Alliteration: The use of words with the same initial letter within a short space. For example, "lithe little lark" ("The Song of Manchán the Hermit").

Anaphora: Words or phrases that are repeated at the beginning of successive lines. See "The Deer's Cry" by St. Patrick, "Columcille Fecit" by St. Columba, and "Saint Isaac's Church, Petrograd" by Claude McKay for examples.

Assonance: A resemblance of sounds between words. For example, "Your Mother is a wonder" from St. Ephrem's "Hymns on the Nativity of Christ in the Flesh." Here the *o* in "mother" and the *o* in "wonder" are an example of assonance.

Ballad: A form of poetry that typically tells a story in short rhyming stanzas.

Blank verse: Poetry written in unrhyming iambic pentameter. (See "Iambic pentameter" below.)

Caesura: A break in the middle of a line, mostly created by punctuation. For example:
"How cool they lie. They hardly ever touch,"
("One Flesh," Elizabeth Jennings)

Enjambment: When one line runs into the next with no break. The sense of that line is completed by the next. For example:

"Where in the world has any voice
Prayed to you Lady . . ."
("To the Immaculate Virgin, on a Winter Night,"
Thomas Merton)

Fourteener: Lines of fourteen syllables and seven stresses.

Free verse: A one-off form of poetry, where the poet organizes sounds (like alliteration and assonance), rhyme, rhythm, and line length to create a music particular to the poem they are writing. Before the twentieth century, most poetry was written within a particular form: lines may have had a certain number of syllables, as was the case in the Greek of St. Gregory of Nazianzus, or a certain rhyme scheme would also be used. (See "Sonnet" below.) Contrary to popular belief, poems rhyming at the ends of lines is the gold standard only to certain languages within certain periods. The Psalms, for example, do not rhyme in the way that we consider rhyme today. In free verse, image, word choice, and placing of words become very important. (The last word of each line is privileged, for example.) Scansion (that is, the stresses and lengths of lines) is also important. In free verse, the poet is relying on their "ear," a little like someone playing the piano without sheet music.

Half rhyme: A rhyme that matches only in terms of vowels or consonants, not both together. Sometimes even these sounds are similar and not exact. For example, "shone" and "come" are examples of half rhyme in Josephine Jacobsen's "The Animals."

Heroic couplets: Couplets of iambic pentameter that rhyme.

Iambic pentameter: Poetry written with five "feet" to a line. An iambic foot is two syllables, the first unstressed, the second stressed.

Iambic tetrameter: As above, but with only four stresses to a line. (See also "Trochaic tetrameter.")

Line: A line of poetry running along the page until it "breaks" and moves down to form another row of words below. Technically, it is called a verse.

Metaphor: A figure of speech that connects two different things. For example, "time itself's a feather" from "One Flesh" by Elizabeth Jennings, presenting time as something tangible and having the lightness of a feather; or "My mangled youth lies dead beneath the heap. / My days have crackled and gone up in smoke" from "The Hound of Heaven" by Francis Thompson, presenting "youth" and "days" as concrete objects that can die and be burnt.

Metaphysical poetry: A loose poetic movement that flourished in the seventeenth century and involved the use of complex and extended metaphors.

Meter: How many stresses a line has and how they are arranged. Iambic pentameter is one kind of meter.

Parallelism: Commonly found in the Psalms, the repetition of content, vocabulary, and/or syntax through various lines.

Rhyme scheme: How rhymes are arranged in a poem. For example, the following stanza from G.K Chesterton's "The Donkey" has the following rhyme scheme: ABAB

"When fishes flew and forests walked (A)

And figs grew upon thorn, (B)

Some moment when the moon was blood (A)

Then surely I was born." (B)"

Simile: A comparison between two things. For example, "His palfrey was as brown as is a berry," from the General Prologue to *The Canterbury Tales* by Geoffrey Chaucer, where the poet likens the brown of the horse (palfrey) to a berry.

Sonnet: A fourteen-line poem. The most recognized forms are the Petrarchan (ABBAABBA CDCDCD or CDECDE) and the Shakespearean (ABABCDCDEFEFGG) written in iambic pentameter. Sonnets usually contain a *volta* (see below) that makes the piece rhetorical, a kind of poetic argument on subjects that are traditionally (but not necessarily) romantic or concerned with the eternal. Some of the most successful sonnets have broken these rules or reworked them (see Gerard Manley Hopkins' "The Windhover"). The translation of Vittoria Colonna's sonnet is a hybrid of the English and Italian forms.

Sprung rhythm: A meter more concerned with stresses than the number of unstressed syllables between them. Named by Gerard Manley Hopkins and exemplified in his work, the effect is of bouncy irregularity and insistence.

Stanza: Lines of poetry, more popularly thought of as a "verse," written together in one chunk. A break will occur on the page before the next stanza. "Quatrains" are a four-line stanza that often rhymes, "tercets" a three-line stanza, and "couplets" a two-line stanza. A couplet also refers to any two lines of poetry that are bonded, often by rhyme. There is a final couplet in a Shakespearean sonnet.

Stress: The natural emphasis we place on a syllable as we read or speak. For example, in the line "As kíngfishers cátch fíre," the stresses fall on the accented syllables.

Terza rima: Three-line stanzas with the rhyme scheme ABA BCB CDC, and so on.

Trochaic tetrameter: A meter with four stressed syllables per line (and usually eight syllables, unless the last is left off). Here the stressed syllable falls before the unstressed. For example, in the first line of "Pangur Bán," "Í and Pángur Bán, my cát."

Verset: A short verse, seen in the Psalms: "Let my prayer come before you; incline your ear to my cry" (Ps. 88:2). Versets are used within this anthology in the poetry of Paul Claudel, Charles Péguy, and Gertrud von Le Fort. In nonscriptural poetry they present as long unrhymed lines that crescendo with feeling.

Volta: An Italian term that refers to the turn within a sonnet, the point at which the poet is beginning to make his or her case for a point of view. In Petrarchan sonnets, like those of Gerard Manley Hopkins, it occurs after the first eight lines; in Shakespearean sonnets, at the final couplet.